Whitaker's Almanack Pocket World 1999

Titles published by Whitaker's Almanack

Whitaker's Almanack 1999
Whitaker's Almanack 1900: Facsimile Edition
Whitaker's Almanack International Sports Records and Results 1998/9

Pocket-books
Whitaker's Almanack Pocket Reference
Whitaker's Almanack Pocket World 1999

Forthcoming
Whitaker's London Almanack 1999: What's What in London

Whitaker's ALMANACK

POCKET WORLD 1999

LONDON: THE STATIONERY OFFICE

© The Stationery Office Ltd 1998

The Stationery Office Ltd
51 Nine Elms Lane, London SW8 5DR

First published 1998

ISBN 0 11 702245 4

A CIP catalogue record for this book is available from the British Library

Editorial Staff
Penny Clarke (Publisher)
Hilary Marsden (Editor)
Daniel Carroll (Assistant Editor, International)
Bridie Macmahon (Assistant Editor, UK)
Neil Mackay (Assistant Editor, UK)
Surekha Davies (Database Co-ordinator)
Allison McKechnie (Freelance Editor)

Text designed by James Crew
Jacket designed by Bob Eames
Jacket photographs © Telegraph Colour Library and © Tony Stone Images
Map by Oxford Cartographers
Typeset by Eclipse Design, Norwich
Printed and bound in Great Britain by BPC Digital Information Ltd, Exeter

Foreword

Who belongs to NATO? What is APEC? Which country's currency is the Nakfa? What is the telephone number of the World Bank? Which country's men have the highest life expectancy in the world?

With *Whitaker's Almanack Pocket World* you have the world at your fingertips.

Every country and major territory in the world is profiled, providing key information at a glance – the head of state and head of government, capital, main languages, embassy details, economic data, hours of business and public holidays, trouble spots – plus information about major political and economic organizations, time zones and telecommunications, travel documents and innoculations. At a glance, *Whitaker's Almanack Pocket World* provides everything the business or armchair traveller might need to know.

Designed to accompany *Whitaker's Almanack Pocket Reference*, it is the essential companion for business and office use, study and general knowledge questions.

Readers' comments and suggestions of additional information that they would find useful are always welcome and should be sent to the Editor at the address below.

Whitaker's Almanack
51 Nine Elms Lane
London
SW8 5DR
Fax: 0171-873 8723
E-mail: whitakers.almanack@theso.co.uk

CONTENTS

Directory of Major International Organizations

COUNTRY PROFILES A–Z

AFGHANISTAN

Area	251,773 sq. miles (652,090 sq. km)
Population	20,141,000 (1994 UN estimate)
Main languages	Dari (a form of Persian), Pushtu
Capital	Kabul (population 1,424,400, 1988)
Currency	Afghani (Af) of 100 puls
Exchange rate (at 29 May)	Af 7745.82
Public holidays	January 30 (3 days); March 21; April 7 (3 days), 17, 28; May 1, 7; July 6; August 19
Usual business hours	Sat.–Wed. 8–12, 13–16.30; Thurs. 8–13.30
Electrical rating	220v AC, 50Hz

Demography
Life expectancy (years)	male 43; female 44
Population density	31 per sq. km (1995)

Government and diplomacy
Political system	Republic
Head of state	None at present
Head of government	None at present
Embassy in UK	31 Prince's Gate, London SW7 1QQ. Tel: 0171-589 8891
British Embassy in Kabul	Karte Parwan. Staff were withdrawn 1989; now resident in Islamabad, Pakistan
Trouble spots	Civil war between several factions in progress

Defence
Military expenditure	15.4% of GDP (1996)

Economy
GDP	US$17,418 million (1994) US$3,937 per capita (1994)
Inflation rate	56.7% (1991); estimated to be 400% in 1996

Education
Enrolment (percentage of age group)	primary 29% (1993); tertiary 1.8% (1990)
Illiteracy rate	68.5%

ALBANIA

Area	11,099 sq. miles (28,748 sq. km)
Population	3,645,000 (1994 UN estimate)
Main language	Albanian
Capital	Tirana (population 244,153, 1990)
Currency	Lek (Lk) of 100 qindarka
Exchange rate (at 29 May)	Lk 252.106
Public holidays	January 1, 2, 30; March 22, 23; April 12, 19; May 1; November 28, 30; December 25
Usual business hours	Mon–Fri. 7.30–15.30
Electrical rating	220v AC, 50Hz

Demography

Life expectancy (years)	male 69.60; female 75.50
Population growth rate	2.3% (1995)
Population density	127 per sq. km (1995)
Urban population	36.7% (1991)

Government and diplomacy

Political system	Republic
Head of state	President Prof. Rexhep Mejdani
Head of government	Fatos Nano
Embassy in UK	4th Floor, 38 Grosvenor Gardens, London SW1W 0EB. Tel: 0171-730 5709
British Embassy in Tirana	Rruga Vaso Pasha, 7–1, Tirana. Tel: Tirana 34973/4/5
Trouble spots	Anti-government protests in early 1997 took the form of armed rebellion, particularly in the south; situation still unstable

Defence

Military expenditure	3.9% of GDP (1996)
Military personnel	Armed forces yet to be reconstituted following civil unrest

Economy

GNP	US$2,705 million (1996) US$820 per capita (1996)
GDP	US$1,689 million (1994) US$700 per capita (1994)
Inflation rate	7.8% (1995)
Total external debt	US$781 million (1996)
Unemployment	9.1% (1991)

Education

Enrolment (percentage of age group)	primary 96% (1995); tertiary 9.6% (1993)

ALGERIA

Area	919,595 sq. miles (2,381,741 sq. km)
Population	28,548,000 (1994 UN estimate)
Main languages	Arabic, Berber, French
Capital	Algiers (population *c*.3,250,000)
Currency	Algerian dinar (DA) of 100 centimes
Exchange rate (at 29 May)	DA 96.5504
Public holidays	January 1, 30 (2 days); April 7 (2 days), 28; May 1, 7; June 19; July 5, 6; November 1
Usual business hours	Sat.–Wed. 8–12, 13–16.30
Electrical rating	220v AC, 50Hz (European plugs)

Demography
Life expectancy (years)	male 65.75; female 66.34
Population growth rate	2.4% (1995)
Population density	12 per sq. km (1995)

Government and diplomacy
Political system	Republic
Head of state	President Brig-Gen. Liamine Zeroual
Head of government	Ahmed Ouyahia
Embassy in UK	54 Holland Park, London W11 3RS. Tel: 0171-221 7800
British Embassy in Algiers	7 Chemin des Glycines, BP08, Alger-Gare 16000, Algiers. Tel: Algiers 692411
Trouble spots	Armed insurgency by Islamic militants; foreign expatriates a prime target

Defence
Military expenditure	4% of GDP (1996)
Military personnel	270,200: Army 107,000, Navy 7,000, Air Force 10,000, Paramilitaries 146,200
Conscription duration	18 months

Economy
GNP	US$43,726 million (1996) US$1,520 per capita (1996)
GDP	US$50,464 million (1994) US$563 per capita (1994)
Annual average growth of GDP	-5.3% (1982)
Inflation rate	32.2% (1995)
Unemployment	23.8% (1992)
Total external debt	US$33,260 million (1996)

Education

Enrolment (percentage of age group)	primary 95% (1995); secondary 56% (1995); tertiary 10.9% (1995)
Illiteracy rate	38.4%

AMERICAN SAMOA, see USA

ANDORRA

Area	175 sq. miles (453 sq. km)
Population	68,000 (1996)
Main languages	Catalan, French, Spanish
Capital	Andorra la Vella (population 16,151, 1986)
Currency	French and Spanish currencies in use
Public holidays	January 1, 6; February 23; March 14; April 9, 10, 13; May 1, 21; June 1, 24; August 15; September 8; November 1, 4; December 8, 24–26, 31
Usual business hours	Vary; banking hours: Mon.–Fri. 9–13, 15–17; Sat. 9–12
Electrical rating	Sockets 240v AC, 50Hz/Lights 125v AC

Demography

Population growth rate	5.1% (1995)
Population density	150 per sq. km (1995)
Urban population	95.6% (1991)

Government and diplomacy

Political system	Constitutional co-principality
Heads of state	The President of France and the Bishop of Urgel, Spain (co-princes)
Head of government	Marc Forné Molné
Delegation in UK	63 Westover Road, London SW18 2RF. Tel: 0181-874 4806
British Embassy	Madrid, Spain

Economy

GDP	US$781 million (1994) US$11,462 per capita (1994)

ANGOLA

Area	481,354 sq. miles (1,246,700 sq. km)
Population	11,072,000 (1994 UN estimate)
Main language	Portuguese
Capital	Luanda (population 475,328, 1970)
Currency	Readjusted kwanza (Kzrl) of 100 lwei
Exchange rate (at 29 May)	Kzrl 435605.3
Public holidays	January 1, 4; February 4, 24; March 8; April 10; May 1; June 1; September 17; November 11; December 25
Usual business hours	Mon.–Thurs. 7.30–12.30, 14.30–18.30; Fri. 7.30–12.30, 14.30–17.30
Electrical rating	220v AC, 60Hz (European plugs)

Demography

Life expectancy (years)	male 44.90; female 48.10
Population growth rate	2% (1995)
Population density	9 per sq. km (1995)

Government and diplomacy

Political system	Republic
Head of state and of government	President José Eduardo dos Santos
Embassy in UK	98 Park Lane, London W1Y 3TA. Tel: 0171-495 1752
British Embassy in Luanda	Rua Diogo Cão 4 (Caixa Postal 1244), Luanda. Tel: Luanda 334582/3
Trouble spots	Civil war between government and UNITA ended with peace agreement in 1994 but fighting resumed in 1997. Situation currently peaceful

Defence

Military expenditure	6.4% of GDP (1996)
Military personnel	126,000: Army 98,000, Navy 2,000, Air Force 11,000, Paramilitaries 15,000

Economy

GNP	US$2,972 million (1996)
	US$270 per capita (1996)
GDP	US$8,524 million (1994)
	US$384 per capita (1994)
Total external debt	US$10,612 million (1996)

Education

Enrolment (percentage of age group)	tertiary 0.7% (1991)

ANGUILLA

Area	37 sq. miles (96 sq. km)
Population	8,000 (1994 UN estimate)
Main language	English
Capital	The Valley (population 1,400, 1994)
Currency	East Caribbean dollar (EC$) of 100 cents
Exchange rate (at 29 May)	EC$ 4.4029
Usual business hours	Mon.–Fri. 8–12, 13–16
Electrical rating	110/220v AC, 60Hz

Demography

Population growth rate	2.7% (1995)
Population density	83 per sq. km (1995)

Government

Political system	UK Overseas Territory
Governor	Robert Harris

Economy

GDP	US$67 million (1994)
	US$9,933 per capita (1994)

ANTIGUA AND BARBUDA

Area	171 sq. miles (442 sq. km); Antigua 108 sq. miles (279 sq. km); Barbuda 62 sq.miles (160 sq. km)
Population	66,000 (1994 UN estimate)
Main language	English
Capital	St John's (population 22,342, 1991)
Currency	East Caribbean dollar (EC$) of 100 cents
Exchange rate (at 29 May)	EC$ 4.4029
Usual business hours	Mon.–Fri. 8–12, 13–16.30
Electrical rating	110/220v AC, 60Hz (US plugs); some hotels also have 240v AC outlets (European plugs)

Demography

Population growth rate	0.6% (1995)
Population density	149 per sq. km (1995)

Government and diplomacy

Political system	Constitutional monarchy
Head of state	Queen Elizabeth II
Governor-General	Sir James Carlisle

Head of government	Lester Bird
High Commission in UK	15 Thayer Street, London W1M 5LD. Tel: 0171-486 7073/5
British High Commission in St John's	11 Old Parham Road (PO 483), St John's. Tel: St John's 4620 008/9

Defence

Military expenditure	0.8% of GDP (1996)
Military personnel	150: Army 125, Navy 25

Economy

GNP	US$482 million (1996)
	US$7,330 per capita (1996)
GDP	US$377 million (1994)
	US$5,666 per capita (1994)
Annual average growth of GDP	3.4% (1993)
Inflation rate	1% (1985)

ARGENTINA

Area	1,073,518 sq. miles (2,780,400 sq. km)
Population	34,587,000 (1994 UN estimate)
Main language	Spanish
Capital	Buenos Aires (population 10,686,163, 1991)
Currency	Peso of 10,000 australes
Exchange rate (at 29 May)	Pesos 1.6299
Public holidays	January 1; April 9, 10; May 1, 25; June 8, 15, 20; July 9; August 17; October 12; December 8, 25, 31
Usual business hours	Mon.–Fri. 9–19
Electrical rating	220v AC, 60Hz

Demography

Life expectancy (years)	male 68.17; female 73.09
Population growth rate	1.2% (1995)
Population density	12 per sq. km (1995)

Government and diplomacy

Political system	Republic; federal state
Head of state and of government	President Carlos Menem
Embassy in UK	65 Brook Street, London W1Y 1YE. Tel: 0171-318 1300
British Embassy in Buenos Aires	Dr Luis Agote 2412, 1425 Buenos Aires. Tel: Buenos Aires 8037 070/1

Defence

Military expenditure	1.5% of GDP (1996)
Military personnel	104,240: Army 41,000, Navy 20,000, Air Force 12,000, Paramilitaries 31,240

Economy

GNP	US$295,131 million (1996)
	US$8,380 per capita (1996)
GDP	US$190,523 million (1994)
	US$8,248 per capita (1994)
Annual average growth of GDP	4.3% (1996)
Inflation rate	0.2% (1996)
Unemployment	18.8% (1995)
Total external debt	US$93,841 million (1996)

Education

Enrolment (percentage of age group)	primary 95% (1991); secondary 59% (1991); tertiary 35.8% (1994)
Illiteracy rate	3.8%

ARMENIA

Area	11,506 sq. miles (29,800 sq. km)
Population	3,762,000 (1994 UN estimate)
Main languages	Armenian, Russian
Capital	Yerevan (population 1,254,400, 1990)
Currency	Dram of 100 louma
Exchange rate (at 29 May)	Dram 819.231★
Public holidays	January 1, 2, 6; April 7, 24; May 9, 28; July 5; September 21; December 7, 31
Usual business hours	Banking hours: Mon.–Fri. 9.30–17.30
Electrical rating	220v AC, 50Hz

Demography

Life expectancy (years)	male 68.66; female 75.51
Population growth rate	1.2% (1995)
Population density	126 per sq. km (1995)
Urban population	68.5% (1992)

Government and diplomacy

Political system	Republic
Head of state	President Robert Kocharian
Head of government	Armen Darbinian
Embassy in UK	25A Cheniston Gardens, London W8 6TG. Tel: 0171-938 5415
British Embassy in Yerevan	28 Charents Street, Yerevan. Tel: Yerevan 151 841/2
Trouble spots	Armenia supported ethnic Armenians in Azeri region of Nagorny-Karabakh in war of 1992–4; cease-fire in place since 1994 but region unstable

Defence

Military expenditure	5.6% of GDP (1996)
Military personnel	59,600: Army 58,600, Paramilitaries 1,000
Conscription duration	18 months

Economy

GNP	US$2,387 million (1996)
	US$630 per capita (1996)
GDP	US$5,487 million (1994)
	US$117 per capita (1994)
Total external debt	US$552 million (1996)

Education

Enrolment (percentage of age group)	tertiary 41.8% (1990)
Illiteracy rate	0.4%

ARUBA, see NETHERLANDS

ASCENSION ISLAND, see ST HELENA

AUSTRALIA

Area	2,988,902 sq. miles (7,741,220 sq. km)
Population	18,054,000 (1996 estimate)
Main language	English
Capital	Canberra (population 307,100, 1996 estimate)
Currency	Australian dollar ($A) of 100 cents
Exchange rate (at 29 May)	$A 2.6035
Public holidays	January 1, 26; April 10, 13, 25; December 25, 26
Usual business hours	Mon.–Fri. 9–17.30
Electrical rating	240/250v AC, 50Hz (Australian 3-pin plugs; adaptor usually needed)

Demography

Life expectancy (years)	male 75.04; female 80.94
Population growth rate	1.1% (1995)
Population density	2 per sq. km (1995)
Urban population	85.4% (1986)

Government and diplomacy

Political system	Constitutional monarchy; federal state
Head of state	Queen Elizabeth II
Governor-General	Sir William Deane
Head of government	John Howard
High Commission in UK	Australia House, Strand, London WC2B 4LA. Tel: 0171-379 4334

| British High Commission in Canberra | Commonwealth Avenue, Yarralumla, Canberra, ACT 2600. Tel: Canberra 270 6666 |

Defence

Military expenditure	2.2% of GDP (1996)
Military personnel	57,400: Army 25,400, Navy 14,300, Air Force 17,700

Economy

GNP	US$367,802 million (1996)
	US$20,090 per capita (1996)
GDP	US$335,527 million (1994)
	US$18,561 per capita (1994)
Annual average growth of GDP	4% (1996)
Inflation rate	2.6% (1996)
Unemployment	8.5% (1995)

Education

Enrolment (percentage of age group)	primary 98% (1995); secondary 89% (1995); tertiary 71.7% (1995)

AUSTRIA

Area	32,378 sq. miles (83,859 sq. km)
Population	8,053,000
Main language	German
Capital	Vienna (population 1,806,737)
Currency	Schilling of 100 Groschen
Exchange rate (at 29 May)	Schilling 20.4569
Public holidays	January 1, 6; April 13; May 1, 21; June 1, 11; August 15; October 26; December 8, 24–26
Usual business hours	Mon.–Fri. 8–12.30, 13.30–17.30
Electrical rating	220v AC, 50Hz (European plugs)

Demography

Life expectancy (years)	male 73.34; female 79.73
Population growth rate	0.8% (1995)
Population density	96 per sq. km (1995)
Urban population	64.6% (1991)

Government and diplomacy

Political system	Republic; federal state
Head of state	President Dr Thomas Klestil
Head of government	Viktor Klima
Embassy in UK	18 Belgrave Mews West, London SW1X 8HU. Tel: 0171-235 3731
British Embassy in Vienna	Jaurèsgasse 12, 1030 Vienna. Tel: Vienna 716130

Defence

Military expenditure	0.9% of GDP (1996)
Military personnel	49,750: Army 45,500, Air Force 4,250
Conscription duration	Seven to eight months, plus refresher training

Economy

GNP	US$226,510 million (1996)
	US$28,110 per capita (1996)
GDP	US$170,558 million (1994)
	US$24,823 per capita (1994)
Annual average growth of GDP	1.8% (1995)
Inflation rate	1.8% (1996)
Unemployment	4.5% (1995)

Education

Enrolment (percentage of age group)	primary 100% (1994); secondary 90% (1994); tertiary 44.8% (1994)

AZERBAIJAN

Area	33,436 sq. miles (86,600 sq. km)
Population	7,499,000 (1996 estimate)
Main language	Azerbaijani
Capital	Baku (population 1,149,000, 1990)
Currency	Manat of 100 gopik
Exchange rate (at 29 May)	Manat 6441.26★
Public holidays	January 1, 30; March 8, 21; April 9; May 7, 9, 28; June 15; October 9, 18; November 17; December 31
Usual business hours	Banking hours: Mon.–Fri. 9.30–17.30
Electrical rating	220v AC, 50Hz

Demography

Life expectancy (years)	male 66.60; female 74.20
Population growth rate	0.9% (1995)
Population density	87 per sq. km (1995)
Urban population	54.2% (1989)

Government and diplomacy

Political system	Republic
Head of state	President Heydar Aliyev
Head of government	Artur Rasizade
Embassy in UK	4 Kensington Court, London W8 5DL. Tel: 0171-938 3412
British Embassy in Baku	2 Izmir Street, Baku 370065/ Tel: Baku 985558
Trouble spots	Following war of 1992–4, 20% of Azeri territory held by Nagorny-Karabakh (ethnic Armenian) forces

pursuing unification with Armenia; cease-fire in place since 1994 but region unstable

Defence

Military expenditure	5.3% of GDP (1996)
Military personnel	106,700: Army 53,300, Navy 2,200, Air Force 11,200, Paramilitaries 40,000
Conscription duration	17 months

Economy

GNP	US$3,642 million (1996)
	US$480 per capita (1996)
GDP	US$10,148 million (1994)
	US$176 per capita (1994)
Total external debt	US$435 million (1996)

Education

Enrolment (percentage of age group)	tertiary 19.8% (1993)
Illiteracy rate	0.4%

THE BAHAMAS

Area	5,358 sq. miles (13,878 sq. km)
Population	278,000 (1996 estimate)
Main language	English
Capital	Nassau (population 172,196, 1996 estimate)
Currency	Bahamian dollar (B$) of 100 cents
Exchange rate (at 29 May)	B$ 1.6307
Public holidays	January 1; April 10, 13; May 29; June 1, 5; July 10; August 3; October 12; December 25
Usual business hours	Mon.–Fri. 9–17
Electrical rating	120v AC, 60Hz

Demography

Life expectancy (years)	male 68.32; female 75.28
Population growth rate	1.7% (1995)
Population density	20 per sq. km (1995)
Urban population	83.5% (1990)

Government and diplomacy

Political system	Constitutional monarchy
Head of state	Queen Elizabeth II
Governor-General	Sir Orville Turnquest
Head of government	Hubert A. Ingraham
High Commission in UK	Bahamas House, 10 Chesterfield Street, London W1X 8AH. Tel: 0171-408 4488

British High Commission in Nassau	PO Box N-7516, Nassau. Tel: Nassau 325 7471

Defence

Military expenditure	0.5% of GDP (1996)
Military personnel	860 Navy

Economy

GNP	US$3,297 million (1995)
	US$11,940 per capita (1995)
GDP	US$3,229 million (1994)
	US$12,342 per capita (1994)
Annual average growth of GDP	4.9% (1987)
Inflation rate	1.4% (1994)
Unemployment	13.3% (1994)

Education

Enrolment (percentage of age group)	primary 95% (1993); secondary 87% (1993); tertiary 17.7% (1985)
Illiteracy rate	1.8%

BAHRAIN

Area	268 sq. miles (694 sq. km)
Population	586,000 (1994 UN estimate)
Main languages	Arabic, English
Capital	Manama (population 140,401, 1991 census)
Currency	Bahraini dinar (BD) of 1,000 fils
Exchange rate (at 29 May)	BD 0.6148
Public holidays	January 1, 30 (3 days); April 7 (3 days), 28; May 7 (2 days); July 6; December 16
Usual business hours	Sat.–Tues. 7–14.15; Wed. 7–14
Electrical rating	230v AC, single-phase and 400v AC, 50Hz/Awali 110v AC, 60Hz

Demography

Life expectancy (years)	male 66.83; female 69.43
Population growth rate	3.1% (1995)
Population density	844 per sq. km (1995)
Urban population	88.4% (1991)

Government and diplomacy

Political system	Constitutional monarchy
Head of state	Shaikh Isa bin Sulman Al-Khalifa (Amir)
Head of government	Shaikh Khalifa bin Salman Al-Khalifa
Embassy in UK	98 Gloucester Road, London SW7 4AU. Tel: 0171-370 5132
British Embassy in Manama	21 Government Avenue, Manama 306, PO Box 114. Tel: Manama 534404

Trouble spots	Bombing campaign by opponents of government

Defence

Military expenditure	5.6% of GDP (1996)
Military personnel	20,850: Army 8,500, Navy 1,000, Air Force 1,500, Paramilitaries 9,850

Economy

GNP	US$4,525 million (1995) US$7,840 per capita (1995)
GDP	US$4,455 million (1994) US$8,223 per capita (1994)
Annual average growth of GDP	2.2% (1995)
Inflation rate	-0.3% (1996)

Education

Enrolment (percentage of age group)	primary 100% (1995); secondary 85% (1994); tertiary 20.2% (1993)
Illiteracy rate	14.8%

BANGLADESH

Area	55,598 sq. miles (143,998 sq. km)
Population	120,433,000 (1994 UN estimate)
Main languages	Bengali, English
Capital	Dhaka (population 3,397,187, 1991 census)
Currency	Taka (Tk) of 100 poisha
Exchange rate (at 29 May)	Tk 75.5015
Public holidays	January 27, 30; February 21; March 26; April 7 (3 days), 14; May 1, 7, 10; July 1, 6; August 15; September 4; October 22; December 6, 16, 25, 31
Usual business hours	Sat.–Thurs. 8–14.30
Electrical rating	220/240v AC, 50Hz

Demography

Life expectancy (years)	male 56.91; female 55.97
Population growth rate	2.2% (1995)
Population density	836 per sq. km (1995)
Urban population	13.8% (1986)

Government and diplomacy

Political system	Republic
Head of state	President Shahabuddin Ahmed
Head of government	Sheikh Hasina Wajed
High Commission in UK	28 Queen's Gate, London SW7 5JA. Tel: 0171-584 0081
British High Commission in Dhaka	United Nations Road, Baridhara Dhaka. PO Box 6079, Dhaka-12. Tel: Dhaka 882705

Defence

Military expenditure	1.7% of GDP (1996)
Military personnel	170,700: Army 101,000, Navy 10,500, Air Force 9,500, Paramilitaries 49,700

Economy

GNP	US$31,217 million (1996) US$260 per capita (1996)
GDP	US$28,734 million (1994) US$234 per capita (1994)
Annual average growth of GDP	5.3% (1996)
Inflation rate	2.7% (1996)
Total external debt	US$16,083 million (1996)

Education

Enrolment (percentage of age group)	primary 62% (1990); secondary 20% (1990); tertiary 4.4% (1990)
Illiteracy rate	61.9%

BARBADOS

Area	166 sq. miles (430 sq. km)
Population	264,000 (1994 UN estimate)
Main language	English
Capital	Bridgetown (population 108,000, 1990)
Currency	Barbados dollar (BD$) of 100 cents
Exchange rate (at 29 May)	BD$ 3.2798
Public holidays	January 1, 21; April 10, 13; May 1; June 1; August 1, 3; October 5; November 30; December 25, 26
Usual business hours	Mon.–Fri. 8–16
Electrical rating	110v AC, 50Hz (US plugs)

Demography

Life expectancy (years)	male 67.15; female 72.46
Population growth rate	0.5% (1995)
Population density	614 per sq. km (1995)

Government and diplomacy

Political system	Constitutional monarchy
Head of state	Queen Elizabeth II
Governor-General	Sir Clifford Husbands
Head of government	Owen Arthur
High Commission in UK	1 Great Russell Street, London WC1B 3JY. Tel: 0171-631 4975
British High Commission in Bridgetown	Lower Collymore Rock, PO Box 676, Bridgetown C. Tel: Bridgetown 436 6694

Defence

Military expenditure	0.7% of GDP (1996)

Military personnel	610: Army 500, Navy 110

Economy

GNP	US$1,745 million (1995)
	US$6,560 per capita (1995)
GDP	US$1,641 million (1994)
	US$6,505 per capita (1994)
Annual average growth of GDP	2.7% (1995)
Inflation rate	2.4% (1996)
Unemployment	19.7% (1995)
Total external debt	US$581 million (1996)

Education

Enrolment (percentage of age group)	primary 78% (1991); secondary 75% (1989); tertiary 28.1% (1994)
Illiteracy rate	2.6%

BELARUS

Area	80,155 sq. miles (207,600 sq. km)
Population	10,141,000 (1995 official estimate)
Main languages	Belarusian, Russian
Capital	Minsk (population 1,687,400, 1993 estimate)
Currency	Rouble of 100 kopeks
Exchange rate (at 29 May)	Roubles 108441.5★
Public holidays	January 1, 7; March 8, 15; April 13, 20, 28; May 1, 9; July 3; November 2, 7; December 25
Usual business hours	Mon.–Fri. 9–18
Electrical rating	220v, 50Hz

Demography

Life expectancy (years)	male 63.75; female 74.43
Population growth rate	-0.2% (1995)
Population density	49 per sq. km (1995)
Urban population	68.1% (1993)

Government and diplomacy

Political system	Republic
Head of state	President Aleksandr Lukashenko
Head of government	Syargei Ling
Embassy in UK	6 Kensington Court, London W8 5DL. Tel: 0171-937 3288
British Embassy in Minsk	37 Karl Marx Street, Minsk 220030. Tel: Minsk 292303/4/5

Defence

Military expenditure	4.2% of GDP (1996)
Military personnel	80,500: Army 50,500, Air Force 22,000, Paramilitaries 8,000
Conscription duration	18 months

Economy
GNP	US$22,452 million (1996)
	US$2,070 per capita (1996)
GDP	US$40,342 million (1994)
	US$517 per capita (1994)
Inflation rate	52.7% (1996)
Unemployment	2.7% (1995)
Total external debt	US$1,071 million (1996)

Education
Enrolment (percentage of age group)	primary 95% (1994); tertiary 42.6% (1995)
Illiteracy rate	0.5%

BELGIUM

Area	11,783 sq. miles (30,519 sq. km)
Population	10,113,000 (1994 UN estimate)
Main languages	Flemish (Dutch), French
Capital	Brussels (population 960,324, 1991 estimate)
Currency	Belgian franc (or frank) of 100 centimes (centiemen)
Exchange rate (at 29 May)	Francs 59.9193
Public holidays	January 1; April 13; May 1, 21, 22; June 1; July 11, 21; August 15, 17; September 27; November 1, 2, 11; December 25
Usual business hours	Mon.–Fri. 8.30–17.30
Electrical rating	220v AC, 50Hz (2-pin plugs)

Demography
Life expectancy (years)	male 72.43; female 79.13
Population growth rate	0.3% (1995)
Population density	331 per sq. km (1995)

Government and diplomacy
Political system	Constitutional monarchy; federal state
Head of state	King Albert II
Head of government	Jean-Luc Dehaene
Embassy in UK	103–105 Eaton Square, London SW1W 9AB. Tel: 0171-470 3700
British Embassy in Brussels	Rue d'Arlon 85, 1040 Brussels. Tel: Brussels 287 6211

Defence
Military expenditure	1.6% of GDP (1996)
Military personnel	43,200: Army 28,500, Navy 2,700, Air Force 12,000

Economy
GNP	US$268,633 million (1996)
	US$26,440 per capita (1996)

GDP	US$201,125 million (1994)
	US$21,765 per capita (1994)
Annual average growth	2.2% (1994)
of GDP	
Inflation rate	2.1% (1996)
Unemployment	9.3% (1995)

Education

Enrolment (percentage	primary 98% (1993); secondary
of age group)	98% (1993); tertiary 49.1% (1993)

BELIZE

Area	8,763 sq. miles (22,696 sq. km)
Population	217,000 (1994 UN estimate)
Main languages	English, Spanish, Creole
Capital	Belmopan (population 44,087, 1991)
Currency	Belize dollar (BZ$) of 100 cents
Exchange rate (at 29 May)	BZ$ 3.2614
Public holidays	January 1; March 9; April 10, 11, 13; May 1, 24; September 10, 21; October 12; November 19; December 25, 26
Usual business hours	Mon.–Thurs. 8–12, 13–17; Fri. 8–12, 13–16.30
Electrical rating	110v AC, 60Hz (US plugs)

Demography

Life expectancy (years)	male 69.95; female 74.07
Population growth rate	2.7% (1995)
Population density	10 per sq. km (1995)
Urban population	47.5% (1994)

Government and diplomacy

Political system	Constitutional monarchy
Head of state	Queen Elizabeth II
Governor-General	Sir Colville Norbert Young
Head of government	Manuel Esquivel
High Commission in UK	22 Harcourt House, 19 Cavendish Square, London W1M 9AD. Tel: 0171-499 9728
British High Commission in Belmopan	PO Box 91, Belmopan. Tel: Belmopan 22146/7

Defence

Military expenditure	2.4% of GDP (1996)
Military personnel	1,000 Army

Economy

GNP	US$600 million (1996)
	US$2,700 per capita (1996)

GDP	US$422 million (1994)
	US$2,630 per capita (1994)
Annual average growth of GDP	1.4% (1996)
Inflation rate	6.4% (1996)
Unemployment	11.1% (1994)
Total external debt	US$288 million (1996)

Education

Enrolment (percentage of age group)	primary 99% (1994); secondary 36% (1992)

BENIN

Area	43,484 sq. miles (112,622 sq. km)
Population	5,561,000 (1994 UN estimate)
Main language	French
Capital	Porto Novo (population 179,138, 1992)
Currency	Franc CFA of 100 centimes
Exchange rate (at 29 May)	Francs 975.610
Public holidays	January 1, 10, 30; April 7, 13; May 1, 21; June 1; July 6; August 1, 15; November 1; December 25
Usual business hours	Mon.–Fri. 8–12.30, 15–18.30
Electrical rating	220v AC, 50Hz

Demography

Life expectancy (years)	male 45.92; female 49.29
Population growth rate	3.2% (1995)
Population density	49 per sq. km (1995)
Urban population	35.7% (1992)

Government and diplomacy

Political system	Republic
Head of state	President Mathieu Kérékou
Head of government	Adrien Houngbedji
Embassy	87 rue du Cherche Midi, 75006 Paris, France. Tel: Paris 4222 3191
Honorary Consulate in UK	Dolphin House, 16 The Broadway, Stanmore, Middx HA7 4DW. Tel: 0181-954 8800
British Embassy	Lagos, Nigeria

Defence

Military expenditure	1.2% of GDP (1996)
Military personnel	7,300: Army 4,500, Navy 150, Air Force 150, Paramilitaries 2,500
Conscription duration	18 months

Economy

GNP	US$1,998 million (1996)
	US$350 per capita (1996)

GDP	US$2,032 million (1994)
	US$278 per capita (1994)
Annual average growth of GDP	6% (1995)
Inflation rate	4.8% (1996)
Total external debt	US$1,594 million (1996)

Education

Enrolment (percentage of age group)	primary 59% (1995); tertiary 2.6% (1995)
Illiteracy rate	63%

BERMUDA

Area	20 sq. miles (53 sq. km)
Population	63,000 (1994 UN estimate)
Main language	English
Capital	Hamilton (population 2,277, 1994)
Currency	Bermuda dollar of 100 cents
Exchange rate (at 29 May)	$1.6307
Public holidays	January 1; April 10; May 25; June 15; July 30, 31; September 7; November 11; December 25, 26
Usual business hours	Mon.–Fri. 9–17
Electrical rating	110v AC, 60Hz (US plugs)

Demography

Life expectancy (years)	male 70.23; female 78.01
Population growth rate	0.8% (1995)
Population density	1,189 per sq. km (1995)

Government

Political system	UK Overseas Territory
Governor	Thorold Masefield

Economy

GDP	US$1,684 million (1994)
	US$29,859 per capita (1994)

BHUTAN

Area	18,147 sq. miles (47,000 sq. km)
Population	1,638,000 (1994 UN estimate)
Main languages	Dzongkha, English
Capital	Thimphu (population 15,000, 1987 estimate)
Currency	Ngultrum of 100 chetrum (Indian currency is also legal tender)
Exchange rate (at 29 May)	Ngultrum 67.9594
Public holidays	January 1, 30 (3 days); April 6, 7 (4 days), 28; June 25, 26; July 6, 26, 27; September 24; November 3, 11, 12, 20
Electrical rating	220v AC, 50Hz

Demography

Life expectancy (years)	male 49.10; female 52.40
Population growth rate	1.2% (1995)
Population density	35 per sq. km (1995)

Government and diplomacy

Political system	Absolute monarchy; no political parties permitted
Head of state and of government	King Jigme Singye Wangchuk
Diplomatic representation	Diplomatic affairs conducted by Indian government
British High Commission	New Delhi, India
Trouble spots	Unrest in south by ethnic Nepalis protesting at measures discriminating against Nepalis

Economy

GNP	US$282 million (1996) US$390 per capita (1996)
GDP	US$345 million (1994) US$163 per capita (1994)
Annual average growth of GDP	6.4% (1996)
Inflation rate	8.4% (1995)
Total external debt	US$87 million (1996)

Education

Illiteracy rate	57.8%

BOLIVIA

Area	424,165 sq. miles (1,098,581 sq.km)
Population	7,414,000 (1994 UN estimate)
Main languages	Spanish, Quechua, Aymará
Capital	La Paz (population 784,976, 1993 estimate)
Currency	Boliviano ($b) of 100 centavos
Exchange rate (at 29 May)	$b 8.9852
Public holidays	January 1; February 23, 24; April 10; May 1; June 11; August 6; November 1, 2; December 25
Usual business hours	Mon.–Fri. 8.30–12, 14.30–18.30; some Sats. 9–12
Electrical rating	110/220v AC in La Paz; 220v AC, 50Hz elsewhere (2-pin plugs)

Demography

Life expectancy (years)	male 57.74; female 61
Population growth rate	2.4% (1995)
Population density	7 per sq. km (1995)
Urban population	57.5% (1992)

Government and diplomacy

Political system	Republic
Head of state and of government	President Hugo Bánzer Suárez
Embassy in UK	106 Eaton Square, London SW1W 9AD. Tel: 0171-235 2257/4248
British Embassy in La Paz	Avenida Arce 2732, (Casilla 694) La Paz. Tel: La Paz 357424

Defence

Military expenditure	2% of GDP (1996)
Military personnel	70,600: Army 25,000, Navy 4,500, Air Force 4,000, Paramilitaries 37,100
Conscription duration	12 months

Economy

GNP	US$6,302 million (1996) US$830 per capita (1996)
GDP	US$6,229 million (1994) US$867 per capita (1994)
Annual average growth of GDP	4.4% (1995)
Inflation rate	12.4% (1996)
Unemployment	3.6% (1995)
Total external debt	US$5,174 million (1996)

Education

Enrolment (percentage of age group)	primary 91% (1990); secondary 29% (1990); tertiary 22.2% (1990)
Illiteracy rate	16.9%

BOSNIA-HERCEGOVINA

Area	19,741 sq. miles (51,129 sq. km)
Population	4,484,000 (1994 UN estimate)
Main languages	Serbo-Croat, Croato-Serb
Capital	Sarajevo (population 415,631)
Currency	Convertible marka
Public holidays	January 1; March 1; May 1; November 25
Electrical rating	220v AC, 50Hz

Demography

Life expectancy (years)	male 69.55; female 75.11
Population growth rate	0% (1995)
Population density	88 per sq. km (1995)
Urban population	39.6% (1991)

Government and diplomacy

Political system	Republic with presidency rotating among triumvirate; federal state of Federation of Bosnia-Hercegovina and Republika Srpska (Serb)
Heads of state (for all Bosnia)	Alija Izetbegovic (Bosnian); Momcilo Krajisnik (Serb); Kresimir Zubak (Croat)
Heads of government (for all Bosnia)	Haris Silajdzic (Bosnian); Boro Bosic (Serb)
Embassy in UK	4th Floor, Morley House, 314–322 Regent Street, London W1R 5AB. Tel: 0171-255 3758
British Embassy in Sarajevo	8 Tina Ujevica, Sarajevo. Tel: Sarajevo 663922
Trouble spots	Tension between Muslims and Serbs in many areas

Defence

Military expenditure	6.25% of GDP (1996)
Military personnel	Bosnian Muslim Army (BiH): 40,000; Croat Defence Council (HVO): 16,000; Bosnian Serb Army: 30,000

Economy

GDP	US$7,768 million (1994) U$1,307 per capita (1994)

BOTSWANA

Area	224,607 sq. miles (581,730 sq. km)
Population	1,456,000 (1994 UN estimate)
Main languages	Setswana, English
Capital	Gaborone (population 133,468, 1991)
Currency	Pula (P) of 100 thebe
Exchange rate (at 29 May)	P 6.4334
Public holidays	January 1, 2; April 10, 11, 13; May1, 21; July 1, 20, 21; September 30; December 25, 26
Usual business hours	Oct–April 7.30–16.30; April–Oct 8–17
Electrical rating	220–240v AC, 50Hz

Demography

Life expectancy (years)	male 52.32; female 59.70
Population growth rate	2.3% (1995)
Population density	3 per sq. km (1995)
Urban population	48.1% (1995)

Government and diplomacy

Political system	Republic
Head of state and of government	President Festus Mogae
High Commission in UK	6 Stratford Place, London W1N 9AE. Tel: 0171-499 0031
British High Commission in Gaborone	Private Bag 0023, Gaborone. Tel: Gaborone 352841/2/3

Defence

Military expenditure	5.2% of GDP (1996)
Military personnel	8,500: Army 7,000, Air Wing 500, Paramilitaries 1,000

Economy

GNP	US$4,381 million (1995) US$3,020 per capita (1995)
GDP	US$3,959 million (1994) US$2,666 per capita (1994)
Annual average growth of GDP	7% (1996)
Inflation rate	10.1% (1996)
Total external debt	US$613 million (1996)

Education

Enrolment (percentage of age group)	primary 96% (1994); secondary 45% (1994); tertiary 4.1% (1994)
Illiteracy rate	30.2%

BRAZIL

Area	3,300,171 sq. miles (8,547,403 sq. km)
Population	155,822,000 (1994 UN estimate)
Main language	Portuguese
Capital	Brasilia (population 1,601,094, 1994)
Currency	Real of 100 centavos
Exchange rate (at 29 May)	Real 1.8756
Public holidays	January 1; February 23–25; April 9–11, 21; May 1; June 11; September 7; October 12; November 1, 2, 15; December 24, 25, 31
Usual business hours	Mon.–Fri. 9–18
Electrical rating	Bahia and Manaus 127v AC; Brasilia and Recife 220v AC, 60Hz; Rio de Janeiro and São Paulo 110/220v AC, 60Hz (2-pin plugs)

Demography
Life expectancy (years)	male 63.81; female 70.38
Population growth rate	1.5% (1995)
Population density	18 per sq. km (1995)
Urban population	75.6% (1991)

Government and diplomacy
Political system	Republic; federal state
Head of state and of government	President Fernando Cardoso
Embassy in UK	32 Green Street, London W1Y 4AT. Tel: 0171-499 0877
British Embassy in Brasilia	Sector de Embaixadus Sul, Quadra 801, Conjunto K, CEP 70.408 Brasilia DF. Tel: Brasilia 225 2710

Defence
Military expenditure	2.8% of GDP (1996)
Military personnel	314,700: Army 200,000, Navy 64,700, Air Force 50,000
Conscription duration	12 months (can be extended to 18)

Economy
GNP	US$709,591 million (1996) US$4,400 per capita (1996)
GDP	US$523,392 million (1994) US$3,786 per capita (1994)
Annual average growth of GDP	4.1% (1995)
Inflation rate	18.2% (1996)
Unemployment	6.2% (1993)
Total external debt	US$179,047 million (1996)

Education

Enrolment (percentage of age group)	primary 90% (1994); secondary 19% (1994); tertiary 11.3% (1994)
Illiteracy rate	16.7%

BRITISH VIRGIN ISLANDS

Area	58 sq. miles (151 sq. km)
Population	19,107 (1994 UN estimate)
Main language	English
Capital	Road Town (population 3,983, 1994)
Currency	US dollar (US$) (£ sterling and EC$ also circulate)
Exchange rate (at 29 May)	US$ 1.6307
Usual business hours	Mon.–Fri. 9–17
Electrical rating	110/60v AC, 60Hz (US plugs)

Demography

Population growth rate	3.4% (1995)
Population density	126 per sq. km (1995)

Government

Political system	UK Overseas Territory
Governor	Frank Savage

Economy

GDP	US$171 million (1994) US$10,730 per capita (1994)

BRUNEI

Area	2,226 sq. miles (5,765 sq. km)
Population	285,000 (1996 estimate)
Main languages	Malay, English
Capital	Bandar Seri Begawan (population 49,902, 1994)
Currency	Brunei dollar (B$) of 100 sen (fully interchangeable with Singapore currency)
Exchange rate (at 29 May)	$ 2.7298
Public holidays	January 1, 30 (2 days); April 7, 10, 13, 26; May 1; July 6, 7; September 8; December 9, 25, 26
Usual business hours	Mon.–Thurs. 7.45–12.15, 13.30–16.30; Sat. 9–12
Electrical rating	220/240v AC, 50Hz (3-pin plugs)

Demography

Life expectancy (years)	male 70.13; female 72.69
Population growth rate	2.4% (1995)
Population density	49 per sq. km (1995)
Urban population	66.6% (1991)

Government and diplomacy

Political system	Absolute monarchy
Head of state and of government	Sultan Haji Hassanal Bolkiah Mu'izzaddin Waddaullah
Embassy in UK	19–20 Belgrave Square, London SW1X 8PG. Tel: 0171-581 0521
British High Commission in Bandar Seri Begawan	2/01 2nd Floor Block D, Kompleks Bangunan Yayasan, Sultan Haji Hassanal Bolkiah, Jalan Pretty, PO Box 2197 Bandar Seri Begawan. Tel: Bandar Seri Begawan 222231

Defence

Military expenditure	6.5% of GDP (1996)
Military personnel	9,050: Army 3,900, Navy 700, Air Force 400, Paramilitaries 4,050

Economy

GNP	US$3,975 million (1994)
	US$14,240 per capita (1994)
GDP	US$3,731 million (1994)
	US$16,270 per capita (1994)

Education

Enrolment (percentage of age group)	primary 91% (1994); secondary 68% (1994); tertiary 6.6% (1994)
Illiteracy rate	11.8%

BULGARIA

Area	42,823 sq. miles (110,912 sq. km)
Population	8,402,000 (1994 UN estimate)
Main language	Bulgarian
Capital	Sofia (population 1,188,563, 1992 estimate)
Currency	Lev of 100 stotinki
Exchange rate (at 29 May)	Leva 2892.78
Public holidays	January 1, 2; March 3; April 17, 20; May 1, 24; December 24–26
Usual business hours	Mon.–Fri. 8–18
Electrical rating	220v AC, 50Hz (2-pin plugs)

Demography

Life expectancy (years)	male 67.71; female 74.72
Population growth rate	-1.4% (1995)
Population density	76 per sq. km (1995)
Urban population	67.4% (1993)

Government and diplomacy

Political system	Republic
Head of state	President Petar Stoyanov
Head of government	Ivan Kostov
Embassy in UK	186–188 Queen's Gate, London SW7 5HL. Tel: 0171-584 9400/9433
British Embassy in Sofia	38 Boulevard Vassil Levski, Sofia. Tel: Sofia 492 3361/2

Defence

Military expenditure	3.3% of GDP (1996)
Military personnel	109,800: Army 50,400, Navy 6,100, Air Force 19,300, Paramilitaries 34,000
Conscription duration	18 months

Economy

GNP	US$9,924 million (1996) US$1,190 per capita (1996)
GDP	US$16,985 million (1994) US$1,106 per capita (1994)
Unemployment	11.1% (1995)
Total external debt	US$9,819 million (1996)

Education

Enrolment (percentage of age group)	primary 97% (1995); secondary 75% (1995); tertiary 39.4% (1995)
Illiteracy rate	1.7%

BURKINA FASO

Area	105,792 sq. miles (274,000 sq. km)
Population	10,200,000 (1994 UN estimate)
Main language	French
Capital	Ouagadougou (population 634,479, 1991 estimate)
Currency	Franc CFA
Exchange rate (at 29 May)	Francs 975.610
Public holidays	January 1, 3, 30; March 8; April 7, 13; May 1, 21; July 6; August 4, 5, 15; October 15; November 1; December 11, 25
Usual business hours	Mon.–Fri. 7–12.30, 15–17.30
Electrical rating	220v AC, 50Hz (2-pin plugs)

Demography

Life expectancy (years)	male 45.84; female 49.01
Population growth rate	2.5% (1995)
Population density	37 per sq. km (1995)
Urban population	15% (1995)

Government and diplomacy

Political system	Republic; regime seized power 1987
Head of state	President Blaise Compaoré
Head of government	Kadré Désiré Ouedraogo
Embassy	16 Place Guy d'Arezzo, 1060 Brussels, Belgium. Tel: Brussels 345 9912
Honorary Consulate in UK	5 Cinnamon Row, Plantation Wharf, London SW11 3TW. Tel: 0171-738 1800
British Embassy	Abidjan, Côte d'Ivoire

Defence

Military expenditure	2% of GDP (1996)
Military personnel	10,000: Army 5,600, Air Force 200, Paramilitaries 4,200

Economy

GNP	US$2,410 million (1996) US$230 per capita (1996)
GDP	US$2,798 million (1994) US$186 per capita (1994)
Annual average growth of GDP	2.7% (1992)
Inflation rate	6.2% (1996)
Total external debt	US$1,294 million (1996)

Education

Enrolment (percentage of age group)	primary 31% (1994); secondary 7% (1993); tertiary 1.1% (1994)
Illiteracy rate	80.8%

BURUNDI

Area	10,747 sq. miles (27,834 sq. km)
Population	5,982,000 (1994 UN estimate)
Main languages	Kirundi, French, Kiswahili
Capital	Bujumbura (population 235,440, 1994)
Currency	Burundi franc of 100 centimes
Exchange rate (at 29 May)	Francs 661.045
Public holidays	January 1; February 5; May 1, 21; July 1; August 15; October 13, 21; November 1; December 25
Usual business hours	Mon.–Fri. 7.30–12, 14–17.30
Electrical rating	220v AC, 50Hz

Demography

Life expectancy (years)	male 48.42; female 51.92
Population growth rate	1.8% (1995)
Population density	215 per sq. km (1995)
Urban population	5% (1990)

Government and diplomacy

Political system	Republic; military regime
Head of state	President Maj. Pierre Buyoya
Head of government	Pascal Firmin Ndimira
Embassy	Square Marie Louise 46, 1040 Brussels, Belgium. Tel: Brussels 230 4535
British Embassy	Kigali, Rwanda
Trouble spots	Ethnic conflict between Hutus and Tutsis

Defence

Military expenditure	4.8% of GDP (1996)
Military personnel	22,000: Army 18,500, Paramilitaries 3,500

Economy

GNP	US$1,066 million (1996) US$170 per capita (1996)
GDP	US$1,264 million (1994) US$172 per capita (1994)
Annual average growth of GDP	2.3% (1992)
Inflation rate	26.4% (1996)
Total external debt	US$1,127 million (1996)

Education

Enrolment (percentage of age group)	primary 52% (1992); secondary 5% (1992); tertiary 0.9% (1992)
Illiteracy rate	64.7%

CAMBODIA

Area	69,898 sq. miles (181,035 sq. km)
Population	9,836,000 (1997 estimate)
Main languages	Khmer, Chinese, Vietnamese, French
Capital	Phnom Penh (population 832,000, 1997)
Currency	Riel of 100 sen
Exchange rate (at 29 May)	Riel 6547.26
Usual business hours	Mon.–Fri. 7–11.30, 14–17.30
Electrical rating	220v AC, 50Hz; outside Phnom Penh power only available 18.30–21.30

Demography

Life expectancy (years)	male 50.10; female 52.90
Population growth rate	2.8% (1995)
Population density	54 per sq. km (1995)
Urban population	12.6% (1990)

Government and diplomacy

Political system	Constitutional monarchy; one-party government since 1997 coup
Head of state	King Norodom Sihanouk
Heads of government	Ing Huot, Hun Sen (election due 26 July 1998)
British Embassy in Phnom Penh	29, Street 75, Phnom Penh. Tel: Phnom Penh 427124
Trouble spots	Khmer Rouge guerrillas control 5% of territory in north; fighting continues on northern border with Thailand

Defence

Military expenditure	3.9% of GDP (1996)
Military personnel	140,500: Army 84,000, Navy 5,000, Air Force 1,500, Provincial Forces 50,000

Economy

GNP	US$3,088 million (1996) US$300 per capita (1996)
GDP	US$1,036 million (1994) US$422 per capita (1994)
Inflation rate	10.1% (1996)
Total external debt	US$2,111 million (1996)

Education

Enrolment (percentage of age group)	tertiary 1.6% (1994)
Illiteracy rate	34.7%

CAMEROON

Area	183,569 sq. miles (475,442 sq. km)
Population	13,277,000 (1994 UN estimate)
Main languages	French, English
Capital	Yaoundé (population 653,670, 1986 estimate)
Currency	Franc CFA of 100 centimes
Exchange rate (at 29 May)	Francs 975.610
Public holidays	January 1, 30; February 11; April 7, 10; May 1, 20, 21; August 15; December 25
Usual business hours	Banking hours: Mon.–Fri. 7.30–15.30
Electrical rating	220v AC, 50Hz

Demography

Life expectancy (years)	male 54.50; female 57.50
Population growth rate	2.8% (1995)
Population density	28 per sq. km (1995)

Government and diplomacy

Political system	Republic
Head of state and of government	President Paul Biya
Embassy in UK	84 Holland Park, London W11 3SB. Tel: 0171-727 0771/3
British High Commission in Yaoundé	Avenue Winston Churchill, BP 547 Yaoundé. Tel: Yaoundé 220545
Trouble spots	Conflict in north-west because of border dispute with Nigeria

Defence

Military expenditure	2.4% of GDP (1996)
Military personnel	22,100: Army 11,500, Navy 1,300, Air Force 300, Paramilitaries 9,000

Economy

GNP	US$8,356 million (1996) US$610 per capita (1996)
GDP	US$10,481 million (1994) US$526 per capita (1994)
Annual average growth of GDP	2.1% (1990)
Inflation rate	4.5% (1996)
Total external debt	US$9,515 million (1996)

Education

Enrolment (percentage of age group)	secondary 15% (1980); tertiary 3.3% (1990)
Illiteracy rate	36.6%

CANADA

Area	3,849,674 sq. miles (9,970,610 sq. km)
Population	29,606,000 (1994 UN estimate)
Main languages	English, French
Capital	Ottawa (population 1,010,288, 1992 estimate)
Currency	Canadian dollar (C$) of 100 cents
Exchange rate (at 29 May)	C$ 2.3726
Public holidays	January 1; April 10, 13; May 18; July 1; September 7; October 12; November 11; December 25, 26, 28
Usual business hours	Mon.–Fri. 9–17
Electrical rating	110v AC, 60Hz (US plugs)

Demography

Life expectancy (years)	male 73.02; female 79.79
Population growth rate	2.2% (1995)
Population density	3 per sq. km (1995)
Urban population	76.6% (1991)

Government and diplomacy

Political system	Constitutional monarchy; federal state
Head of state	Queen Elizabeth II
Governor-General	Roméo Le Blanc
Head of government	Jean Chrétien
High Commission in UK	Macdonald House, 1 Grosvenor Street, London W1X 0AB. Tel: 0171-258 6600
British High Commission in Ottawa	80 Elgin Street, Ottawa K1P 5K7. Tel: Ottawa 237 1530

Defence

Military expenditure	1.5% of GDP (1996)
Military personnel	57,000: Army 21,900, Navy 9,400, Air Force 14,600, Other 11,100

Economy

GNP	US$569,899 million (1996) US$19,020 per capita (1996)
GDP	US$599,578 million (1994) US$18,635 per capita (1994)
Annual average growth of GDP	1.5% (1996)
Inflation rate	1.6% (1996)
Unemployment	9.5% (1995)

Education

Enrolment (percentage of age group)	primary 95% (1994); secondary 92% (1994); tertiary 102.9% (1993)

CAPE VERDE

Area	1,557 sq. miles (4,033 sq. km)
Population	392,000 (1995 estimate)
Main languages	Portuguese, Creole
Capital	Praia (population 80,000, 1995 estimate)
Currency	Escudo Caboverdiano of 100 centavos
Exchange rate (at 29 May)	Esc 163.241
Public holidays	January 1, 20; May 1, 19; August 15; November 1; December 24, 25
Usual business hours	Mon.–Fri. 8–12.30, 14.30–18
Electrical rating	220v AC, 50Hz

Demography

Life expectancy (years)	male 63.53; female 71.33
Population growth rate	2.8% (1995)
Population density	97 per sq. km (1995)
Urban population	44.1% (1990)

Government and diplomacy

Political system	Republic
Head of state	President António Mascarenhas Monteiro
Head of government	Carlos Veiga
Embassy	44 Koninginnegracht, 2514 AD, The Hague, The Netherlands. Tel: The Hague 346 9623
Honorary Consulate in UK	43 Upper Grosvenor Street, London W1X 9PG. Tel: 0171-493 4840
British Embassy	Dakar, Senegal

Defence

Military expenditure	1.7% of GDP (1996)
Military personnel	1,100: Army 1,000, Air Force 100

Economy

GNP	US$393 million (1996) US$1,010 per capita (1996)
GDP	US$382 million (1994) US$900 per capita (1994)
Total external debt	US$211 million (1996)

Education

Enrolment (percentage of age group)	primary 100% (1993); secondary 22% (1993)
Illiteracy rate	28.4%

CAYMAN ISLANDS

Area	102 sq. miles (264 sq. km)
Population	35,000 (1994 UN estimate)
Main language	English
Capital	George Town (population 20,000, 1994)
Currency	Cayman Islands dollar (CI$) of 100 cents
Exchange rate (at 29 May)	CI$ 1.3506
Public holidays	January 1; February 25; April 10, 13; May 18; June 16; July 6; November 9; December 25, 26, 28
Usual business hours	Mon.–Fri. 9–17
Electrical rating	110v AC, 60Hz (US plugs)

Demography

Population growth rate	3.3% (1995)
Population density	117 per sq. km (1995)

Government

Political system	UK Overseas Territory
Governor	John W. Owen
Cayman Islands Office in UK	6 Arlington Street, London SW1A 1RE. Tel: 0171-491 7772

Economy

GDP	US$536 million (1994)
	US$19,351 per capita (1994)

CENTRAL AFRICAN REPUBLIC

Area	240,535 sq. miles (622,984 sq. km)
Population	3,315,000 (1994 UN estimate)
Main languages	French, Sango
Capital	Bangui (population 473,817, 1984 estimate)
Currency	Franc CFA of 100 centimes
Exchange rate (at 29 May)	Francs 975.610
Public holidays	January 1; March 29; April 13; May 1, 21; June 1; August 13, 15; November 1; December 1, 25
Usual business hours	Mon.–Fri. 6.30–13.30; Sat. 7–12
Electrical rating	220/380v AC, 50Hz

Demography

Life expectancy (years)	male 46.87; female 51.88
Population growth rate	2.5% (1995)
Population density	5 per sq. km (1995)

Government and diplomacy

Political system	Republic
Head of state	President Ange-Felix Patasse
Head of government	Michel Gbezera-Bria
Embassy	30 rue des Perchamps, 75016 Paris, France. Tel: Paris 4224 4256
British Embassy	Yaoundé, Cameroon
Trouble spots	Army divided between northerners loyal to President Patasse and southerners loyal to ex-President Kolingba; frequent outbursts of fighting in Bangui; situation deteriorating elsewhere

Defence

Military expenditure	2.7% of GDP (1996)
Military personnel	4,950: Army 2,500, Air Force 150, Paramilitaries 2,300
Conscription duration	Two years

Economy

GNP	US$1,024 million (1996)
	US$310 per capita (1996)
GDP	US$1,642 million (1994)
	US$313 per capita (1994)
Inflation rate	19.2% (1995)
Total external debt	US$928 million (1996)

Education

Enrolment (percentage of age group)	primary 54% (1990); tertiary 1.4% (1991)
Illiteracy rate	40%

CHAD

Area	495,755 sq. miles (1,284,000 sq. km)
Population	6,361,000 (1994 UN estimate)
Main languages	French, Arabic, Sara
Capital	N'Djaména (population 179,000, 1972 estimate)
Currency	Franc CFA of 100 centimes
Exchange rate (at 29 May)	Francs 975.610
Public holidays	January 1, 30; April 7, 13; May 1, 25; July 6; August 11; November 1, 28; December 1, 25
Usual business hours	Mon.–Sat. 7–15.30; Fri. 7–12
Electrical rating	220/380v AC, 50Hz

Demography

Life expectancy (years)	male 45.93; female 49.12
Population growth rate	2.2% (1995)
Population density	5 per sq. km (1995)
Urban population	21.7% (1993)

Government and diplomacy

Political system	Republic
Head of state	President Idriss Déby
Head of government	Nassour Owaido Guelendouksia
Embassy	Boulevard Lambermont 52, 1030 Brussels, Belgium. Tel: Brussels 215 1975
British Embassy	Abuja, Nigeria

Defence

Military expenditure	3.8% of GDP (1996)
Military personnel	29,850: Army 25,000, Air Force 350, Paramilitaries 4,500

Economy

GNP	US$1,035 million (1996)
	US$160 per capita (1996)
GDP	US$1,535 million (1994)
	US$162 per capita (1994)
Annual average growth of GDP	-5.6% (1987)
Inflation rate	9.1% (1995)
Total external debt	US$997 million (1996)

Education

Enrolment (percentage of age group)	tertiary 0.8% (1994)
Illiteracy rate	51.9%

CHILE

Area	292,135 sq. miles (756,626 sq. km)
Population	14,210,000 (1994 UN estimate)
Main language	Spanish
Capital	Santiago (population 5,257,937)
Currency	Chilean peso of 100 centavos
Exchange rate (at 29 May)	Pesos 741.887
Public holidays	January 1; April 10, 11; May 1, 21; June 11, 29; August 15; September 11, 18, 19; October 12; November 1; December 8, 25, 31
Usual business hours	Mon.–Fri. 9–18.30
Electrical rating	220v AC, 50Hz (3-pin plugs)

Demography

Life expectancy (years)	male 71.83; female 77.77
Population growth rate	1.6% (1995)
Population density	19 per sq. km (1995)
Urban population	84.5% (1995)

Government and diplomacy

Political system	Republic
Head of state and of government	President Eduardo Frei Ruiz-Tagle
Embassy in UK	12 Devonshire Street, London W1N 2DS. Tel: 0171-580 6392
British Embassy in Santiago	Avenida El Bosque Norte 0125, Casilla 72-D, Santiago 9. Tel: Santiago 231 3737

Defence

Military expenditure	3.4% of GDP (1996)
Military personnel	125,500: Army 51,000, Navy 29,800, Air Force 13,500, Paramilitaries 31,200
Conscription duration	12–22 months

Economy

GNP	US$70,060 million (1996) US$4,860 per capita (1996)
GDP	US$39,365 million (1994) US$3,685 per capita (1994)
Annual average growth of GDP	7.2% (1996)
Inflation rate	7.4% (1996)
Unemployment	4.7% (1995)
Total external debt	US$27,411 million (1996)

Education

Enrolment (percentage of age group)	primary 86% (1995); secondary 55% (1995); tertiary 30.3% (1996)
Illiteracy rate	4.8%

CHINA

Area	3,705,408 sq. miles (9,596,961 sq. km).
Population	1,221,462,000 (1994 UN estimate)
Main languages	Mandarin Chinese, Cantonese, Fukienese, Xiamenhua, Hakka
Capital	Beijing (Peking) (population 7,362,426, 1990)
Currency	Renminbi Yuan of 10 jiao or 100 fen
Exchange rate (at 29 May)	Yuan 13.5011
Public holidays	January 1, 2, 28; May 1, 2; October 1, 2
Usual business hours	Mon.–Fri. 8–11.30, 13–17
Electrical rating	220/240v AC, 50Hz (mainly 2-pin plugs)

Demography

Life expectancy (years)	male 66.70; female 70.45
Population growth rate	1.1% (1995)
Population density	127 per sq. km (1995)
Urban population	26.2% (1990)

Government and diplomacy

Political system	Republic; one-party (Communist) state
Head of state	President Jiang Zemin
Head of government	Zhu Rongji
Embassy in UK	49–51 Portland Place, London W1N 4JL. Tel: 0171-636 0288/5726
British Embassy in Beijing	11 Guang Hua Lu, Jian Guo Men Wai, Beijing 100 600. Tel: Beijing 6532 1961/4

Defence

Military expenditure	6.2% of GDP (1996)
Military personnel	3,640,000: Army 2,090,000, Navy 280,000, Air Force 470,000, Paramilitaries 800,000
Conscription duration	Three to four years

Economy

GNP	US$906,079 million (1996) US$750 per capita (1996)
GDP	US$613,617 million (1994) US$440 per capita (1994)
Annual average growth of GDP	10.5% (1995)
Inflation rate	8.3% (1996)
Unemployment	2.8% (1994)
Total external debt	US$128,817 million (1996)

Education

Enrolment (percentage of age group)	primary 99% (1995); tertiary 5.7% (1996)
Illiteracy rate	18.5%

HONG KONG

Area	415 sq. miles (1,075 sq. km)
Population	6,190,000 (1996)
Main languages	Chinese, English
Currency	Hong Kong dollar (HK$) of 100 cents
Exchange rate (at 29 May)	HK$ 12.6363
Public holidays	January 1, 28; April 6, 10, 11, 13; May 30; July 1; August 17; October 1, 2, 6, 28; December 25, 26
Usual business hours	Mon.–Fri. 9–13, 14–17; Sat. 9–13; some Chinese offices open before 9 and close later than 17
Electrical rating	220v AC, 50Hz

Demography

Life expectancy (years)	male 75.84; female 81.16
Population growth rate	1.6% (1995)
Population density	5,758 per sq. km (1995)
Urban population	93.1% (1986)

Government and diplomacy

Political system	Special Administrative Region of the People's Republic of China
Chief Executive	Tung Chee-hwa
Hong Kong Office in UK	6 Grafton Street, London W1X 3LB. Tel: 0171-499 9821
British Consulate in Hong Kong	1 Supreme Court Road, Central, (PO Box 528), Hong Kong. Tel: Hong Kong 2901 3000

Economy

GNP	US$153,288 million (1996) US$24,290 per capita (1996)
GDP	US$93,223 million (1994) US$22,590 per capita (1994)
Inflation rate	6% (1996)
Unemployment	3.2% (1995)

Education

Enrolment (percentage of age group)	primary 91% (1995); secondary 71% (1995); tertiary 21.9% (1993)
Illiteracy rate	7.8%

COLOMBIA

Area	439,737 sq. miles (1,138,914 sq. km)
Population	35,099,000 (1994 UN estimate)
Main language	Spanish
Capital	Bogotá (population 8,000,000, 1992)
Currency	Colombian peso of 100 centavos
Exchange rate (at 29 May)	Pesos 2279.07
Public holidays	January 1, 12; February 25; March 23; April 9–11; May 1, 25; June 15, 22, 29; July 20; August 7, 17; October 12; November 2, 16; December 8, 25
Usual business hours	Mon.–Fri. 8–12, 14–17
Electrical rating	110/120v AC, 60Hz (US plugs common)

Demography

Life expectancy (years)	male 66.36; female 72.26
Population growth rate	1.7% (1995)
Population density	31 per sq. km (1995)
Urban population	67.2% (1985)

Government and diplomacy

Political system	Republic
Head of state and of government	President Andres Pastrana
Embassy in UK	Flat 3A, 3 Hans Crescent, London SW1X 0LR. Tel: 0171-589 9177/5037
British Embassy in Bogotá	Edificio Ing Barings, Carrera 9 No 76-49 Piso 9, Bogotá. Tel: Bogotá 218 5111
Trouble spots	Terrorism by left-wing guerrillas; violence by drugs cartels; opportunistic kidnappings

Defence

Military expenditure	2.2% of GDP (1996)
Military personnel	146,300: Army 121,000, Navy 18,000, Air Force 7,300
Conscription duration	12–18 months

Economy

GNP	US$80,174 million (1996) US$2,140 per capita (1996)
GDP	US$46,145 million (1994) US$1,847 per capita (1994)
Annual average growth of GDP	2.1% (1996)
Inflation rate	20.2% (1996)
Total external debt	US$28,859 million (1996)

Education

Enrolment (percentage of age group)	primary 85% (1995); secondary 50% (1995); tertiary 17.2% (1995)
Illiteracy rate	8.7%

THE COMOROS

Area	863 sq. miles (2,235 sq. km)
Population	653,000 (1994 UN estimate)
Main languages	French, Arabic, Comoran
Capital	Moroni (population 17,267, 1980)
Currency	Comorian franc (KMF) of 100 centimes
Exchange rate (at 29 May)	Francs 731.246
Usual business hours	Mon.–Thurs. 7.30–14.30; Fri. 7.30–11
Electrical rating	220v AC, 50Hz

Demography

Life expectancy (years)	male 55.50; female 56.50
Population growth rate	3.7% (1995)
Population density	292 per sq. km (1995)
Urban population	28.5% (1991)

Government and diplomacy

Political system	Republic; federal state
Head of state	President Mohammad Taki Abdoulkarim
Head of government	Nourdine Bourhane
British Embassy	Antananarivo, Madagascar

Economy

GNP	US$228million (1996)
	US$450 per capita (1996)
GDP	US$259 million (1994)
	US$301 per capita (1994)
Total external debt	US$206 million (1996)

Education

Enrolment (percentage of age group)	primary 53% (1993); tertiary 0.6% (1995)
Illiteracy rate	42.7%

DEMOCRATIC REPUBLIC OF CONGO

Area	905,355 sq. miles (2,344,858 sq.km)
Population	43,901,000 (1994 UN estimate)
Main languages	Swahili, Lingala, French
Capital	Kinshasa (population 2,664,309, 1985)
Currency	Congolese franc
Exchange rate (at 29 May)	Zaïre 216883
Public holidays	January 1, 4 ; May 1; June 24, 30; August 1; October 14, 27; November 17; December 25
Usual business hours	Mon.–Fri. 7.30–15; Sat. 7.30–12
Electrical rating	220v AC, 50Hz

Demography

Life expectancy (years)	male 50.40; female 53.66
Population growth rate	4.2% (1995)
Population density	19 per sq. km (1995)
Urban population	39.5% (1985)

Government and diplomacy

Political system	Republic; new constitution to be drafted following 1997 civil war
Head of state and government	President Laurent Kabila
Embassy in UK	26 Chesham Place, London SW1X 8HH. Tel: 0171-235 6137
British Embassy in Kinshasa	Avenue des Trois 'Z', Gombe, Kinshasa. Tel: Kinshasa 34775
Trouble spots	Situation still fragile after 1997 civil war; armed clashes continue, especially in east Secession in southern region of Shaba (Katanga) since 1993. Ethnic tension between Katangans and Kasais

Defence

Military expenditure	2.8% of GDP (1996)
Military personnel	20,000–40,000: Army being reorganized following change of government

Economy

GNP	US$5,727 million (1996) US$130 per capita (1996)
GDP	US$9,642 million (1994) at current prices US$227 per capita (1994)
Annual average growth of GDP	-10.5% (1992)
Inflation rate	658.8% (1996)
Total external debt	US$12,826 million (1996)

Education

Enrolment (percentage of age group)	primary 61% (1994); secondary 23% (1994); tertiary 2.3% (1994)
Illiteracy rate	22.7%

REPUBLIC OF THE CONGO

Area	132,047 sq. miles (342,000 sq. km)
Population	2,590,000 (1994 UN estimate)
Main languages	French, Lingala, Kikongo
Capital	Brazzaville (population 596,200, 1984)
Currency	Franc CFA of 100 centimes
Exchange rate (at 29 May)	Francs 975.610
Public holidays	January 1, 4; May 1; June 30; November 2; December 25
Usual business hours	Usually Mon.–Fri. 7–14; Sat. 7–12
Electrical rating	220v AC, 50Hz

Demography

Life expectancy (years)	male 48.91; female 53.77
Population growth rate	3% (1995)
Population density	8 per sq. km (1995)

Government and diplomacy

Political system	Republic
Head of state and de facto head of government	President Denis Sassou-Nguesso
Embassy	37 bis Rue Paul Valéry, 75116 Paris, France. Tel: Paris 4500 6057
Honorary Consulate in UK	Alliance House, 12 Caxton Street, London SW1H OQS. Tel: 0171-222 7575
British Embassy	Kinshasa, Democratic Republic of Congo
Trouble spots	Civil war since 1997

Defence

Military expenditure	2.3% of GDP (1996)
Military personnel	12,000: Army 8,000, Navy 800, Air Force 1,200, Paramilitaries 2,000

Economy

GNP	US$1,813 million (1996) US$670 per capita (1996)
GDP	US$2,832 million (1994) US$860 per capita (1994)
Annual average growth of GDP	1.8% (1989)
Inflation rate	21.4% (1995)
Total external debt	US$5,240 million (1996)

Education

Enrolment (percentage of age group)	primary 96% (1980); tertiary 5.3% (1990)
Illiteracy rate	25.1%

COSTA RICA

Area	19,730 sq. miles (51,100 sq. km)
Population	3,333,000 (1994 UN estimate)
Main language	Spanish
Capital	San José (population 1,186,417, 1994 estimate)
Currency	Costa Rican colón (₡) of 100 céntimos
Exchange rate (at 29 May)	₡ 414.287
Public holidays	January 1; April 9–11; May 1; July 25; August 2, 15; September 15; October 12; December 25, 29–31
Usual business hours	Mon.–Fri. 8–12, 14–16
Electrical rating	110/220v AC, 60Hz (2-pin plugs)

Demography

Life expectancy (years)	male 72.89; female 77.60
Population growth rate	3.5% (1995)
Population density	65 per sq. km (1995)
Urban population	44% (1994)

Government and diplomacy

Political system	Republic
Head of state and of government	President Miguel Angel Rodríguez
Embassy in UK	Flat 1, 14 Lancaster Gate, London W2 3LH. Tel: 0171-706 8844
British Embassy in San José	Apartado 815, Edificio Centro Colón (11th Floor), San José 1007. Tel: San José 221 5566

Defence

Military expenditure	0.5% of GDP (1996)
Military personnel	7,000 Paramilitaries

Economy

GNP	US$9,081 million (1996) US$2,640 per capita (1996)
GDP	US$6,996 million (1994) US$2,463 per capita (1994)
Annual average growth of GDP	-0.7% (1996)
Inflation rate	17.5% (1996)
Unemployment	5.2% (1995)
Total external debt	US$3,454 million (1996)

Education

Enrolment (percentage of age group)	primary 92% (1995); secondary 43% (1995); tertiary 31.9% (1994)
Illiteracy rate	5.2%

CÔTE D'IVOIRE

Area	124,504 sq. miles (322,463 sq. km)
Population	14,230,000 (1994 estimate)
Main language	French
Capital	Yamoussoukro (population 126,191, 1988)
Currency	Franc CFA of 100 centimes
Exchange rate (at 29 May)	Francs 975.610
Public holidays	January 30 (2 days); April 7 (2 days); May 1, 21; June 1; July 6; August 7, 15; November 1, 15; December 7, 25
Usual business hours	Mon.–Fri. 7.30–12, 14.30–18; Sat. 8–12
Electrical rating	220v AC, 50Hz (2-pin plugs)

Demography

Life expectancy (years)	male 49.69; female 52.38
Population growth rate	3.9% (1995)
Population density	44 per sq. km (1995)
Urban population	45.6% (1993)

Government and diplomacy

Political system	Republic
Head of state	President Henri Konan-Bédié
Head of government	Daniel Kablan Duncan
Embassy in UK	2 Upper Belgrave Street, London SW1X 8BJ. Tel: 0171-235 6991
British Embassy in Abidjan	Immeuble Les Harmonies, 01 BP 2581, Abidjan 01. Tel: Abidjan 226850

Defence

Military expenditure	0.9% of GDP (1996)
Military personnel	15,400: Army 6,800, Navy 900, Air Force 700, Paramilitaries 7,000
Conscription duration	Six months

Economy

GNP	US$9,434 million (1996)
	US$660 per capita (1996)
GDP	US$11,645 million (1994)
	US$544 per capita (1994)
Inflation rate	2.5% (1996)
Total external debt	US$19,713 million (1996)

Education

Enrolment (percentage of age group)	primary 47% (1990); tertiary 4.4% (1993)
Illiteracy rate	59.9%

CROATIA

Area	34,022 sq. miles (88,117 sq. km)
Population	4,495,000 (1994 UN estimate)
Main languages	Croato-Serb, Serbo-Croat
Capital	Zagreb (population 867,717, 1991)
Currency	Kuna of 100 lipas
Exchange rate (at 29 May)	Kuna 10.5640
Public holidays	January 1, 6; April 13; May 1, 30; June 22; August 5, 15; November 1; December 25, 26
Usual business hours	Mon.–Fri. 8–16
Electrical rating	220v AC, 50Hz

Demography

Life expectancy (years)	male 68.29; female 75.63
Population growth rate	-1.2% (1995)
Population density	51 per sq. km (1995)
Urban population	54.3% (1991)

Government and diplomacy

Political system	Republic
Head of state	President Franjo Tudjman
Head of government	Zlatko Matesa
Embassy in UK	21 Conway Street, London W1P 5HL. Tel: 0171-387 2022
British Embassy in Zagreb	Vlaska 121/III Floor, PO Box 454, 4100 Zagreb. Tel: Zagreb 455 5310

Defence

Military expenditure	6.9% of GDP (1996)
Military personnel	98,000: Army 50,000, Navy 3,000, Air Force 5,000, Paramilitaries 40,000
Conscription duration	Ten months

Economy

GNP	US$18,130 million (1996)
	US$3,800 per capita (1996)
GDP	US$16,915 million (1994)
	US$3,867 per capita (1994)
Inflation rate	4.3% (1996)
Total external debt	US$4,634 million (1996)
Unemployment	16.8% (1993)

Education

Enrolment (percentage of age group)	primary 82% (1994); secondary 66% (1994); tertiary 28.3% (1995)
Illiteracy rate	2.4%

CUBA

Area	42,804 sq. miles (110,861 sq. km)
Population	11,041,000 (1994 estimate)
Main language	Spanish
Capital	Havana (population 2,175,888, 1992 estimate)
Currency	Cuban peso of 100 centavos
Exchange rate (at 29 May)	Pesos 37.5061
Public holidays	January 1, 28; February 24; March 13, 28; April 16, 19; May 1, 17; July 25, 30; August 12; October 8, 10, 28; November 27; December 2, 7
Usual business hours	Mon.–Fri. 8.30–12.30, 13.30–16.30
Electrical rating	110/120v AC, 60Hz (mainly US plugs)

Demography

Life expectancy (years)	male 72.89; female 76.80
Population growth rate	0.8% (1995)
Population density	100 per sq. km (1995)
Urban population	74.4% (1993)

Government and diplomacy

Political system	Republic; one-party (Communist) state
Head of state and of government	President Fidel Castro Ruz
Embassy in UK	167 High Holborn, London WC1V 6PA. Tel: 0171-240 2488
British Embassy in Havana	e7 ma Y 17, Miramar, Havana. Tel: Havana 33 1771

Defence

Military expenditure	5.4% of GDP (1996)
Military personnel	72,000: Army 38,000, Navy 5,000, Air Force 10,000, Paramilitaries 19,000
Conscription duration	Two years

Economy

GDP	US$14,131 million (1994) US$1,627 per capita (1994)

Education

Enrolment (percentage of age group)	primary 99% (1995); secondary 59% (1993); tertiary 12.7% (1995)
Illiteracy rate	4.3%

CYPRUS

Area	3,572 sq. miles (9,251 sq. km)
Population	742,000 (1994 estimate)
Main languages	Greek, Turkish
Capital	Nicosia (Lefkosia) (population in the government-controlled area 188,800)
Currency	Cyprus pound (C£) of 100 cents
Exchange rate (at 29 May)	C£ 0.8559
Public holidays	January 1, 6; March 2, 25; April 1, 17, 20, 21; May 1; June 8; August 15; October 1, 28; December 25, 26
Usual business hours	Summer: Mon.–Fri. 8–13, 16–19; winter: Mon.–Fri. 8–13, 15–18. All offices closed half-day Wed.
Electrical rating	240v AC, 50Hz

Demography

Life expectancy (years)	male 74.64; female 79.05
Population growth rate	1.7% (1995)
Population density	80 per sq. km (1995)
Urban population	67.7% (1992)

Government and diplomacy

Political system	Republic
Head of state and of government	President Glafcos Clerides
High Commission in UK	93 Park Street, London W1Y 4ET. Tel: 0171-499 8272
British High Commission in Nicosia	Alexander Pallis Street (PO Box 1978), Nicosia. Tel: Nicosia 2-473131
Trouble spots	Cyprus divided between largely Greek Cypriot and Turkish Cypriot communities; northern third of island is self-declared 'Turkish Republic of Northern Cyprus'

Defence

Military expenditure	5% of GDP (1996)
Military personnel	10,000 National Guard
Conscription duration	26 months

Economy

GDP	US$6,620 million (1994) US$9,754 per capita (1994)
Annual average growth of GDP	5% (1995)
Inflation rate	3% (1996)
Unemployment	2.6% (1995)

Education

Enrolment (percentage) *of age group*	primary 96% (1995); secondary 93% (1995); tertiary 20% (1995)

CZECH REPUBLIC

Area	30,450 sq. miles (78,864 sq. km)
Population	10,331,000 (1994 estimate)
Main language	Czech
Capital	Prague (population 1,216,568, 1994 estimate)
Currency	Koruna (Kčs) of 100 haléřu
Exchange rate (at 29 May)	Kčs 53.7601
Public holidays	January 1; April 13; May 1, 8; July 5, 6; October 28; December 24–26
Usual business hours	Mon.–Fri. 8–16
Electrical rating	Mainly 220v AC, 50Hz

Demography

Life expectancy (years)	male 69.53; female 76.55
Population growth rate	-0.1% (1995)
Population density	131 per sq. km (1995)
Urban population	74.7% (1993)

Government and diplomacy

Political system	Republic
Head of state	President Václav Havel
Head of government	Milos Zeman
Embassy in UK	26–30 Kensington Palace Gardens, London W8 4QY. Tel: 0171-243 1115
British Embassy in Prague	Thunovská 14, 11800 Prague 1. Tel: Prague 10439

Defence

Military expenditure	1.9% of GDP (1996)
Military personnel	49,600: Army 27,000, Air Force 17,000, Paramilitaries 5,600
Conscription duration	12 months

Economy

GNP	US$48,861 million (1996) US$4,740 per capita (1996)
GDP	US$25,777 million (1994) US$3,498 per capita (1994)
Annual average growth *of GDP*	4.4% (1996)
Inflation rate	8.8% (1996)
Unemployment	3.4% (1995)
Total external debt	US$20,094 million (1996)

Education

Enrolment (percentage of age group)	primary 98% (1994); secondary 88% (1994); tertiary 20.8% (1994)

DENMARK

Area	16,639 sq. miles (43,094 sq. km)
Population	5,228,000 (1996 estimate)
Main language	Danish
Capital	Copenhagen (population 1,353,333, 1996 estimate)
Currency	Danish krone of 100 øre
Exchange rate (at 29 May)	Kroner 11.0753
Public holidays	January 1; April 9, 10, 13; May 8, 21; June 1, 5; December 24–26
Usual business hours	Mon.–Fri. 8 or 9–16 or 17
Electrical rating	220v AC, 50Hz

Demography

Life expectancy (years)	male 72.49; female 77.76
Population growth rate	0.3% (1995)
Population density	121 per sq. km (1995)

Government and diplomacy

Political system	Constitutional monarchy
Head of state	Queen Margrethe II
Head of government	Poul Nyrup Rasmussen
Embassy in UK	55 Sloane Street, London SW1X 9SR. Tel: 0171-333 0200
British Embassy in Copenhagen	36–40 Kastelsvej, DK-2100 Copenhagen. Tel: Copenhagen 3526 4600

Defence

Military expenditure	1.7% of GDP (1996)
Military personnel	32,900: Army 19,000, Navy 6,000, Air Force 7,900
Conscription duration	Four to 12 months

Economy

GNP	US$168,917 million (1996) US$32,100 per capita (1996)
GDP	US$139,826 million (1994) US$ 28,245 per capita (1994)
Annual average growth of GDP	2.4% (1996)
Inflation rate	2.1% (1996)
Unemployment	7% (1995)

Education

Enrolment (percentage of age group)	primary 99% (1994); secondary 86% (1994); tertiary 45% (1994)

FARÖE ISLANDS

Area	540 sq. miles (1,399 sq. km)
Population	47,000 (1996 estimate)
Main language	Danish
Capital	Tórshavn (population 16,218, 1996 estimate)
Currency	Currency is that of Denmark

Demography

Life expectancy (years)	male 73.30; female 79.60
Population growth rate	-0.2% (1995)
Population density	34 per sq. km (1995)

Government

Political system	Self-government
Head of government	Edmund Joensen

GREENLAND

Area	840,004 sq. miles (2,175,600 sq. km)
Population	58,000 (1996 estimate)
Main language	Danish
Capital	Godthåb (population 12,483, 1996 estimate)
Currency	Currency is that of Denmark
Usual business hours	Mon.–Fri. 9–15
Electrical rating	220v AC, 50Hz

Demography

Life expectancy (years)	male 60.40; female 66.30
Population growth rate	0.8% (1995)
Urban population	80.6% (1994)

Government

Political system	Self-government
Head of government	Jonathan Motzfeldt

DJIBOUTI

Area	8,958 sq. miles (23,200 sq. km)
Population	577,000 (1994 estimate)
Main languages	Arabic, French
Capital	Djibouti (population 340,700, 1991)
Currency	Djibouti franc of 100 centimes
Exchange rate (at 29 May)	Francs 289.808
Public holidays	January 1, 30 (2 days); April 7 (2 days), 12, 28; May 1; June 27; July 6; November 17; December 25
Usual business hours	Sat.–Thurs. 6.20–13
Electrical rating	220v AC, 50Hz

Demography

Life expectancy (years)	male 46.72; female 50
Population growth rate	2.2% (1995)
Population density	25 per sq. km (1995)

Government and diplomacy

Political system	Republic
Head of state	President Hassan Gouled Aptidon
Head of government	Barkat Gourad Hamadou
Embassy	26 rue Emile Ménier, 75116 Paris, France. Tel: Paris 4727 4922
British Consulate in Djibouti	PO Box 81, 9–11 Rue de Geneve, Djibouti
Trouble spots	Rebel attacks in north
	Affected by border conflict between Eritrea and Ethiopia since June 1998

Defence

Military expenditure	5.1% of GDP (1996)
Military personnel	11,400: Army 8,000, Navy 200, Air Force 200, Paramilitaries 3,000

Economy

GDP	US$493 million (1994)
	US$926 per capita (1994)
Total external debt	US$241 million (1996)

Education

Enrolment (percentage of age group)	primary 32% (1995); secondary 11% (1985); tertiary 0.2% (1995)
Illiteracy rate	53.8%

DOMINICA

Area	290 sq. miles (751 sq. km)
Population	71,000 (1994 UN estimate)
Main languages	English, Creole
Capital	Roseau (population 16,243, 1991)
Currency	East Caribbean dollar (EC$) of 100 cents
Exchange rate (at 29 May)	EC$ 4.4029
Public holidays	January 1; February 24; April 10, 13; May 1; June 1; August 3; November 4, 5; December 25, 26
Usual business hours	Government offices: Mon. 8–13, 14–17; Tues.–Fri. 8–13, 14–16
Electrical rating	220/240v AC, 50Hz

Demography
Population growth rate	-0.1% (1995)
Population density	95 per sq. km (1995)

Government and diplomacy
Political system	Republic
Head of state	President Crispin Sorhaindo
Head of government	Edison James
High Commission in UK	1 Collingham Gardens, London SW5 0HW. Tel: 0171-370 5194/5
British Consulate in Roseau	PO Box 6, Roseau

Economy
GNP	US$228 million (1996)
	US$3,090 per capita (1996)
GDP	US$204 million (1994)
	US$2,902 per capita (1994)
Annual average growth of GDP	1.8% (1993)
Inflation rate	1.7% (1996)
Total external debt	US$111 million (1996)

DOMINICAN REPUBLIC

Area	18,816 sq. miles (48,734 sq. km)
Population	7,915,000 (1994 UN estimate)
Main language	Spanish
Capital	Santo Domingo (population 2,134,779, 1981)
Currency	Dominican Republic peso (RD$) of 100 centavos
Exchange rate (at 29 May)	RD$ 24.3790
Public holidays	January 1, 6, 21, 26; February 27; April 10; May 1, 16; June 11; August 16; September 24; December 25
Usual business hours	Mon.–Fri. 8.30–12, 14–18
Electrical rating	110v AC, 60Hz (US plugs)

Demography

Life expectancy (years)	male 67.63; female 71.69
Population growth rate	2% (1995)
Population density	162 per sq. km (1995)
Urban population	61.7% (1995)

Government and diplomacy

Political system	Republic
Head of state and of government	President Leonel Fernández
Embassy in UK	139 Inverness Terrace, London W2. Tel: 0171-727 6285
British Embassy in Santo Domingo	Edificio Corominas Pepin, Ave 27 de Fabrero No 233, Santo Domingo. Tel: Santo Domingo 472 7671/7373

Defence

Military expenditure	1.1% of GDP (1996)
Military personnel	39,500: Army 15,000, Navy 4,000, Air Force 5,500, Paramilitaries 15,000

Economy

GNP	US$12,765 million (1996) US$1,600 per capita (1996)
GDP	US$8,892 million (1994) US$1,347 per capita (1994)
Annual average growth of GDP	7.3% (1996)
Inflation rate	12.5% (1995)
Total external debt	US$4,310 million (1996)

Education

Enrolment (percentage of age group)	primary 81% (1994); secondary 22% (1994); tertiary 18% (1985)
Illiteracy rate	17.9%

ECUADOR

Area	109,484 sq. miles (283,561 sq. km)
Population	11,460,000 (1994 estimate)
Main languages	Spanish, Quechua
Capital	Quito (population 1,387,887, 1991 estimate)
Currency	Sucre of 100 centavos
Exchange rate (at 29 May)	Sucres 8539.15★
Public holidays	January 1; April 10; May 1; August 10; October 9; November 2, 3; December 25
Usual business hours	Banking hours: Mon.–Fri. 9–13.30, 14.30–18.30
Electrical rating	110/120v AC, 60Hz

Demography

Life expectancy (years)	male 67.32; female 72.49
Population growth rate	2.2% (1995)
Population density	40 per sq. km (1995)
Urban population	59.2% (1995)

Government and diplomacy

Political system	Republic
Head of state and of government	President Jamil Mahaud
Embassy in UK	Flat 3B, 3 Hans Crescent, London SW1X 0LS. Tel: 0171-584 1367
British Embassy in Quito	Av. González Suárez, 111 (Casilla 314), Quito. Tel: Quito 560670

Defence

Military expenditure	2.8% of GDP (1996)
Military personnel	57,370: Army 50,000, Navy 4,100, Air Force 3,000, Paramilitaries 270
Conscription duration	12 months

Economy

GNP	US$17,531 million (1996) US$1,500 per capita (1996)
GDP	US$12,322 million (1994) US$1,597 per capita (1994)
Annual average growth of GDP	2.9% (1996)
Inflation rate	24.4% (1996)
Unemployment	7.1% (1994)
Total external debt	US$14,491 million (1996)

Education

Enrolment (percentage of age group)	primary 92% (1994); tertiary 20% (1990)
Illiteracy rate	9.9%

EGYPT

Area	386,662 sq. miles (1,001,449 sq. km)
Population	59,226,000 (1995 estimate)
Main language	Arabic
Capital	Cairo (population 13,000,000, 1994 estimate)
Currency	Egyptian pound (£E) of 100 piastres or 1,000 millièmes
Exchange rate (at 29 May)	£E 5.5627
Public holidays	January 7, 30 (2 days); April 6, 7 (2 days), 19, 20 (2 days), 25, 28; May 1; July 1, 6, 23; October 6
Usual business hours	Banking hours: Sun.–Thurs. 8.30–15
Electrical rating	Mainly 220v AC, 50Hz

Demography

Life expectancy (years)	male 62.86; female 66.39
Population growth rate	2.1% (1995)
Population density	59 per sq. km (1995)
Urban population	44% (1994)

Government and diplomacy

Political system	Republic
Head of state	President Muhammad Hosni Mubarak
Head of government	Ahmed Kamal el-Ganzouri
Embassy in UK	12 Curzon Street, London W1Y 7FJ. Tel: 0171-499 2401
British Embassy in Cairo	Ahmed Ragheb Street, Garden City, Cairo. Tel: Cairo 354 0850
Trouble spots	Attacks by Muslim fundamentalists, mainly in Upper Egypt and Cairo

Defence

Military expenditure	3.5% of GDP (1996)
Military personnel	680,000: Army 320,000, Navy 20,000, Air Force 30,000, Air Defence Command 80,000, Paramilitaries 230,000
Conscription duration	Three years

Economy

GNP	US$64,275 million (1996) US$1,080 per capita (1996)
GDP	US$48,691 million (1994) US$760 per capita (1994)
Annual average growth of GDP	5.1% (1996)
Inflation rate	7.2% (1996)
Unemployment	11% (1994)
Total external debt	US$31,407 million (1996)

Education

Enrolment (percentage of age group)	primary 89% (1993); secondary 65% (1993); tertiary 18.1% (1994)
Illiteracy rate	48.6%

EL SALVADOR, see SALVADOR

EQUATORIAL GUINEA

Area	10,831 sq. miles (28,051 sq. km)
Population	400,000 (1994 estimate)
Main languages	French, Spanish
Capital	Malabo (population 30,418, 1983 estimate)
Currency	Franc CFA of 100 centimes
Exchange rate (at 29 May)	Francs 975.610
Public holidays	January 1; April 10; May 1; June 5, 11; July 25; August 3, 15; October 12; November 17; December 10, 25
Usual business hours	Banking hours: Mon.–Sat. 8–12
Electrical rating	220/240v AC

Demography

Life expectancy (years)	male 44.86; female 47.78
Population growth rate	2.8% (1995)
Population density	14 per sq. km (1995)
Urban population	37% (1991)

Government and diplomacy

Political system	Republic
Head of state	President Brig.-Gen. Teodoro Obiang Nguema Mbasogo
Head of government	Angel Serafin Seriche Dougan
Embassy	6 rue Alfred de Vigny, 75008 Paris, France. Tel: Paris 4766 4433
British Embassy	Yaoundé, Cameroon

Defence

Military expenditure	1.1% of GDP (1996)
Military personnel	1,320: Army 1,100, Navy 120, Air Force 100

Economy

GNP	US$217million (1996) US$530 per capita (1996)
GDP	US$174 million (1994) US$342 per capita (1994)
Inflation rate	4% (1993)
Total external debt	US$282 million (1996)

Education

Illiteracy rate	21.5%

ERITREA

Area	45,406 sq. miles (117,600 sq. km)
Population	3,531,000 (1994 estimate)
Main languages	English, Arabic
Capital	Asmara (population 358,100, 1990 estimate)
Currency	Nakfa
Usual business hours	Mon.–Fri. 8–12, 14–17; Sat. 8–12
Electrical rating	110/220v AC

Demography

Life expectancy (years)	male 48.85; female 52.06
Population growth rate	2.7% (1995)
Population density	30 per sq. km (1995)

Government and diplomacy

Political system	Republic
Head of state and of government	President Isaias Afewerki
Consulate	96 White Lion Street, London N1 9PF. Tel: 0171-713 0096
British Consulate in Asmara	PO Box 997, Asmara. Tel: Asmara 411 4242
Trouble spots	Fighting against Ethiopian forces on common border; border with Djibouti also affected

Defence

Military expenditure	8.4% of GDP (1996)
Military personnel	No figures available on division of armed forces between Eritrea and Ethiopia following Eritrean independence
Conscription duration	Two years

Economy

GDP	US$581 million (1994) US$96 per capita (1994)
Total external debt	US$46 million (1996)

Education

Enrolment (percentage of age group)	primary 31% (1995); secondary 15% (1995); tertiary 1.1% (1994)

ESTONIA

Area	17,413 sq. miles (45,100 sq. km)
Population	1,530,000 (1997 estimate)
Main languages	Estonian, Russian
Capital	Tallinn (population 447,672, 1996 estimate)
Currency	Kroon of 100 sents
Exchange rate (at 29 May)	Kroons 23.2401
Public holiday	January 1; February 24; April 10, 12; May 1, 31; June 23, 24; December 25, 26
Usual business hours	Mon.–Fri. 8.30–18.30
Electrical rating	220v AC, 50Hz (European plugs)

Demography

Life expectancy (years)	male 64.05; female 75.03
Population growth rate	-0.5% (1995)
Population density	34 per sq. km (1995)
Urban population	70.4% (1993)

Government and diplomacy

Political system	Republic
Head of state	President Lennart Meri
Head of government	Mart Siimann
Embassy in UK	16 Hyde Park Gate, London SW7 5DG. Tel: 0171-589 3428
British Embassy in Tallinn	Kentmanni 20, Tallinn EE0100. Tel: Tallinn 631 3353

Defence

Military expenditure	2.4% of GDP (1996)
Military personnel	3,510: Army 3,350, Navy 160
Conscription duration	12 months

Economy

GNP	US$4,509 million (1996)
	US$3,080 per capita (1996)
GDP	US$85,956 million (1994)
	US$1,510 per capita (1994)
Annual average growth of GDP	2.9% (1995)
Inflation rate	23.1% (1996)
Unemployment	8.9% (1994)
Total external debt	US$405 million (1996)

Education

Enrolment (percentage of age group)	primary 94% (1995); secondary 77% (1995); tertiary 38.1% (1995)
Illiteracy rate	0.2%

ETHIOPIA

Area	426,373 sq. miles (1,104,300 sq. km)
Population	56,677,000 (1994 estimate)
Main language	Amharic
Capital	Addis Ababa (population 2,316,400, 1994 estimate)
Currency	Ethiopian birr (EB) of 100 cents
Exchange rate (at 29 May)	EB 11.3872
Public holidays	January 7, 19, 30; March 2; April 7, 17, 19; May 1, 28; July 6; September 11, 27
Usual business hours	Mon.–Fri. 8–12, 13–17
Electrical rating	220v AC, 50Hz

Demography

Life expectancy (years)	male 45.93; female 49.06
Population growth rate	3.2% (1995)
Population density	51 per sq. km (1995)
Urban population	15.3% (1995)

Government and diplomacy

Political system	Republic; federal state
Head of state	President Negasso Gidada
Head of government	Meles Zenawi
Embassy in UK	17 Prince's Gate, London SW7 1PZ. Tel: 0171-589 7212/3/4/5
British Embassy in Addis Ababa	Fikre Mariam Abatechan Street (PO Box 858), Addis Ababa. Tel: Addis Ababa 161 2354
Trouble spots	Fighting against Eritrean forces on common border; Tigray, northern Gondar and Afar regions affected Tension on borders with Sudan and Somalia

Defence

Military expenditure	2% of GDP (1996)
Military personnel	120,000

Economy

GNP	US$6,042 million (1996) US$100 per capita (1996)
GDP	US$8,941 million (1994) US$96 per capita (1994)
Annual average growth of GDP	-6% (1991)
Inflation rate	-5.1% (1996)
Total external debt	US$10,077 million (1996)

Education

Enrolment (percentage of age group)	primary 24% (1994); tertiary 0.7% (1994)
Illiteracy rate	64.5%

FALKLAND ISLANDS

Area	4,700 sq. miles (12,173 sq. km)
Population	2,000 (1994 UN estimate)
Main language	English
Capital	Stanley (population 1,636, 1994)
Currency	Falkland pound of 100 pence
Exchange rate (29 May)	At parity with £ sterling
Usual business hours	Banking hours: Mon.–Fri. 8–12, 13.30–15
Electrical rating	240v AC, 50Hz

Demography

Population growth rate	0% (1995)
Urban population	76% (1991)

Government

Political system	UK Overseas Territory
Governor	Richard Ralph
Falkland Islands Office in UK	Falkland House, 14 Broadway, London SW1H 0BH. Tel: 0171-222 2542

FARÖE ISLANDS, see DENMARK

FIJI

Area	7,056 sq. miles (18,274 sq. km)
Population	796,000 (1994 estimate)
Main languages	Fijian, Hindi
Capital	Suva (population 141,273, 1986)
Currency	Fiji dollar (F$) of 100 cents
Exchange rate (at 29 May)	F$ 3.2746
Public holidays	January 1; March 13; April 10, 11, 13; May 29; June 15; July 6, 27; October 12, 19; December 25, 26
Usual business hours	Mon.–Fri. 8.30–16.30
Electrical rating	240v AC, 50Hz

Demography

Life expectancy (years)	male 60.72; female 63.87
Population growth rate	1.7% (1995)
Population density	44 per sq. km (1995)
Urban population	38.7% (1987)

Government and diplomacy

Political system	Republic
Head of state	President Kamisese Mara
Head of government	Maj.-Gen. Sitiveni Rabuka
Embassy in UK	34 Hyde Park Gate, London SW7 5DN. Tel: 0171-584 3661
British Embassy in Suva	Victoria House, 47 Gladstone Road, PO Box 1355, Suva. Tel: Suva 311033

Defence

Military expenditure	2.3% of GDP (1996)
Military personnel	3,600: Army 3,300, Navy 300

Economy

GNP	US$1,983 million (1996)
	US$2,470 per capita (1996)
GDP	US$1,466 million (1994)
	US$2,369 per capita (1994)
Annual average growth of GDP	6.7% (1990)
Inflation rate	3.1% (1996)
Unemployment	5.4% (1995)
Total external debt	US$217 million (1996)

Education

Enrolment (percentage of age group)	primary 99% (1992); tertiary 11.9% (1991)
Illiteracy rate	8.4%

FINLAND

Area	130,559 sq. miles (338,145 sq. km)
Population	5,108,000 (1994 estimate)
Main languages	Finnish, Swedish
Capital	Helsinki (Helsingfors) (population 1,016,291, 1993 estimate)
Currency	Markka (Mk) of 100 penniä
Exchange rate (at 29 May)	Mk 8.8351
Public holidays	January 1, 6; April 9, 10, 13; May 1, 21; June 19; December 6, 24–26, 31
Usual business hours	Mon.–Fri. 8–16.15
Electrical rating	220v AC, 50Hz (European plugs)

Demography

Life expectancy (years)	male 72.82; female 80.15
Population growth rate	0.5% (1995)
Population density	15 per sq. km (1995)
Urban population	64.2% (1994)

Government and diplomacy

Political system	Republic
Head of state	President Martti Ahtisaari
Head of government	Paavo Lipponen
Embassy in UK	38 Chesham Place, London SW1X 8HW. Tel: 0171-838 6200
British Embassy in Helsinki	Itäinen Puistotie 17, 00140 Helsinki. Tel: Helsinki 2286 5100

Defence

Military expenditure	1.8% of GDP (1996)
Military personnel	31,000: Army 27,000, Navy 2,100, Air Force 1,900

Conscription duration	Eight to 11 months

Economy

GNP	US$119,086 million (1996)
	US$23,240 per capita (1996)
GDP	US$123,720 million (1994)
	US$19,048 per capita (1994)
Annual average growth of GDP	3.7% (1996)
Inflation rate	0.6% (1996)
Unemployment	17.4% (1995)

Education

Enrolment (percentage of age group)	primary 99% (1994); secondary 93% (1994); tertiary 66.9% (1994)

FRANCE

Area	212,935 sq. miles (551,500 sq. km)
Population	58,143,000, including overseas departments (1994 estimate)
Main language	French
Capital	Paris (population 9,319,367, 1990)
Currency	Franc of 100 centimes
Exchange rate (at 29 May)	Francs 9.7561
Public holidays	January 1; April 11, 13; May 1, 8, 21; June 1; July 13, 14; August 15; November 1, 11; December 24, 25
Usual business hours	Mon.–Fri. 9–12, 14–18
Electrical rating	220v AC, 50Hz (European plugs)

Demography

Life expectancy (years)	male 72.94; female 81.15
Population growth rate	0.5% (1995)
Population density	105 per sq. km (1995)
Urban population	73.9% (1992)

Government and diplomacy

Political system	Republic
Head of state	President Jacques Chirac
Head of government	Lionel Jospin
Embassy in UK	58 Knightsbridge, London SW1X 7JT. Tel: 0171-201 1000
British Embassy in Paris	35 rue du Faubourg St Honoré, 75383 Paris Cedex 08. Tel: Paris 4451 3100

Defence

Military expenditure	3.1% of GDP (1996)
Military personnel	469,320: Army 219,900, Strategic Nuclear Forces 10,400, Navy 63,300, Air Force 83,420, Paramilitaries 92,300

| *Conscription duration* | Ten to 24 months; to be phased out by 2003 |

Economy

GNP	US$1,533,619 million (1996)
	US$26,270 per capita (1996)
GDP	US$1,241,147 million (1994)
	US$24,608 per capita (1994)
Annual average growth of GDP	1.5% (1996)
Inflation rate	2% (1996)
Unemployment	11.6% (1995)

Education

| *Enrolment (percentage of age group)* | primary 99% (1993); secondary 92% (1993); tertiary 49.6% (1993) |

OVERSEAS DEPARTMENTS

FRENCH GUIANA

Area	34,749 sq. miles (90,000 sq. km)
Population	147,000 (1994)
Capital	Cayenne (population 41,164, 1990)
Prefect	P. Dartout

GUADELOUPE

Area	658 sq. miles (1,705 sq. km)
Population	428,000 (1994 estimate)
Capital	Basse Terre (population 29,522, 1990)
Prefect	M. Diefenbacher

MARTINIQUE

Area	425 sq. miles (1,102 sq. km)
Population	379,000 (1994 estimate)
Capital	Fort de France (population 97,814, 1990)
Prefect	J.-F. Cordet

RÉUNION

Area	969 sq. miles (2,510 sq. km)
Population	653,000
Capital	St Denis (population 121,999)
Prefect	R. Pommies

TERRITORIAL COLLECTIVITÉS

MAYOTTE

Area	144 sq. miles (372 sq. km)
Population	94,410 (1994 estimate)
Capital	Mamoundzou (population 12,000, 1990)
Prefect	P. Boisadam

ST PIERRE AND MIQUELON

Area	93 sq. miles (242 sq. km)
Population	6,000 (1994 estimate)
Capital	St Pierre (population 5,416, 1990)
Prefect	J.-F. Carenco

OVERSEAS TERRITORIES

FRENCH POLYNESIA

Area	1,544 sq. miles (4,000 sq. km)
Population	220,000 (1994 estimate)
Capital	Papeete (population 36,784, 1990)
High Commissioner	P. Roncière

NEW CALEDONIA

Area	7,172 sq. miles (18,575 sq. km)
Population	186,000 (1994 estimate)
Capital	Nouméa (population 97,581, 1990)
High Commissioner	D. Bur

WALLIS AND FUTUNA ISLANDS

Area	77 sq. miles (200 sq. km)
Population	14,000 (1994 estimate)
Capital	Mata-Utu
Supreme Administrator	C. Pierret

GABON

Area	103,347 sq. miles (267,668 sq. km)
Population	1,320,000 (1994 UN estimate)
Main languages	French, Fang, Eshira
Capital	Libreville (population 251,000)
Currency	Franc CFA of 100 centimes
Exchange rate (at 29 May)	Francs 975.610
Public holidays	January 1, 30; April 7, 13; May 1; June 1; August 15, 16; November 1; December 25
Usual business hours	Mon.–Fri. 7.30–12, 14.30–18
Electrical rating	220v AC, 50Hz

Demography

Life expectancy (years)	male 51.86; female 55.18
Population growth rate	2.8% (1995)
Population density	5 per sq. km (1995)
Urban population	73.2% (1993)

Government and diplomacy

Political system	Republic
Head of state	President El Hadj Omar Bongo
Head of government	Paulin Obame-Nguema
Embassy in UK	27 Elvaston Place, London SW7 5NL. Tel: 0171-823 9986
British Embassy	Yaoundé, Cameroon

Defence

Military expenditure · 2.2% of GDP (1996)

Military personnel · 9,500: Army 3,200, Navy 500, Air Force 1,000, Paramilitary 4,800

Economy

GNP · US$4,444 million (1996)
US$3,950 per capita (1996)

GDP · US$5,851 million (1994)
US$3,086 per capita (1994)

Inflation rate · 4.2% (1996)

Total external debt · US$4,213 million (1996)

Education

Illiteracy rate · 36.8%

THE GAMBIA

Area · 4,361 sq. miles (11,295 sq. km)

Population · 1,118,000 (1994 estimate)

Main languages · English, Mandinka, Fula, Wollof

Capital · Banjul (population 109,986, 1980 estimate)

Currency · Dalasi (D) of 100 butut

Exchange rate (at 29 May) · D 16.5602

Public holidays · January 1, 30 (2 days); February 18; April 7 (2 days), 10; May 1, 7; July 6, 22; August 15; December 25

Usual business hours · Mon.–Thurs. 8–16; Fri. 8–12.30

Electrical rating · 220v AC, 50Hz

Demography

Life expectancy (years) · male 43.41; female 46.63

Population growth rate · 3.8% (1995)

Population density · 99 per sq. km (1995)

Government and diplomacy

Political system · Republic

Head of state and of government President Capt. Yayah Jammeh

High Commission in UK · 57 Kensington Court, London W8 5DG. Tel: 0171-937 6316

British High Commission in Banjul · 48 Atlantic Road, Fajara (PO Box 507), Banjul. Tel: Banjul 495133

Defence

Military expenditure · 3.9% of GDP (1996)

Military personnel · 800 Army

Economy

GNP · US$354 million (1995)
US$320 per capita (1995)

GDP · US$330 million (1994)
US$332 per capita (1994)

Annual average growth of GDP	-4.1% (1995)
Inflation rate	1.1% (1996)
Total external debt	US$452 million (1996)

Education

Enrolment (percentage of age group)	primary 55% (1992); secondary 18% (1992); tertiary 1.7% (1994)
Illiteracy rate	61.4%

GEORGIA

Area	26,911 sq. miles (69,700 sq. km)
Population	5,457,000 (1995 official estimate)
Main languages	Georgian, Russian, Armenian
Capital	Tbilisi (population 1,268,000, 1990 estimate)
Currency	Lari of 100 tetri
Public holidays	January 1; March 3; April 9, 15; May 9, 26; August 15, 28; October 14; November 23
Usual business hours	Mon.–Fri. 9.30–17.30
Electrical rating	220v AC, 50Hz

Demography

Life expectancy (years)	male 68.10; female 75.70
Population growth rate	0% (1995)
Population density	78 per sq. km (1995)
Urban population	55.4% (1989)

Government and diplomacy

Political system	Republic; federal state
Head of state and government	President Eduard Shevardnadze
Embassy in UK	3 Hornton Place, London W8 4LZ. Tel: 0171-937 8233
British Embassy in Tbilisi	Metechi Palace Hotel, 380003 Tbilisi. Tel: Tbilisi 955497
Trouble spots	Secession of South Ossetia 1992; status unresolved and situation unstable Secession of Abkhazia 1992; fighting continues and neighbouring districts affected

Defence

Military expenditure	3.4% of GDP (1996)
Military personnel	17,600: Army 12,600, Navy 2,000, Air Force 3,000
Conscription duration	Two years

Economy

GNP	US$4,590 million (1996) US$850 per capita (1996)

GDP	US$4,547 million (1994)
	US$256 per capita (1994)
Total external debt	US$1,356 million (1996)

Education

Enrolment (percentage of age group)	primary 82% (1995); secondary 71% (1995); tertiary 38.1% (1995)
Illiteracy rate	0.5%

GERMANY

Area	137,735 sq. miles (356,733 sq. km)
Population	81,642,000 (1994 estimate)
Main language	German
Capital	Berlin (population 3,472,009, 1996). Seat of government and parliament to transfer from Bonn to Berlin by 2000
Currency	Deutsche Mark (DM) of 100 Pfennig
Exchange rate (at 29 May)	DM 2.9072
Public holidays	January 1; April 10, 13; May 1, 21; June 1; October 3; December 24–26, 31
Usual business hours	Mon.–Fri. 8–16
Electrical rating	220v AC, 50Hz

Demography

Life expectancy (years)	male 72.77; female 79.30
Population growth rate	0.6% (1995)
Population density	229 per sq. km (1995)
Urban population	76.3% (1990)

Government and diplomacy

Political system	Republic; federal state
Head of state	President Roman Herzog
Head of government	Helmut Kohl
Embassy in UK	23 Belgrave Square, London SW1X 8PZ. Tel: 0171-824 1300
British Embassy in Bonn	Friedrich-Ebert-Allée 77, 53113 Bonn. Tel: Bonn 91670

Defence

Military expenditure	1.7% of GDP (1996)
Military personnel	344,610: Army 239,950, Navy 27,760, Air Force 76,900 Under the Treaty of Unification, active armed forces limited to 370,000
Conscription duration	Ten to 23 months

Economy

GNP	US$2,364,632 million (1996)
	US$28,870 per capita (1996)
GDP	US$1,767,217 million (1994)
	US$25,179 per capita (1994)
Annual average growth of GDP	1.3% (1996)
Inflation rate	1.5% (1996)
Unemployment	12.9% (1995)

Education

Enrolment (percentage of age group)	primary 100% (1994); secondary 88% (1994); tertiary 42.7% (1994)

GHANA

Area	92,098 sq. miles (238,533 sq. km)
Population	17,453,000 (1997 estimate)
Main languages	English, Twi, Fanti
Capital	Accra (population 738,498, 1970)
Currency	Cedi of 100 pesewas
Exchange rate (at 29 May)	Cedi 3799.54
Public holidays	January 1, 30 (2 days); March 6; April 7, 10, 13; May 1; June 4; July 1; December 4, 25, 26
Usual business hours	Mon.–Fri. 8–12, 14–17; Sat. 8.30–12
Electrical rating	220v AC, 50Hz (mainly 3-pin plugs)

Demography

Life expectancy (years)	male 54.22; female 57.84
Population growth rate	3% (1995)
Population density	73 per sq. km (1995)

Government and diplomacy

Political system	Republic; military regime
Head of state and government	President Jerry Rawlings
High Commission in UK	13 Belgrave Square, London SW1 8PN. Tel: 0171-235 4142
British High Commission in Accra	PO Box 296, Osu Link, Accra. Tel: Accra 221665

Defence

Military expenditure	1.9% of GDP (1996)
Military personnel	7,800: Army 5,000, Navy 1,000, Air Force 1,000, Paramilitaries 800

Economy

GNP	US$6,223 million (1996)
	US$360 per capita (1996)
GDP	US$7,710 million (1994)
	US$333 per capita (1994)

Annual average growth of GDP	4.5% (1995)
Inflation rate	34% (1996)
Total external debt	US$6,202 million (1996)

Education

Enrolment (percentage of age group)	tertiary 1.4% (1990)
Illiteracy rate	35.5%

GIBRALTAR

Area	2.3 sq. miles (6 sq. km)
Population	28,000 (1994 UN estimate)
Main languages	English, Spanish
Capital	Gibraltar
Currency	Gibraltar pound of 100 pence
Exchange rate (at 29 May)	At parity with £ sterling
Public holidays	January 1; March 9; April 10, 13; May 1, 25; June 15; August 31; September 10; December 25, 28
Usual business hours	Mon.–Fri. 9–17 (8–14 in summer)
Electrical rating	220/240v AC, 50Hz

Demography

Population growth rate	-1.9% (1995)
Population density	4,667 per sq. km (1995)

Government

Political system	UK Overseas Territory
Governor	Sir Richard Luce

GREECE

Area	50,949 sq. miles (131,957 sq. km)
Population	10,458,000 (1994 estimate)
Main language	Greek
Capital	Athens (population 3,027,922, 1981)
Currency	Drachma of 100 leptae
Exchange rate (at 29 May)	Drachmae 496.548
Public holidays	January 1, 6; March 2, 25; April 17, 20; May 1; June 8; August 15; October 28; December 25, 26
Usual business hours	Banking hours: Mon.–Thurs. 8–14; Fri. 8–13.30
Electrical rating	220v AC, 50Hz

Demography
Life expectancy (years)	male 74.61; female 79.96
Population growth rate	0.6% (1995)
Population density	79 per sq. km (1995)
Urban population	58.9% (1991)

Government and diplomacy
Political system	Republic
Head of state	President Constantine Stephanopoulos
Head of government	Costas Simitis
Embassy in UK	1A Holland Park, London W11 3TP. Tel: 0171-229 3850
British Embassy in Athens	1 Ploutarchou Street, 10675 Athens. Tel: Athens 723 6211

Defence
Military expenditure	4.7% of GDP (1996)
Military personnel	166,300: Army 116,000, Navy 19,500, Air Force 26,800, Paramilitaries 4,000
Conscription duration	Up to 21 months

Economy
GNP	US$120,021 million (1996)
	US$11,460 per capita (1996)
GDP	US$70,897 million (1994)
	US$7,465 per capita (1994)
Annual average growth of GDP	1.5% (1994)
Inflation rate	8.2% (1996)
Unemployment	10% (1995)

Education
Enrolment (percentage of age group)	primary 98% (1990); secondary 85% (1994); tertiary 38.1% (1994)
Illiteracy rate	3.3%

GREENLAND, see DENMARK

GRENADA

Area	133 sq. miles (344 sq. km)
Population	92,000 (1994 UN estimate)
Main language	English
Capital	St George's (population 4,788, 1981)
Currency	East Caribbean dollar (EC$) of 100 cents
Exchange rate (at 29 May)	EC$ 4.4029
Public holidays	January 1; February 7; April 10, 13; May 1; June 1, 11; August 3, 4, 10, 11; October 25, 26; December 25, 26
Usual business hours	Mon.–Thurs. 8–13.30; Fri. 8–16
Electrical rating	220/240v AC, 50Hz

Demography
Population growth rate	0.2% (1995)
Population density	267 per sq. km (1995)

Government and diplomacy
Political system	Constitutional monarchy
Head of state	Queen Elizabeth II
Governor-General	Sir Daniel Williams
Head of government	Dr Keith Mitchell
High Commission in UK	1 Collingham Gardens, London SW5 0HW. Tel: 0171-373 7809
British High Commission	Bridgetown, Barbados

Economy
GNP	US$285 million (1996)
	US$2,880 per capita (1996)
GDP	US$208 million (1994)
	US$2,437 per capita (1994)
Annual average growth of GDP	0.6% (1992)
Inflation rate	3% (1995)
Total external debt	US$120 million (1996)

GUADELOUPE, see FRANCE

GUAM, see USA

GUATEMALA

Area	42,042 sq. miles (108,889 sq. km)
Population	10,621,000 (1994 UN estimate)
Main languages	Spanish, but 40% of the population speaks an Indian language
Capital	Guatemala City (population 1,675,589, 1990 estimate)
Currency	Quetzal (Q) of 100 centavos
Exchange rate (at 29 May)	Q 10.2312
Public holidays	January 1; April 8–11; May 1, 10, 11; June 30; July 1; August 15; September 15; October 12, 20; November 1, 2; December 24, 25, 31
Usual business hours	Mon.–Fri. 8–18; Sat. 8–12
Electrical rating	110v AC, 60Hz; some regional variations

Demography

Life expectancy (years)	male 55.11; female 59.43
Population growth rate	2.9% (1995)
Population density	98 per sq. km (1995)
Urban population	38.7% (1995)

Government and diplomacy

Political system	Republic
Head of state and of government	President Alvaro Arzú Irigoyen
Embassy in UK	13 Fawcett Street, London SW10 9HN. Tel: 0171-351 3042
British Embassy in Guatemala City	Edificio Centro Financiero (7th Floor), Seventh Avenue 5–10, Zone 4, Guatemala City. Tel: Guatemala City 332 1601

Defence

Military expenditure	1.3% of GDP (1996)
Military personnel	50,500: Army 38,500, Navy 1,500, Air Force 700, Paramilitaries 9,800
Conscription duration	30 months

Economy

GNP	US$16,018 million US$1,470 per capita (1996)
GDP	US$8,969 million (1994) US$1,252 per capita (1994)
Annual average growth of GDP	3% (1996)
Inflation rate	11.1% (1996)
Total external debt	US$3,785 million (1996)

Education

Enrolment (percentage of age group)	primary 58% (1980); secondary 13% (1980); tertiary 8.1% (1995)
Illiteracy rate	44.4%

GUINEA

Area	94,926 sq. miles (245,857 sq. km)
Population	6,700,000 (1994 UN estimate)
Main languages	French, Susu, Malinké, Fula
Capital	Conakry (population 763,000)
Currency	Guinea franc of 100 centimes
Exchange rate (at 29 May)	Francs 2002.50
Public holidays	January 1, 30; April 3, 7, 13; May 1; July 6; August 15; October 2; December 25
Usual business hours	Mon.–Thurs. 8–16.30; Fri. 8–13
Electrical rating	220v AC, 50Hz

Demography

Life expectancy (years)	male 44; female 45
Population growth rate	3% (1995)
Population density	27 per sq. km (1995)

Government and diplomacy

Political system	Republic
Head of state and of government	President Maj.-Gen. Lansana Conté
Embassy	51 rue de la Faisanderie, 75061 Paris, France. Tel: Paris 4704 8148/4553 8545
Honorary Consulate in UK	20 Upper Grosvenor Street, London W1X 9PB. Tel: 0171-333 0044
British Consulate in Conakry	BP 834 Conakry, Guinea

Defence

Military expenditure	1.4% of GDP (1996)
Military personnel	12,300: Army 8,500, Navy 400, Air Force 800, Paramilitaries 2,600
Conscription duration	Two years

Economy

GNP	US$3,804 million (1996) US$560 per capita (1996)
GDP	US$3,223 million (1994) US$461 per capita (1994)
Total external debt	US$3,240 million (1996)

Education

Enrolment (percentage of age group)	primary 37% (1993); secondary 9% (1985); tertiary 1.1% (1990)
Illiteracy rate	64.1%

GUINEA–BISSAU

Area	13,948 sq. miles (36,125 sq. km)
Population	1,073,000 (1994 UN estimate)
Main languages	Portuguese, Creole
Capital	Bissau (population 109,214, 1979)
Currency	Franc CFA
Exchange rate (at 29 May)	Francs 975.610
Public holidays	January 1, 20, 30; March 8; April 7; May 1; August 3; September 24; November 14; December 25
Usual business hours	Banking hours: Mon.–Fri. 7.30–14.30
Electrical rating	Limited supply on 220v AC, 50Hz

Demography

Life expectancy (years)	male 41.92; female 45.12
Population growth rate	2.1% (1995)
Population density	30 per sq. km (1995)

Government and diplomacy

Political system	Republic
Head of state and of government	Chairman of the Republic Brig.-Gen. João Bernardo Vieira
Embassy	94 Rue St Lazare, Paris 9, France. Tel: Paris 4526 1851
British Consulate in Bissau	Mavegro Int., CP100, Bissau
Trouble spots	Attempted military coup in June 1998; widespread fighting between factions continues

Defence

Military expenditure	2.8% of GDP (1996)
Military personnel	9,250: Army 6,800, Navy 350, Air Force 100, Paramilitaries 2,000

Economy

GNP	US$270 million (1996) US$250 per capita (1996)
GDP	US$262 million (1994) US$182 per capita (1994)
Annual average growth of GDP	3% (1993)
Inflation rate	50.7% (1996)
Total external debt	US$937 million (1996)

Education

Enrolment (percentage of age group)	primary 46% (1986); secondary 3% (1980); tertiary 0.5% (1988)
Illiteracy rate	45.1%

GUYANA

Area	83,000 sq. miles (214,969 sq. km)
Population	835,000 (1994 UN estimate)
Main languages	English, Creole
Capital	Georgetown (population 250,000)
Currency	Guyana dollar (G$) of 100 cents
Exchange rate (at 29 May)	G$ 235.310
Public holidays	January 1; February 23; March 24; April 7, 10, 13; May 1; July 6, 7; August 1; October 19; December 25, 26
Usual business hours	Mon.–Fri. 8–11.30, 13–16.30
Electrical rating	110v AC, 60Hz

Demography

Life expectancy (years)	male 62.44; female 68.02
Population growth rate	1% (1995)
Population density	4 per sq. km (1995)

Government and diplomacy

Political system	Republic
Head of state	President Janet Jagan
Head of government	Sam Hinds
High Commission in UK	3 Palace Court, Bayswater Road, London W2 4LP. Tel: 0171-229 7684
British High Commission in Georgetown	44 Main Street (PO Box 10849), Georgetown. Tel: Georgetown 65881/4

Defence

Military expenditure	1% of GDP (1996)
Military personnel	1,500: Army 1,400, Air Force 100

Economy

GNP	US$582 million (1996)
	US$690 per capita (1996)
GDP	US$531 million (1994)
	US$655 per capita (1994)
Annual average growth of GDP	8.2% (1993)
Inflation rate	2.6% (1992)
Total external debt	US$1,631 million (1996)

Education

Enrolment (percentage of age group)	primary 90% (1994); secondary 66% (1992); tertiary 8.6% (1994)
Illiteracy rate	1.9%

HAITI

Area	10,714 sq. miles (27,750 sq. km)
Population	7,180,000 (1994 UN estimate)
Main language	Creole
Capital	Port-au-Prince (population 690,168, 1990 estimate)
Currency	Gourde of 100 centimes
Exchange rate (at 29 May)	Gourdes 27.6382
Public holidays	January 1, 2; February 24; April 10; May 1, 18; August 15; October 17; November 1, 2, 18; December 25
Usual business hours	Mon.–Fri. 7–16
Electrical rating	110v AC, 60Hz

Demography

Life expectancy (years)	male 54.95; female 58.34
Population growth rate	2% (1995)
Population density	259 per sq. km (1995)
Urban population	32.6% (1995)

Government and diplomacy

Political system	Republic
Head of state	President René Préval
Head of government	Vacant
British Embassy	Kingston, Jamaica

Defence

Military expenditure	3.5% of GDP (1996)

Economy

GNP	US$2,282 million (1996) US$310 per capita (1996)
GDP	US$1,959 million (1994) US$266 per capita (1994)
Annual average growth of GDP	2.8% (1996)
Inflation rate	17.1% (1996)
Total external debt	US$897 million (1996)

Education

Enrolment (percentage of age group)	primary 26% (1990); tertiary 1.1% (1985)
Illiteracy rate	55%

HONDURAS

Area	43,277 sq. miles (112,088 sq. km)
Population	5,953,000 (1994 UN estimate)
Main languages	Spanish, English
Capital	Tegucigalpa (population 670,100, 1991 estimate)
Currency	Lempira of 100 centavos
Exchange rate (at 29 May)	Lempiras 21.7046
Public holidays	January 1; April 9, 10, 14; May 1; September 15; October 3, 12, 21; December 25
Usual business hours	Mon.–Fri. 8–12, 14–17; Sat. 8–11
Electrical rating	110/120/220v AC, 60Hz

Demography

Life expectancy (years)	male 65.43; female 70.06
Population growth rate	3.1% (1995)
Population density	53 per sq. km (1995)
Urban population	47.5% (1995)

Government and diplomacy

Political system	Republic
Head of state and of government	President Carlos Flores
Embassy in UK	115 Gloucester Place, London W1H 3PJ. Tel: 0171-486 4880
British Embassy in Tegucigalpa	Apartado Postal 290, Tegucigalpa. Tel: Honduras 320612/18

Defence

Military expenditure	1.1% of GDP (1996)
Military personnel	24,300: Army 16,000, Navy 1,000, Air Force 1,800, Paramilitaries 5,500

Economy

GNP	US$4,012 million (1996) US$660 per capita (1996)
GDP	US$7,136 million (1994) US$532 per capita (1994)
Annual average growth of GDP	3% (1996)
Inflation rate	23.8% (1996)
Unemployment	3.2% (1995)
Total external debt	US$4,453 million (1996)

Education

Enrolment (percentage of age group)	primary 90% (1993); secondary 21% (1991); tertiary 10% (1994)
Illiteracy rate	27.3%

HONG KONG, see CHINA

HUNGARY

Area	35,920 sq. miles (93,032 sq. km)
Population	10,225,000 (1994 UN estimate)
Main languages	Magyar (Hungarian), German
Capital	Budapest (population, 2,002,121, 1993 estimate)
Currency	Forint of 100 fillér
Exchange rate (at 29 May)	Forints 349.076
Public holidays	January 1; March 15; April 13; May 1; June 1; August 20; October 23; December 25, 26
Usual business hours	Mon.–Fri. 8–16.30
Electrical rating	230v AC, 50 Hz

Demography
Life expectancy (years)	male 64.84; female 74.23
Population growth rate	-0.3% (1995)
Population density	110 per sq. km (1995)
Urban population	63.3% (1994)

Government and diplomacy
Political system	Republic
Head of state	President Árpád Göncz
Head of government	Gyula Horn
Embassy in UK	35 Eaton Place, London SW1X 8BY. Tel: 0171-235 4048/7191
British Embassy in Budapest	Harmincad Utca 6, Budapest V. Tel: Budapest 266 2888

Defence
Military expenditure	1.2% of GDP (1996)
Military personnel	63,200: Army 31,600, Air Force 17,500, Paramilitaries 14,100
Conscription duration	Nine months

Economy
GNP	US$44,274 million (1996) US$4,340 per capita (1996)
GDP	US$31,155 million (1994) US$4,072 per capita (1994)
Annual average growth of GDP	2.9% (1994)
Inflation rate	23.5% (1996)
Unemployment	10.3% (1995)
Total external debt	US$26,958 million (1996)

Education
Enrolment (percentage of age group)	primary 93% (1994); secondary 73% (1994); tertiary 19.1% (1994)
Illiteracy rate	0.8%

ICELAND

Area	39,769 sq. miles (103,000 sq. km)
Population	269,000 (1996)
Main languages	Icelandic, Danish
Capital	Reykjavik (population 153,210, 1995)
Currency	Icelandic króna (Kr) of 100 aurar
Exchange rate (at 29 May)	Kr 116.563
Public holidays	January 1; April 9, 10, 13, 23; May 1, 21; June 1, 17; August 3; December 24–26, 31
Usual business hours	Mon.–Fri. 9–17
Electrical rating	220v AC, 50Hz

Demography
Life expectancy (years)	male 76.85; female 80.75
Population growth rate	1.1% (1995)
Population density	3 per sq. km (1995)
Urban population	91.3% (1993)

Government and diplomacy
Political system	Republic
Head of state	President Olafur Ragnar Grimsson
Head of government	David Oddsson
Embassy in UK	1 Eaton Terrace, London SW1W 8EY. Tel: 0171-730 5131
British Embassy in Reykjavik	Laufásvegur 49, 101 Reykjavik. Tel: Reykjavik 551 15883/4

Defence
Military expenditure	0.1% of GDP (1996)
Military personnel	120 Paramilitaries

Economy
GNP	US$7,175 million (1996)
	US$26,580 per capita (1996)
GDP	US$6,345 million (1994)
	US$23,280 per capita (1994)
Annual average growth of GDP	5.7% (1996)
Inflation rate	2.3% (1996)
Unemployment	4.9% (1995)

Education
Enrolment (percentage of age group)	tertiary 35.2% (1994)

INDIA

Area	1,269,346 sq. miles (3,287,590 sq. km)
Population	935,744,000 (1994 UN estimate)
Main languages	Hindi in the Devanagari script, English, 17 regional languages
Capital	New Delhi (population 301,297; 8,419,084 including Delhi/Dilli, 1991)
Currency	Indian rupee (Rs) of 100 paisa
Exchange rate (at 29 May)	Rs 67.9594
Public holidays	January 26, 30; March 31; August 15; September 30; October 2, 11, 19; December 25
Usual business hours	Mon.–Fri. 9.30–17; Sat. 9.30–13
Electrical rating	Mainly 220v AC, 50Hz; some areas have DC supply

Demography

Life expectancy (years)	male 57.70; female 58.10
Population growth rate	2.3% (1995)
Population density	285 per sq. km (1995)
Urban population	26.3% (1993)

Government and diplomacy

Political system	Republic; federal state
Head of state	President Kocheril Raman Narayanan
Head of government	Atal Behari Vajpayee
High Commission in UK	India House, Aldwych, London WC2B 4NA. Tel: 0171-836 8484
British High Commission in New Delhi	Chanakyapuri, New Delhi 110021. Tel: New Delhi 687 2161
Trouble spots	Tension with Pakistan over Jammu and Kashmir and nuclear arms race Muslim separatists in Jammu and Kashmir fighting Indian security forces Bodo separatists in Assam fighting for a separate Bodoland Ethnic tensions between Hindus and Muslims, and Sikhs in Punjab

Defence

Military expenditure	2.8% of GDP (1996)
Military personnel	1,145,000: Army 980,000, Navy 55,000, Air Force 110,000

Economy

GNP	US$357,759 million (1996) US$380 per capita (1996)
GDP	US$349,071 million (1994) US$309 per capita (1994)

Annual average growth of GDP	7.3% (1995)
Inflation rate	9% (1996)
Total external debt	US$89,827 million (1996)

Education

Enrolment (percentage of age group)	tertiary 6.4% (1995)
Illiteracy rate	48%

INDONESIA

Area	735,358 sq. miles (1,904,569 sq. km)
Population	193,750,000 (1994 UN estimate)
Main languages	Bahasa Indonesian (250 dialects), Dutch, English
Capital	Jakarta (population 9,160,500)
Currency	Rupiah (Rp) of 100 sen
Exchange rate (at 29 May)	Rp 18427
Public holidays	January 1, 30 (2 days); March 29; April 7, 10, 28; May 11, 21; July 6; August 17; November 17; December 25
Usual business hours	Mon.–Fri. 8–16 or 9–17
Electrical rating	Mainly 220v AC, 50Hz; 110v AC, 50Hz in some areas

Demography

Life expectancy (years)	male 61; female 64.50
Population growth rate	1.5% (1995)
Population density	102 per sq. km (1995)
Urban population	30.9% (1990)

Government and diplomacy

Political system	Republic; *de facto* military rule; possible reforms following civil unrest
Head of state and of government	President Bacharuddin Jusuf Habibie
Embassy in UK	38 Grosvenor Square, London W1X 9AD. Tel: 0171-499 7661
British Embassy in Jakarta	Jalan M. H. Thamrin 75, Jakarta 10310. Tel: Jakarta 330904
Trouble spots	Armed campaign for independence in East Timor since 1975. The UN does not recognize Indonesia's annexation
	Secessionist movements in Irian Jaya (Papua Independent Organization guerrillas) and in northern Sumatra (Free Aceh Movement)

Defence

Military expenditure	2.1% of GDP (1996)

Military personnel	284,000: Army 220,000, Navy 43,000, Air Force 21,000
Conscription duration	Two years

Economy

GNP	US$213,384 million (1996)
	US$1,080 per capita (1996)
GDP	US$136,934 million (1994)
	US$792 per capita (1994)
Annual average growth of GDP	7.8% (1996)
Inflation rate	7.9% (1996)
Total external debt	US$129,033 million (1996)

Education

Enrolment (percentage of age group)	primary 97% (1994); secondary 42% (1994); tertiary 11.1% (1994)
Illiteracy rate	16.2%

IRAN

Area	630,577 sq. miles (1,633,188 sq. km)
Population	67,283,000 (1996 census)
Main languages	Persian, Turkish, Kurdish, Arabic, Lori, Guilani, Mazandarani, Baluchi
Capital	Tehran (population 6,750,043, 1994 estimate)
Currency	Rial
Exchange rate (at 29 May)	Rials 4892.10
Public holidays	January 20, 30; February 11, 23; March 10, 20, 21 (4 days); April 1, 2, 8, 16; May 6, 7; June 4, 5, 15, 23; July 6; November 13, 17; December 5
Usual business hours	Sat.–Wed. 8–16; Thurs. 9–12
Electrical rating	220v AC, 50Hz

Demography

Life expectancy (years)	male 58.38; female 59.70
Population growth rate	4.2% (1995)
Population density	41 per sq. km (1995)
Urban population	57.5% (1993)

Government and diplomacy

Political system	Republic
Head of state	Leader of the Islamic Republic Ayatollah Seyed Ali Khamenei
Head of government	Seyed Mohammad Khatami
Embassy in UK	16 Prince's Gate, London SW7 1PT. Tel: 0171-225 3000
British Embassy in Tehran	143 Ferdowsi Avenue, PO Box 113654474, Tehran 11344. Tel: Tehran 675011

Defence

Military expenditure	2.1% of GDP (1996)
Military personnel	668,000: Army 350,000, Revolutionary Guard Corps 120,000, Navy 18,000, Air Force 30,000, Paramilitaries 150,000
Conscription duration	Two years

Economy

GDP	US$656,589 million (1994) US$1,151 per capita (1994)
Annual average growth of GDP	4.2% (1995)
Inflation rate	28.9% (1996)
Total external debt	US$21,183 million (1996)

Education

Enrolment (percentage of age group)	primary 79% (1985); tertiary 14.8% (1994)
Illiteracy rate	27.9%

IRAQ

Area	169,235 sq. miles (438,317 sq. km)
Population	20,449,000 (1994 UN estimate)
Main languages	Arabic, Kurdish, Turkic, Aramaic
Capital	Baghdad (population 3,841,268, 1987)
Currency	Iraqi dinar (ID) of 1,000 fils
Exchange rate (at 29 May)	ID 0.5070★
Public holidays	January 1, 6, 30 (3 days); February 8; March 21; April 7 (4 days), 17, 28; May 1, 7; July 6, 14, 17; August 8
Usual business hours	Sat.–Wed. 8–14; Thurs. 8–13
Electrical rating	220v AC, 50Hz

Demography

Life expectancy (years)	male 77.43; female 78.22
Population growth rate	3.3% (1995)
Population density	47 per sq. km (1995)
Urban population	69.9% (1990)

Government and diplomacy

Political system	Republic; *de facto* dictatorship
Head of state and of government	President Saddam Hussein
Iraqi Embassy in UK	Since 1991 the Jordanian Embassy has handled Iraqi interests in the UK
British Embassy	Since 1991 the Russian Embassy in Baghdad has handled British interests in Iraq

Trouble spots	UN safe haven in northern Iraq and air exclusion zone north of the 36th parallel to protect Kurds. *De facto* Kurdish administration with its capital at Arbil
	Air exclusion zone south of the 32nd parallel to protect Shi'ites in southern marshlands
	Systematic drainage of southern marshes by regime effectively ended Shi'ite rebellion in 1994
	Frequent stand-offs with UN weapons inspectors in Iraq and UN forces policing exclusion zones

Defence

Military expenditure	8.7% of GDP (1996)
Military personnel	437,500: Army 350,000, Navy 2,500, Air Force 35,000, Paramilitaries 50,000
Conscription duration	18–24 months

Economy

GDP	US$25,219 million (1994)
	US$2,855 per capita (1994)
Annual average growth of GDP	-7.2% (1989)

Education

Enrolment (percentage of age group)	primary 79% (1992); secondary 37% (1992); tertiary 12.6% (1990)
Illiteracy rate	42%

REPUBLIC OF IRELAND

Area	27,137 sq. miles (70,284 sq. km)
Population	3,582,000 (1996 census)
Main languages	English, Irish
Capital	Dublin (Baile Atha Cliath) (population 952,700, 1996)
Currency	Punt (IR£) of 100 pence
Exchange rate (at 29 May)	IR£ 1.1522
Public holidays	January 1; March 17; April 10, 13; May 1, 4; June 1; August 3; October 25; December 25, 26, 28, 29
Usual business hours	Banking hours: Mon.–Fri. 10–16
Electrical rating	220v AC, 50Hz

Demography
Life expectancy (years)	male 72.30; female 77.87
Population growth rate	0.4% (1995)
Population density	51 per sq. km (1995)
Urban population	57% (1991)

Government and diplomacy
Political system	Republic
Head of state	President Mary McAleese
Head of government	Bertie Ahern
Embassy in UK	17 Grosvenor Place, London SW1X 7HR. Tel: 0171-235 2171
British Embassy in Dublin	31 Merrion Road, Dublin 4. Tel: Dublin 205 3700

Defence
Military expenditure	1.1% of GDP (1996)
Military personnel	12,700: Army 10,500, Navy 1,100, Air Force 1,100
Conscription duration	Three-year terms

Economy
GNP	US$62,040 million (1996) US$17,110 per capita (1996)
GDP	US$53,727 million (1994) US$14,735 per capita (1994)
Annual average growth of GDP	7.7% (1996)
Inflation rate	1.7% (1996)
Unemployment	12.15% (1995)

Education
Enrolment (percentage of age group)	primary 100% (1994); secondary 85% (1994); tertiary 37% (1994)

ISRAEL

Area	8,130 sq. miles (21,056 sq. km)
Population	5,545,000 (1994 UN estimate)
Main languages	Hebrew, Arabic
Capital	Tel Aviv (population 1,880,200). Jerusalem (population 662,700, 1995) declared the capital in 1950 but not recognized by the UN because the UN and international law rejects the Israeli annexation of East Jerusalem
Currency	Shekel of 100 agora
Exchange rate (at 29 May)	Shekels 5.9593
Public holidays	January 1, 8; February 11; March 11; April 11, 17, 23, 29, 30; May 14, 24, 31; July 12; August 2; September 21–23, 30; October 5, 12; December 13, 20
Usual business hours	Office hours vary; banking hours: Mon., Tues., Thurs. 8.30–12.30, 16–17.30; Wed., Fri. 8.30–12.30
Electrical rating	220v AC, 50Hz

Demography

Life expectancy (years)	male 75.33; female 79.10
Population growth rate	3.5% (1995)
Population density	263 per sq. km (1995)
Urban population	89.7% (1994)

Government and diplomacy

Political system	Republic
Head of state	President Ezer Weizmann
Head of government	Benjamin Netanyahu
Embassy in UK	2 Palace Green, Kensington, London W8 4QB. Tel: 0171-957 9500
British Embassy in Tel Aviv	192 Hayarkon Street, Tel Aviv 63405. Tel: Tel Aviv 524 9171
Trouble spots	Tension between Jews and Palestinians regularly flares into violence, especially over building of Jewish settlements on West Bank Tension with neighbouring Arab states, especially over continuing Israeli occupation of West Bank and Golan Heights, and client groups in Southern Lebanon Security Zone

Defence

Military expenditure	10.2% of GDP (1996)
Military personnel	181,050: Army 134,000, Navy 9,000, Air Force 32,000, Paramilitaries 6,050

Conscription duration	21–48 months (Jews and Druze only)

Economy

GNP	US$90,310 million (1996)
	US$15,870 per capita (1996)
GDP	US$69,831 million (1994)
	US$14,333 per capita (1994)
Annual average growth of GDP	4.4% (1996)
Inflation rate	11.3% (1996)
Unemployment	6.9% (1995)

Education

Enrolment (percentage of age group)	tertiary 41.1% (1995)
Illiteracy rate	4.4%

PALESTINIAN AUTONOMOUS AREAS

Area	2,406 sq. miles (6,231 sq. km): fully autonomous, 159 sq. miles (412 sq. km) (Gaza Strip 136 sq. miles (352 sq. km), Jericho enclave 23 sq. miles (60 sq. km)); partially autonomous, 2,247 sq. miles (5,819 sq. km) (remainder of the West Bank)
Population	1,635,000 (1994 UN estimate): Gaza Strip, 660,000; Jericho, 40,000; remainder of West Bank, 935,000
Administrative capital	Gaza City (population 120,000). Palestinians claim East Jerusalem as their capital

Government and diplomacy

Political system	Self-government; Jewish settlers in the West Bank (141,000) and Gaza Strip (4,000) remain under Israeli administration and jurisdiction
Palestinian National Authority Leader	Yasser Arafat
British Consulate-General	19 Nashashibi Street, PO Box 19690, East Jerusalem 97200

ITALY

Area	116,320 sq. miles (301,268 sq. km)
Population	57,187,000 (1994 UN estimate)
Main language	Italian; there are numerous dialects
Capital	Rome (population 2,693,383, 1991)
Currency	Lira of 100 centesimi
Exchange rate (at 29 May)	Lire 2864.81
Public holidays	January 1, 6; April 13, 25; May 1; June 29; August 14, 15; November 1; December 7, 8, 24–26, 31
Usual business hours	Mon.–Fri. 9–17
Electrical rating	220v AC, 50Hz

Demography

Life expectancy (years)	male 73.79; female 80.36
Population growth rate	-0.2% (1995)
Population density	190 per sq. km (1995)
Urban population	96.6% (1991)

Government and diplomacy

Political system	Republic
Head of state	President Oscar Scalfaro
Head of government	Romano Prodi
Embassy in UK	14 Three Kings Yard, Davies Street, London W1Y 2EH. Tel: 0171-312 2200
British Embassy in Rome	Via XX Settembre 80A, 00187 Rome. Tel: Rome 482 5441

Defence

Military expenditure	1.9% of GDP (1996)
Military personnel	551,600: Army 188,300, Navy 44,000, Air Force 63,600, Paramilitaries 255,700
Conscription duration	Ten months

Economy

GNP	US$1,140,484 million (1996) US$19,880 per capita (1996)
GDP	US$1,134,661 million (1994) US$17,921 per capita (1994)
Annual average growth of GDP	0.7% (1996)
Inflation rate	4% (1996)
Unemployment	12% (1995)

Education

Enrolment (percentage of age group)	primary 97% (1994); tertiary 40.6% (1994)
Illiteracy rate	1.9%

JAMAICA

Area	4,243 sq. miles (10,990 sq. km)
Population	2,530,000 (1994 UN estimate)
Main language	English
Capital	Kingston (population 103,962, 1991)
Currency	Jamaican dollar (J$) of 100 cents
Exchange rate (at 29 May)	J$ 58.7052
Public holidays	January 1; February 25; April 10, 13; May 23, 25; August 1, 6; October 19; December 25, 26
Usual business hours	Mon.–Fri. 8.30–16.30
Electrical rating	110v AC, 50Hz, single phase

Demography

Life expectancy (years)	male 71.41; female 75.82
Population growth rate	0.9% (1995)
Population density	230 per sq. km (1995)

Government and diplomacy

Political system	Constitutional monarchy
Head of state	Queen Elizabeth II
Governor-General	Sir Howard Felix Hanlon Cooke
Head of government	Percival J. Patterson
High Commission in UK	1–2 Prince Consort Road, London SW7 2BZ. Tel: 0171-823 9911
British High Commission in Kingston	PO Box 575, Trafalgar Road, Kingston 10. Tel: Kingston 926 9050

Defence

Military expenditure	0.5% of GDP (1996)
Military personnel	3,320: Army 3,000, Coast Guard 150, Air Wing 170

Economy

GNP	US$4,066 million (1996)
	US$1,600 per capita (1996)
GDP	US$4,484 million (1994)
	US$1,650 per capita (1994)
Annual average growth of GDP	0.8% (1994)
Inflation rate	26.4% (1996)
Unemployment	15.9% (1992)
Total external debt	US$4,041 million (1996)

Education

Enrolment (percentage of age group)	primary 100% (1992); secondary 64% (1992); tertiary 6% (1992)
Illiteracy rate	15%

JAPAN

Area	145,870 sq. miles (377,801 sq. km)
Population	125,197,000 (1994 UN estimate)
Main language	Japanese
Capital	Tokyo (population 11,927,457, 1993 estimate)
Currency	Yen of 100 sen
Exchange rate (at 29 May)	Yen 225.958
Public holidays	January 1–3, 15; February 11; March 21; April 29; May 3–5; July 20; September 15, 23; October 10; November 3, 23; December 23, 31
Usual business hours	Mon.–Fri. 9–17
Electrical rating	100v AC, 60Hz in the west; 100v AC, 50Hz in the east and Tokyo

Demography

Life expectancy (years)	male 76.57; female 82.98
Population growth rate	0.3% (1995)
Population density	331 per sq. km (1995)
Urban population	77.4% (1990)

Government and diplomacy

Political system	Constitutional monarchy
Head of state	Emperor Akihito
Head of government	Keizo Obuchi
Embassy in UK	101–104 Piccadilly, London W1V 9FN. Tel: 0171-465 6500
British Embassy in Tokyo	No. 1 Ichiban-cho, Chiyoda-ku, Tokyo 102. Tel: Tokyo 5211 1100

Defence

Military expenditure	1% of GDP (1996)
Military personnel	246,300: Army 147,700, Navy 42,500, Air Force 44,100, Paramilitaries 12,000

Economy

GNP	US$5,149,185 million (1996) US$40,940 per capita (1996)
GDP	US$3,152,205 million (1994) US$36,782 per capita (1994)
Annual average growth of GDP	3.6% (1996)
Inflation rate	0.1% (1996)
Unemployment	3.2% (1995)

Education

Enrolment (percentage of age group)	primary 100% (1993); secondary 96% (1993); tertiary 40.3% (1994)

JORDAN

Area	37,738 sq. miles (97,740 sq. km)
Population	5,439,000 (1994 UN estimate)
Main languages	Arabic, English, French
Capital	Amman (population 1,270,000, 1994)
Currency	Jordanian dinar (JD) of 1,000 fils
Exchange rate (at 29 May)	JD 1.1594
Public holidays	January 1, 30; April 7, 19, 28; May 1, 25; June 10; July 6; August 11; November 14, 17; December 25
Usual business hours	Sat., Wed., Thurs. 9–17
Electrical rating	220v AC, 50Hz

Demography

Life expectancy (years)	male 66.16; female 69.84
Population growth rate	4.9% (1995)
Population density	56 per sq. km (1995)

Government and diplomacy

Political system	Constitutional monarchy
Head of state	King Hussein
Head of government	Dr Abdel Salam Majali
Embassy in UK	6 Upper Phillimore Gardens, London W8 7HB. Tel: 0171-937 3685
British Embassy in Amman	Abdoun (PO Box 87), Amman. Tel: Amman 823100

Defence

Military expenditure	5.5% of GDP (1996)
Military personnel	114,050: Army 90,000, Navy 650, Air Force 13,400, Paramilitaries 10,000

Economy

GNP	US$7,088 million (1996) US$1,650 per capita (1996)
GDP	US$4,938 million (1994) US$1,095 per capita (1994)
Annual average growth of GDP	5.2% (1996)
Inflation rate	6.5% (1996)
Total external debt	US$8,118 million (1996)

Education

Enrolment (percentage of age group)	primary 89% (1992); secondary 42% (1989); tertiary 24.5% (1989)
Illiteracy rate	13.4%

KAZAKHSTAN

Area	1,049,156 sq. miles (2,717,300 sq. km)
Population	16,590,000 (1994 UN estimate)
Main languages	Kazakh, Russian
Capital	Astana (population 292,000, 1993 estimate)
Currency	Tenge
Exchange rate (at 29 May)	Tenge 125.401
Public holidays	January 1, 2; March 8, 21; May 1, 9; August 30; October 25; December 16
Usual business hours	Banking hours: Mon.–Fri. 9.30–17.30
Electrical rating	220v AC, 50Hz

Demography

Life expectancy (years)	male 63.83; female 736
Population growth rate	-0.1% (1995)
Population density	6 per sq. km (1995)
Urban population	56.7% (1993)

Government and diplomacy

Political system	Republic
Head of state	President Nursultan Nazarbayev
Head of government	Nurlan Balgymbayev
Embassy in UK	33 Thurloe Square, London SW7 2SD. Tel: 0171-581 4646
British Embassy in Alma-Ata	U1 Furmanova 173, Alma-Ata. Tel: Alma-Ata 506191

Defence

Military expenditure	2.7% of GDP (1996)
Military personnel	69,600: Army 20,000, Navy 100, Air Force 15,000, Paramilitaries 34,500
Conscription duration	31 months

Economy

GNP	US$22,213 million (1996) US$1,350 per capita (1996)
GDP	US$37,288 million (1994) US$120 per capita (1994)
Inflation rate	39.2% (1996)
Unemployment	1% (1993)
Total external debt	US$2,920 million (1996)

Education

Enrolment (percentage of age group)	tertiary 32.7% (1995)
Illiteracy rate	0.4%

KENYA

Area	224,081 sq. miles (580,367 sq. km)
Population	30,522,000 (1994 UN estimate)
Main languages	Swahili, English
Capital	Nairobi (population 1,400,000, 1989 estimate)
Currency	Kenya shilling (Ksh) of 100 cents
Exchange rate (at 29 May)	Ksh 102.367
Public holidays	January 1, 30 (3 days); April 10, 13; May 1; June 1; October 10, 20; December 12, 25, 26
Usual business hours	Mon.–Fri. 8–13, 14–17
Electrical rating	220/240v AC, 50Hz

Demography
Life expectancy (years)	male 54.18; female 57.29
Population density	53 per sq. km (1995)

Government and diplomacy
Political system	Republic
Head of state and of government	President Daniel T. arap Moi
High Commission in UK	45 Portland Place, London W1N 4AS. Tel: 0171-636 2371
British High Commission in Nairobi	Bruce House, Standard Street, PO Box 30465 Nairobi. Tel: Nairobi 335944
Trouble spots	Election irregularities and opposition intimidation

Defence
Military expenditure	2.2% of GDP (1996)
Military personnel	29,200: Army 20,500, Navy 1,200, Air Force 2,500, Paramilitaries 5,000

Economy
GNP	US$8,661 million (1996) US$320 per capita (1996)
GDP	US$9,016 million (1994) US$254 per capita (1994)
Annual average growth of GDP	4.2% (1996)
Inflation rate	8.8% (1996)
Total external debt	US$6,893 million (1996)

Education
Enrolment (percentage of age group)	primary 91% (1980); tertiary 1.6% (1990)
Illiteracy rate	21.9%

KIRIBATI

Area	280 sq. miles (726 sq. km)
Population	79,000 (1994 UN estimate)
Main languages	I-Kiribati, English
Capital	Tarawa (population 17,921, 1978)
Currency	Australian dollar ($A) of 100 cents
Exchange rate (at 29 May)	$A 2.6035
Public holidays	January 1; April 10, 13, 18; June 11, 13, 14; August 5; December 10, 25, 26
Usual business hours	Mon.–Fri. 8–12.30, 13.30–16.15
Electrical rating	240v AC, 50Hz

Demography

Population growth rate	1.9% (1995)
Population density	109 per sq. km (1995)

Government and diplomacy

Political system	Republic
Head of state and of government	President Teburoro Tito
Honorary Consulate in UK	The Great House, Llanddewi Rhydderch, Monmouthshire, NP7 9UY. Tel: 01873-840375
British High Commission	Suva, Fiji

Economy

GNP	US$75 million (1996)
	US$920 per capita (1996)
GDP	US$41 million (1994)
	US$602 per capita (1994)

DEMOCRATIC PEOPLE'S REPUBLIC OF KOREA (NORTH KOREA)

Area	46,540 sq. miles (120,538 sq. km)
Population	23,917,000 (1994 UN estimate)
Main language	Korean
Capital	Pyongyang (population *c*.2,000,000)
Currency	Won of 100 chon
Exchange rate (at 29 May)	Won 3.5876
Electrical rating	110/220v AC, 60Hz

Demography

Life expectancy (years)	male 67.70; female 73.95
Population growth rate	1.9% (1995)
Population density	198 per sq. km (1995)
Urban population	58.9% (1993)

Government and diplomacy

Political system	Republic; one-party (Communist) state
Head of state	President, vacant
Head of government	Kang Song-san
Embassies	North Korea has no diplomatic relations with the UK

Defence

Military expenditure	27% of GDP (1996)
Military personnel	1,244,000: Army 923,000, Navy 47,000, Air Force 85,000, Paramilitaries 189,000
Conscription duration	Three to ten years

Economy

GDP	US$19,566 million (1994)
	US$1,155 per capita (1994)

REPUBLIC OF KOREA (SOUTH KOREA)

Area	38,330 sq. miles (99,274 sq. km)
Population	44,851,000 (1996)
Main language	Korean
Capital	Seoul (population 10,776,201, 1995)
Currency	Won of 100 jeon
Exchange rate (at 29 May)	Won 2295.21
Public holidays	January 1, 2, 27–29; March 1; April 5; May 1, 3, 5; June 6; July 17; August 15; October 3–6; December 25
Usual business hours	Mon.–Fri. 9–18; Sat. 9–13
Electrical rating	110/220v AC, 60Hz

Demography

Life expectancy (years)	male 67.66; female 75.67
Population growth rate	0.9% (1995)
Population density	452 per sq. km (1995)
Urban population	74.4% (1990)

Government and diplomacy

Political system	Republic
Head of state	President Kim Dae-jung
Head of government	Vacant pending approval of National Assembly. Kim Jong-Pil (acting)
Embassy in UK	60 Buckingham Gate, London SW1E 6AJ
British Embassy in Seoul	No. 4, Chung-Dong, Chung-Ku, Seoul 100. Tel: Seoul 735 7341/3

Defence

Military expenditure	3.2% of GDP (1996)
Military personnel	676,500: Army 560,000, Navy 60,000, Air Force 52,000, Paramilitaries 4,500
Conscription duration	26–30 months

Economy

GNP	US$483,130 million (1996) US$10,610 per capita (1996)
GDP	US$317,891 million (1994) US$8,519 per capita (1994)
Annual average growth of GDP	7.1% (1996)
Inflation rate	5% (1996)
Unemployment	2% (1995)

Education

Enrolment (percentage of age group)	primary 99% (1993); secondary 96% (1995); tertiary 52% (1995)
Illiteracy rate	2%

KUWAIT

Area	6,880 sq. miles (17,818 sq. km)
Population	1,691,000 (1995 census)
Main languages	Arabic, English
Capital	Kuwait City (population 400,000, 1975)
Currency	Kuwaiti dinar (KD) of 1,000 fils
Exchange rate (at 29 May)	KD 0.4991
Public holidays	January 1, 30 (3 days); February 25, 26; April 7, 28; July 6; November 17
Usual business hours	Sat.–Wed. 7.30–12.30, 16–19
Electrical rating	240v AC, 50Hz, single phase (UK plugs)

Demography
Life expectancy (years)	male 71.77; female 73.32
Population growth rate	-4.7% (1995)
Population density	95 per sq. km (1995)

Government and diplomacy
Political system	Constitutional monarchy
Head of state	Sheikh Jaber al-Ahmad al Jaber Al-Sabah (Amir)
Head of government	Sheikh Saad al-Abdullah al-Salem al-Sabah
Embassy in UK	45–46 Queen's Gate, London SW7 5JN. Tel: 0171-589 4533
British Embassy in Kuwait	PO Box 2 Safat, 13001 Safat, Kuwait. Tel: Kuwait 240 3334/6

Defence
Military expenditure	14.5% of GDP (1996)
Military personnel	20,300: Army 11,000, Navy 1,800, Air Force 2,500, Paramilitaries 5,000
Conscription duration	Two years

Economy
GNP	US$28,941 million (1995) US$17,390 per capita (1995)
GDP	US$22,946 million (1994) US$16,285 per capita (1994)
Annual average growth of GDP	1% (1995)
Inflation rate	3.2% (1996)

Education
Enrolment (percentage of age group)	primary 65% (1995); secondary 54% (1993); tertiary 25.4% (1995)
Illiteracy rate	21.4%

KYRGYZSTAN

Area	76,641 sq. miles (198,500 sq. km)
Population	4,668,000 (1994 UN estimate)
Main languages	Kirghiz, Russian
Capital	Bishkek (population 627,800, 1991 estimate)
Currency	Som
Public holidays	January 1, 7; March 8, 21; May 1, 5, 9; August 31
Usual business hours	Mon.–Sat. 9–18
Electrical rating	220v AC, 50Hz

Demography

Life expectancy (years)	male 64.23; female 72.23
Population growth rate	1.2% (1995)
Population density	24 per sq. km (1995)
Urban population	39.3% (1995)

Government and diplomacy

Political system	Republic
Head of state	President Askar Akaev
Head of government	Kubanychbek Jumaliev
Embassy in UK	Kyrgyz interests are handled by the Russian Embassy
British Embassy	Alma-Ata, Kazakhstan

Defence

Military expenditure	2.6% of GDP (1996)
Military personnel	17,200: Army 9,800, Air Force 2,400, Paramilitaries 5,000
Conscription duration	18 months

Economy

GNP	US$2,486 million (1996) US$550 per capita (1996)
GDP	US$3,117 million (1994) US$222 per capita (1994)
Total external debt	US$789 million (1996)

Education

Enrolment (percentage of age group)	primary 97% (1995); tertiary 12.2% (1995)
Illiteracy rate	0.4%

LAOS

Area	91,429 sq. miles (236,800 sq. km)
Population	4,882,000 (1995 census)
Main languages	Lao, French, Vietnamese
Capital	Vientiane (population 120,000, 1984 estimate)
Currency	Kip (K) of 100 at
Exchange rate (at 29 May)	K 3276.07
Usual business hours	Mon.–Fri. 8–12, 14–17; Sat. 8–12
Electrical rating	220v AC, 50Hz

Demography

Life expectancy (years)	male 49.50; female 52.50
Population growth rate	3% (1995)
Population density	21 per sq. km (1995)

Government and diplomacy

Political system	Republic; one-party (Lao People's Revolutionary Party) state
Head of state	President Gen. Khamtai Siphandone
Head of government	Sisavat Keobounphanh
Embassy	74 Avenue Raymond-Poincaré 75116 Paris, France. Tel: Paris 4553 0298
British Embassy	Bangkok, Thailand

Defence

Military expenditure	3.9% of GDP (1996)
Military personnel	29,000: Army 25,000, Navy 500, Air Force 3,500
Conscription duration	18 months minimum

Economy

GNP	US$1,895 million (1996) US$400 per capita (1996)
GDP	US$990 million (1994) US$290 per capita (1994)
Annual average growth of GDP	6.7% (1996)
Inflation rate	19.6% (1995)
Total external debt	US$2,263 million (1996)

Education

Enrolment (percentage of age group)	primary 68% (1993); secondary 18% (1993); tertiary 1.5% (1993)
Illiteracy rate	43.4%

LATVIA

Area	24,942 sq. miles (64,600 sq. km)
Population	2,515,000 (1995)
Main languages	Latvian, Russian
Capital	Riga (population 847,976, 1995)
Currency	Lats of 100 santimes
Exchange rate (at 29 May)	Lats 0.9674
Public holidays	January 1; April 10, 11; May 1, 10; June 23, 24; November 18; December 25, 26, 31
Usual business hours	Mon.–Fri. 8.30–17.30
Electrical rating	220v AC, 50Hz

Demography

Life expectancy (years)	male 60.72; female 72.87
Population growth rate	-1.2% (1995)
Population density	39 per sq. km (1995)
Urban population	69.1% (1994)

Government and diplomacy

Political system	Republic
Head of state	President Guntis Ulmanis
Head of government	Guntars Krasts
Embassy in UK	45 Nottingham Place, London W1M 3FE. Tel: 0171-312 0040
British Embassy in Riga	5, Alunana Iela Street, Riga LV1010. Tel: Riga 733 8126

Defence

Military expenditure	2.6% of GDP (1996)
Military personnel	8,100: Army 3,400, Navy 980, Air Force 120, Paramilitaries 3,600
Conscription duration	12 months

Economy

GNP	US$5,730 million (1996) US$2,300 per capita (1996)
GDP	US$9,370 million (1994) US$1,173 per capita (1994)
Annual average growth of GDP	2.8% (1996)
Inflation rate	17.6% (1996)
Unemployment	6.6% (1995)
Total external debt	US$472 million (1996)

Education

Enrolment (percentage of age group)	primary 84% (1995); secondary 78% (1995); tertiary 25.7% (1995)
Illiteracy rate	0.3%

LEBANON

Area	4,015 sq. miles (10,400 sq. km)
Population	3,009,000 (1994 UN estimate)
Main languages	Arabic, French, English
Capital	Beirut (population 1,500,000, 1991)
Currency	Lebanese pound (L£) of 100 piastres
Exchange rate (at 29 May)	L£ 2466.43
Public holidays	January 1, 30 (3 days); February 9; April 7 (3 days), 10, 13, 17, 20, 28; May 1, 6, 7; July 6; August 15; November 1, 22; December 25
Usual business hours	Mon.–Fri. 8–17
Electrical rating	110/220v AC, 50Hz

Demography

Life expectancy (years)	male 66.60; female 70.50
Population growth rate	3.3% (1995)
Population density	289 per sq. km (1995)

Government and diplomacy

Political system	Republic
Head of state	President Elias Hrawi
Head of government	Rafic Al-Hariri
Embassy in UK	21 Kensington Palace Gardens, London W8 4QM. Tel: 0171-229 7265/6
British Embassy in Beirut	Autostrade Jal El Dib, Coolrite Building (PO Box 60180), Beirut. Tel: Beirut 406330
Trouble spots	South under control of Israeli client groups
	Area south of Tyre, southern Beka'a valley and border with Southern Lebanon Security Zone volatile

Defence

Military expenditure	3.7% of GDP (1996)
Military personnel	68,100: Army 53,300, Navy 1,000, Air Force 800, Paramilitaries 13,000
Conscription duration	12 months

Economy

GNP	US$12,118 million (1996)
	US$2,970 per capita (1996)
GDP	US$4,977 million (1994)
	US$1,692 per capita (1994)
Inflation rate	6.8% (1994)
Total external debt	US$3,996 million (1996)

Education

Enrolment (percentage of age group)	tertiary 27% (1995)
Literacy rate	7.6%

LESOTHO

Area	11,720 sq. miles (30,355 sq. km)
Population	2,050,000 (1994 UN estimate)
Main languages	Sesotho, English
Capital	Maseru (population 288,951, 1986)
Currency	Loti (M) of 100 lisente
Exchange rate (at 29 May)	M 8.4079
Public holidays	January 1; March 11; April 4, 10, 13; May 1, 21; July 17; October 4; December 25, 26
Usual business hours	Mon.–Fri. 8–12.45, 14–16.30; Sat. 8–13
Electrical rating	220v AC, 50Hz

Demography

Life expectancy (years)	male 58; female 63
Population growth rate	2.7% (1995)
Population density	68 per sq. km (1995)

Government and diplomacy

Political system	Constitutional monarchy
Head of state	King Letsie III
Head of government	Dr Ntsu Mokhehle
High Commission in UK	7 Chesham Place, London SW1X 8HN. Tel: 0171-235 5686
British High Commission in Maseru	PO Box 521, Maseru 100. Tel: Maseru 313961

Defence

Military expenditure	3.3% of GDP (1996)
Military personnel	2,000 Army

Economy

GNP	US$1,331 million (1996)
	US$660 per capita (1996)
GDP	US$684 million (1994)
	US$424 per capita (1994)
Total external debt	US$654 million (1996)

Education

Enrolment (percentage of age group)	primary 65% (1994); secondary 16% (1994); tertiary 2.4% (1994)
Illiteracy rate	28.7%

LIBERIA

Area	43,000 sq. miles (111,369 sq. km)
Population	2,760,000 (1994 UN estimate)
Main languages	English; over 16 ethnic languages are also spoken
Capital	Monrovia (population 421,053, 1984)
Currency	Liberian dollar (L$) of 100 cents
Exchange rate (at 29 May)	L$ 1.6307
Public holidays	January 1; February 11; March 12, 15; April 10, 11; July 26; August 24; November 6, 29; December 25
Usual business hours	Mon.–Fri. 8–12, 14–16
Electrical rating	110v AC, 60Hz

Demography

Life expectancy (years)	male 45.80; female 44
Population growth rate	2.7% (1995)
Population density	25 per sq. km (1995)
Urban population	44.6% (1995)

Government and diplomacy

Political system	Republic
Head of state and of government	President Charles Taylor
Embassy in UK	2 Pembridge Place, London W2 4XB. Tel: 0171-221 1036
British Embassy	Abidjan, Côte d'Ivoire
Trouble spots	Situation unstable following end of civil war in 1997 and withdrawal of ECOMOG peace-keeping troops in 1998
	North-west affected by rebel activity in Sierra Leone

Defence

Military expenditure	3.5% of GDP (1996)

Economy

GDP	US$1,442 million (1994)
	US$718 per capita (1994)
Annual average growth of GDP	2.7% (1987)
Inflation rate	9.1% (1989)
Total external debt	US$2,107 million (1996)

Education

Illiteracy rate	61.7%

LIBYA

Area	679,362 sq. miles (1,759,540 sq. km)
Population	5,407,000 (1994 UN estimate)
Main language	Arabic
Capital	Tripoli (population 1,000,000, 1991 estimate)
Currency	Libyan dinar (LD) of 1,000 dirhams
Exchange rate (at 29 May)	LD 0.6254
Public holidays	January 30 (3 days); March 2; April 7 (4 days); June 11; July 6, 23; September 1
Usual business hours	Generally 7–14
Electrical rating	150/220v AC, 50Hz

Demography

Life expectancy (years)	male 61.58; female 65
Population density	3 per sq. km (1995)

Government and diplomacy

Political system	Republic
Head of state	Col. Muammar al-Gadhafi (Leader of the Revolution)
Head of government	Mohammad Ahmed al-Manqoush
Embassy in UK	Since 1984 the Embassy of Saudi Arabia has handled Libyan interests in Britain
British Embassy in Tripoli	British interests are handled by the British Interests Section of the Italian Embassy, Sharia Uahran 1 (PO Box 4206), Tripoli

Defence

Military expenditure	1.8% of GDP (1996)
Military personnel	65,000: Army 35,000, Navy 8,000, Air Force 22,000
Conscription duration	One to two years

Economy

GDP	US$29,274 million (1994) US$4,220 per capita (1994)

Education

Enrolment (percentage of age group)	primary 97% (1992); secondary 62% (1980); tertiary 16.4% (1991)
Illiteracy rate	23.8%

LIECHTENSTEIN

Area	62 sq. miles (160 sq. km)
Population	31,000 (1994 UN estimate)
Main language	German
Capital	Vaduz (population 5,072, 1993)
Currency	Swiss franc of 100 rappen (or centimes)
Exchange rate (at 29 May)	Francs 2.4112
Public holidays	January 1, 2, 6; February 2, 24; March 19; April 10, 13; May 1, 21; June 1, 11; August 15; September 8; November 1; December 8, 24–26, 31
Usual business hours	Mon.–Fri. 8–12, 13.30–17
Electrical rating	220v AC, 50Hz

Demography

Life expectancy (years)	male 66.07; female 72.94
Population growth rate	1.3% (1995)
Population density	194 per sq. km (1995)

Government and diplomacy

Political system	Constitutional monarchy
Head of state	Prince Hans Adam II
Head of government	Dr Mario Frick
Embassy in UK	Liechtenstein is represented in diplomatic and consular matters by the Swiss Embassy
British Embassy	Berne, Switzerland

Economy

GDP	US$1,296 million (1994) US$49,368 per capita (1994)

LITHUANIA

Area	25,174 sq. miles (65,200 sq. km)
Population	3,715,000 (1997)
Main languages	Lithuanian, Russian; some Polish, Belarusian
Capital	Vilnius (population 581,500, 1997)
Currency	Litas
Exchange rate (at 29 May)	Litas 6.5249
Public holidays	January 1; February 16; March 11; April 12, 13; July 6; November 1; December 25, 26
Usual business hours	Mon.–Fri. 9–13, 14–18
Electrical rating	220v AC, 50Hz

Demography

Life expectancy (years)	male 63.27; female 75.04
Population growth rate	0% (1995)
Population density	57 per sq. km (1995)
Urban population	67.9% (1995)

Government and diplomacy

Political system	Republic
Head of state	President Valdas Adamkus
Head of government	Gediminas Vagnorius
Embassy in UK	84 Gloucester Place, London W1H 3HN. Tel: 0171-486 6401
British Embassy in Vilnius	2 Antakalnio, 2055 Vilnius. Tel: Vilnius 222 2070

Defence

Military expenditure	1.6% of GDP (1996)
Military personnel	5,250: Army 4,200, Navy 500, Air Force 550
Conscription duration	12 months

Economy

GNP	US$8,455 million (1996)
	US$2,280 per capita (1996)
GDP	US$7,596 million (1994)
	US$1,132 per capita (1994)
Annual average growth of GDP	3.6% (1996)
Inflation rate	24.6% (1996)
Unemployment	7.3% (1995)
Total external debt	US$1,286 million (1996)

Education

Enrolment (percentage of age group)	secondary 80% (1994); tertiary 28.2% (1995)
Illiteracy rate	0.5%

LUXEMBOURG

Area	998 sq. miles (2,586 sq. km)
Population	406,000 (1996)
Main languages	Letzebuergesch (Luxembourgish), French, German
Capital	Luxembourg (population 76,446, 1996)
Currency	Luxembourg franc (LF) of 100 centimes. Belgian currency is also legal tender
Exchange rate (at 29 May)	LF 59.9193
Public holidays	January 1; April 13; May 1, 21; June 1, 23; August 15; November 1, 2; December 24–26
Usual business hours	Mon.–Fri. 8.30–12, 14–18
Electrical rating	220v AC, 50Hz

Demography

Life expectancy (years)	male 70.61; female 77.87
Population growth rate	1.2% (1995)
Population density	157 per sq. km (1995)

Government and diplomacy

Political system	Constitutional monarchy
Head of state	Grand Duke Jean
Head of government	Jean-Claude Juncker
Embassy in UK	27 Wilton Crescent, London SW1X 8SD. Tel: 0171-235 6961
British Embassy in Luxembourg	14 Boulevard F. D. Roosevelt, L-2450 Luxembourg Ville. Tel: Luxembourg 229864

Defence

Military expenditure	0.7% of GDP (1996)
Military personnel	1,360: Army 800, Paramilitaries 560

Economy

GNP	US$18,850 million (1996) US$45,360 per capita (1996)
GDP	US$9,973 million (1994) US$27,611 per capita (1994)
Annual average growth of GDP	1.8% (1992)
Inflation rate	1.4% (1996)
Unemployment	2.8% (1995)

Education

Enrolment (percentage of age group)	primary 81% (1985); secondary 66% (1985); tertiary 2.6% (1985)

MACAO, see PORTUGAL

FORMER YUGOSLAV REPUBLIC OF MACEDONIA

Area	9,928 sq. miles (25,713 sq. km)
Population	2,163,000 (1994 UN estimate)
Main language	Macedonian
Capital	Skopje (population 448,229, 1991)
Currency	Dinar of 100 paras
Exchange rate (at 29 May)	Dinars 89.9394
Public holidays	January 1; May 1; August 2; September 8; October 11
Usual business hours	Mon.–Fri. 7–15
Electrical rating	220v AC, 50Hz

Demography
Life expectancy (years)	male 68.80; female 74.95
Population growth rate	1.3% (1995)
Population density	84 per sq. km (1995)
Urban population	58.1% (1991)

Government and diplomacy
Political system	Republic
Head of state	President Milo Djukanovic
Head of government	Filip Vujanovic
Embassy in UK	10 Harcourt House, 19A Cavendish Square, London W1M 9AD. Tel: 0171-499 5152
British Embassy in Skopje	Veljko Vlahovíc 26, 9100 Skopje. Tel: Skopje 116772

Defence
Military expenditure	7.5% of GDP (1996)
Military personnel	22,900: Army 15,400, Paramilitaries 7,500
Conscription duration	Nine months

Economy
GNP	US$1,956 million (1996) US$990 per capita (1996)
GDP	US$3,470 million (1994) US$1,552 per capita (1994)
Unemployment	35.6% (1995)
Total external debt	US$1,659 million (1996)

Education
Enrolment (percentage of age group)	primary 85% (1995); secondary 51% (1995); tertiary 17.5% (1995)

MADAGASCAR

Area	226,658 sq. miles (587,041 sq. km)
Population	14,763,000 (1994 UN estimate)
Main languages	Malagasy, French
Capital	Antananarivo (population 377,600, 1971 estimate)
Currency	Franc malgache (FMG) of 100 centimes
Exchange rate (at 29 May)	FMG 8577.48
Public holidays	January 1; April 10, 13; May 1, 21, 25; June 1, 26; August 15; December 25, 31
Electrical rating	Mainly 220v AC, 50Hz

Demography

Life expectancy (years)	male 55; female 58
Population density	25 per sq. km (1995)

Government and diplomacy

Political system	Republic
Head of state	President Adm. Didier Ratsiraka
Head of government	Pascal Rakotomavo
Embassy	4 avenue Raphael, 75016 Paris, France. Tel: Paris 4504 6211
Honorary Consulate in UK	16 Lanark Mansions, Pennard Road, London W12 8DT. Tel: 0181-746 0133
British Embassy in Antananarivo	1st Floor, Immeuble 'Ny Havana', Cite de 67 Ha, BP 167, Antananarivo. Tel: Antananarivo 27749

Defence

Military expenditure	0.8% of GDP (1996)
Military personnel	28,500: Army 20,000, Navy 500, Air Force 500, Paramilitaries 7,500
Conscription duration	18 months

Economy

GNP	US$3,428 million (1996) US$250 per capita (1996)
GDP	US$2,979 million (1994) US$208 per capita (1994)
Annual average growth of GDP	1.8% (1995)
Inflation rate	19.8% (1996)
Total external debt	US$4,175 million (1996)

Education

Enrolment (percentage of age group)	tertiary 3.4% (1992)
Illiteracy rate	54.3%

MALAWI

Area	45,747 sq. miles (118,484 sq. km)
Population	9,788,000 (1994 UN estimate)
Main languages	Chichewa, English
Capital	Lilongwe (population 233,973, 1987)
Currency	Kwacha (K) of 100 tambala
Exchange rate (at 29 May)	K 42.7162
Public holidays	January 1, 15; March 3; April 10, 13; May 1; June 15; July 6; October 14; December 25, 26, 28
Usual business hours	Mon.–Fri. 7.30–17
Electrical rating	220/240v AC, 50Hz

Demography

Life expectancy (years)	male 43.51; female 46.75
Population growth rate	3.3% (1995)
Population density	83 per sq. km (1995)
Urban population	18.9% (1995)

Government and diplomacy

Political system	Republic
Head of state and of government	President Bakili Muluzi
High Commission in UK	33 Grosvenor Street, London W1X 0DE. Tel: 0171-491 4172/7
British High Commission in Lilongwe	PO Box 30042, Lilongwe 3. Tel: Lilongwe 782400

Defence

Military expenditure	1.2% of GDP (1996)
Military personnel	6,000: Army 5,000, Paramilitaries 1,000

Economy

GNP	US$1,832 million (1996)
	US$180 per capita (1996)
GDP	US$2,079 million (1994)
	US$130 per capita (1994)
Annual average growth of GDP	-9.3% (1994)
Inflation rate	83.3% (1995)
Total external debt	US$2,312 million (1996)

Education

Enrolment (percentage of age group)	primary 100% (1994); secondary 2% (1994); tertiary 0.8% (1993)
Illiteracy rate	43.6%

MALAYSIA

Area	127,320 sq. miles (329,758 sq. km)
Population	20,140,000 (1995)
Main languages	Bahasa Malaysia (Malay), English, various dialects of Chinese, Tamil, indigenous languages in Sabah and Sarawak
Capital	Kuala Lumpur (population 1,145,075, 1991)
Currency	Malaysian dollar (ringgit) (M$) of 100 sen
Exchange rate (at 29 May)	M$ 6.2627
Public holidays	January 28–31; April 28; May 1, 10; June 6; July 6; August 31; December 25
Usual business hours	Generally Mon.–Fri. 8.30–16 or 17.30
Electrical rating	220v AC, 50Hz

Demography

Life expectancy (years)	male 68.68; female 73.04
Population growth rate	2.5% (1995)
Population density	61 per sq. km (1995)
Urban population	50.6% (1991)

Government and diplomacy

Political system	Federation of constitutional monarchies
Head of state	Tuanku Jaafar Ibni Al-Marhum Tuanku Abdul Rahman (Supreme Head of the Federation)
Head of government	Dr Mahathir Mohamad
High Commission in UK	45 Belgrave Square, London SW1X 8QT. Tel: 0171-235 8033
British High Commission in Kuala Lumpur	185 Jalan Ampang (PO Box 11030), 50450 Kuala Lumpur. Tel: Kuala Lumpur 248 2122

Defence

Military expenditure	3.6% of GDP (1996)
Military personnel	131,600: Army 85,000, Navy 14,000, Air Force 12,500, Paramilitaries 20,100

Economy

GNP	US$89,800 million (1996) US$4,370 per capita (1996)
GDP	US$58,941 million (1994) US$3,582 per capita (1994)
Annual average growth of GDP	9.6% (1995)
Inflation rate	3.5% (1996)
Unemployment	2.8% (1995)
Total external debt	US$39,777 million (1996)

Education

Enrolment (percentage of age group)	primary 91% (1994); tertiary 10.6% (1994)
Illiteracy rate	16.5%

MALDIVES

Area	115 sq. miles (298 sq. km)
Population	254,000 (1996)
Main language	Maldivian (Dhivehi)
Capital	Malé (population 62,973, 1995)
Currency	Rufiyaa of 100 laaris
Exchange rate (at 29 May)	Rufiyaa 19.1933
Public holidays	January 1, 30 (4 days); April 7 (4 days), 28; July 6, 26, 27; November 11–13
Usual business hours	Sun.–Thurs. 7.30–14.30
Electrical rating	220v AC, 50Hz

Demography

Life expectancy (years)	male 67.15; female 66.60
Population growth rate	3.3% (1995)
Population density	852 per sq. km (1995)
Urban population	25.9% (1990)

Government and diplomacy

Political system	Republic
Head of state and of government	President Maumoon Abdul Gayoom
High Commission in UK	22 Nottingham Place, London W1M 3FB
British High Commission	Colombo, Sri Lanka

Economy

GNP	US$277 million (1996)
	US$1,080 per capita (1996)
GDP	US$180 million (1994)
	US$1,032 per capita (1994)
Annual average growth of GDP	7.2% (1995)
Inflation rate	6.3% (1996)
Total external debt	US$167 million (1996)

Education

Illiteracy rate	6.8%

MALI

Area	478,841 sq. miles (1,240,192 sq. km)
Population	10,795,000 (1994 UN estimate)
Main languages	French, local dialects
Capital	Bamako (population 658,275, 1987)
Currency	Franc CFA of 100 centimes
Exchange rate (at 29 May)	Francs 975.610
Public holidays	January 1, 20, 30; March 26; April 7, 20; May 1, 25; July 6, 21; September 22; December 25
Usual business hours	Mon.–Thurs. 7.30–12.30, 13–16; Fri. 7.30–12.30, 14.30–17.30
Electrical rating	Bamako 220v AC, 50Hz; other towns have local supply

Demography

Life expectancy (years)	male 55.24; female 58.66
Population density	9 per sq. km (1995)
Urban population	22% (1987)

Government and diplomacy

Political system	Republic
Head of state	President Alpha Oumar Konaré
Head of government	Ibrahim Boubacar Keita
Embassy	Avenue Molière 487, 1060 Brussels, Belgium. Tel: Brussels 345 7432
British Embassy	Dakar, Senegal

Defence

Military expenditure	1.8% of GDP (1996)
Military personnel	12,150: Army 7,350, Paramilitaries 4,800
Conscription duration	Two years

Economy

GNP	US$2,422 million (1996)
	US$240 per capita (1996)
GDP	US$2,895 million (1994)
	US$183 per capita (1994)
Annual average growth of GDP	-0.2% (1991)
Inflation rate	6.8% (1996)
Total external debt	US$3,020 million (1996)

Education

Enrolment (percentage of age group)	primary 25% (1994); secondary 5% (1990); tertiary 0.8% (1990)
Illiteracy rate	69%

MALTA

Area	122 sq. miles (316 sq. km)
Population	371,000 (1995)
Main languages	Maltese, English
Capital	Valletta (population 9,144, 1995 census)
Currency	Maltese lira (LM) of 100 cents or 1,000 mils
Exchange rate (at 29 May)	LM 0.6432
Public holidays	January 1; February 10; March 19, 31; April 10; May 1; June 7, 29; August 15; September 8, 21; December 8, 13, 25
Usual business hours	Mon.–Fri. 8.30–12.45, 14.30–17.30; Sat. 8.30–12
Electrical rating	240v AC, 50Hz

Demography
Life expectancy (years)	male 74.86; female 79.11
Population growth rate	0.9% (1995)
Population density	1,173 per sq. km (1995)

Government and diplomacy
Political system	Republic
Head of state	President Dr Ugo Mifsud Bonnici
Head of government	Dr Alfred Sant
High Commission in UK	Malta House, 36–38 Piccadilly, London W1V 0PQ. Tel: 0171-292 4800
British High Commission in Floriana	7 St Anne Street, Floriana (PO Box 506), Malta. Tel: Floriana 233134/8

Defence
Military expenditure	1.1% of GDP (1996)
Military personnel	1,950

Economy
GDP	US$2,804 million (1994) US$7,394 per capita (1994)
Annual average growth of GDP	9% (1995)
Inflation rate	2.5% (1996)
Unemployment	4.5% (1993)
Total external debt	US$953 million (1996)

Education
Enrolment (percentage of age group)	primary 100% (1994); secondary 84% (1994); tertiary 21.8% (1994)
Illiteracy rate	8.7%

MARSHALL ISLANDS

Area	70 sq. miles (181 sq. km)
Population	56,000 (1994 UN estimate)
Main languages	Marshallese, English
Capital	Dalap-Uliga-Darrit (population 20,000), on Majuro Atoll
Currency	Currency is that of USA
Exchange rate (at 29 May)	US$ 1.6307
Usual business hours	Mon.–Fri. 8–17
Electrical rating	110/120v AC, 60Hz (US plugs)

Demography

Life expectancy (years)	male 596; female 62.96
Population growth rate	3.7% (1995)
Population density	307 per sq. km (1995)

Government and diplomacy

Political system	Republic
Head of state and of government	President Imata Kabua British Embassy Suva, Fiji

Economy

GNP	US$108 million (1996)
	US$1,890 per capita (1996)
GDP	US$72 million (1994)
	US$1,719 per capita (1994)

MARTINIQUE, see FRANCE

MAURITANIA

Area	395,956 sq. miles (1,025,520 sq. km)
Population	2,284,000 (1994 UN estimate)
Main language	Arabic. Pulaar, Soninke, Wolof and French also spoken
Capital	Nouakchott (population 850,000)
Currency	Ouguiya (UM) of 5 khoums
Exchange rate (at 29 May)	UM 289.850
Public holidays	January 1, 30; April 7, 28; May 1, 25; July 6; November 28
Usual business hours	Sat.–Wed. 8–15, Thurs. 8–13
Electrical rating	127/220v AC, 50Hz

Demography

Life expectancy (years)	male 49.90; female 53.10
Population growth rate	2.6% (1995)
Population density	2 per sq. km (1995)

Government and diplomacy

Political system	Republic
Head of state	President Col. Maaouya Ould Sidi Ahmed Taya
Head of government	Mohamed Lemine Ould Guig
Embassy	5 rue de Montevideo, Paris XVIe, France. Tel: Paris 4504 8854
Honorary Consulate in UK	140 Bow Common Lane, London E3 4BH. Tel: 0181-980 4382
British Embassy	Rabat, Morocco

Defence

Military expenditure	2.9% of GDP (1996)
Military personnel	20,650: Army 15,000, Navy 500, Air Force 150, Paramilitaries 5,000
Conscription duration	Two years

Economy

GNP	US$1,089 million (1996)
	US$470 per capita (1996)
GDP	US$1,193 million (1994)
	US$411 per capita (1994)
Inflation rate	4.7% (1996)
Total external debt	US$2,363 million (1996)

Education

Enrolment (percentage of age group)	primary 60% (1995); tertiary 4.1% (1993)
Illiteracy rate	62.3%

MAURITIUS

Area	788 sq. miles (2,040 sq. km)
Population	1,122,000 (1996 estimate)
Main languages	Creole, English, French, several Indian languages
Capital	Port Louis (population 144,776, 1994 estimate)
Currency	Mauritius rupee of 100 cents
Exchange rate (at 29 May)	Rs 38.9982
Public holidays	January 1, 2, 28, 30; February 10, 25; March 12, 29; May 1; August 15, 27; October 19; December 25
Usual business hours	Mon.–Fri. 9–16; Sat. 9–12 (some offices only)
Electrical rating	220v AC, 50Hz (UK plugs common)

Demography
Life expectancy (years)	male 66.44; female 73.95
Population growth rate	1.2% (1995)
Population density	550 per sq. km (1995)
Urban population	43.6% (1994)

Government and diplomacy
Political system	Republic
Head of state	President Cassam Uteem
Head of government	Dr Navinchandra Ramgoolam
High Commission in UK	32–33 Elvaston Place, London SW7 5NW. Tel: 0171-581 0294/5
British High Commission in Port Louis	Les Cascades Building, Edith Cavell Street, Port Louis (PO Box 1063). Tel: Port Louis 211 1361

Defence
Military expenditure	1.4% of GDP (1996)
Military personnel	1,800 Paramilitaries

Economy
GNP	US$4,205 million (1996) US$3,710 per capita (1996)
GDP	US$4,810 million (1994) US$3,134 per capita (1994)
Annual average growth of GDP	5.5% (1996)
Inflation rate	6.6% (1996)
Total external debt	US$1,818 million (1996)

Education
Enrolment (percentage of age group)	primary 96% (1995); tertiary 6.3% (1995)
Illiteracy rate	17.1%

MAYOTTE, see FRANCE

MEXICO

Area	756,066 sq. miles (1,958,201 sq. km)
Population	90,487,000 (1994 UN estimate)
Main languages	Spanish, Indian languages (Náhuatl, Maya, Zapotec, Otomí, Mixtec) and dialects derived from them
Capital	Mexico City (population 15,047,685, 1990)
Currency	Peso of 100 centavos
Exchange rate (at 29 May)	Pesos 14.3763
Public holidays	January 1; February 5; March 21; April 8–10; May 1, 5; September 1, 16; November 2, 20; December 12, 24, 25, 31
Usual business hours	Vary; usually Mon.–Fri. 9–14, 15–18
Electrical rating	110v AC, 60Hz

Demography

Life expectancy (years)	male 62.10; female 66
Population growth rate	1.8% (1995)
Population density	46 per sq. km (1995)

Government and diplomacy

Political system	Republic; federal state
Head of state and of government	President Dr Ernesto Zedillo Ponce de León
Embassy in UK	42 Hertford Street, London W1Y 7TF. Tel: 0171-499 8586
British Embassy in Mexico City	Calle Río Lerma 71, Colonia Cuauhtémoc, 06500 Mexico City. Tel: Mexico City 207 2089
Trouble spots	Armed revolt by the Zapatista National Liberation Army (ZNLA) in southern state of Chiapas in 1994 and 1995 over government corruption, election fraud and indigenous rights led to political reforms. Negotiations on indigenous rights ongoing; area still tense
	New guerrilla groups, the People's Revolutionary Army (EPR) and the Popular Insurgency Revolutionary Army (ERIP), emerged in 1996

Defence

Military expenditure	0.8% of GDP (1996)
Military personnel	175,000: Army 130,000, Navy 37,000, Air Force 8,000

Conscription duration	12 months (four hours per week)

Economy

GNP	US$341,718 million (1996)
	US$3,670 per capita (1996)
GDP	US$270,699 million (1994)
	US$4,041 per capita (1994)
Annual average growth of GDP	5.1% (1996)
Inflation rate	34.4% (1996)
Unemployment	4.7% (1995)
Total external debt	US$157,125 million (1996)

Education

Enrolment (percentage of age group)	primary 100% (1993); secondary 45% (1990); tertiary 14.3% (1994)
Illiteracy rate	10.4%

FEDERATED STATES OF MICRONESIA

Area	271 sq. miles (702 sq. km)
Population	105,000 (1994 UN estimate)
Main languages	English, Yapese, Ulithian, Woleaian, Ponapean, Nukuoran, Kapingamarangi, Trukese, Kosraen
Federal capital	Palikir, on Pohnpei
Currency	Currency is that of USA
Exchange rate (at 29 May)	US$ 1.6307
Usual business hours	Mon.–Fri. 8–17
Electrical rating	110/120v AC, 60Hz (US plugs)

Demography

Population growth rate	1% (1995)
Population density	150 per sq. km (1995)

Government and diplomacy

Political system	Republic; federal state
Head of state and of government	President Jacob Nena
British Embassy	Suva, Fiji

Economy

GNP	US$225 million (1996)
	US$2,070 per capita (1996)
GDP	US$259 million (1994)
	US$2,560 per capita (1994)

MOLDOVA

Area	13,012 sq. miles (33,700 sq. km)
Population	4,432,000 (1996 estimate)
Main languages	Moldovan, Russian, Ukrainian
Capital	Kishinev (population 667,100)
Currency	Leu (plural lei)
Exchange rate (at 29 May)	Leu 7.7295
Public holidays	January 1, 7, 8; March 8; April 19, 20, 26, 27; May 1, 9; August 27, 31
Electrical rating	220v AC, 50Hz

Demography

Life expectancy (years)	male 64.28; female 70.99
Population growth rate	0.3% (1995)
Population density	132 per sq. km (1995)
Urban population	46.9% (1992)

Government and diplomacy

Political system	Republic
Head of state	President Petru Lucinschi
Head of government	Ion Chubuk
Embassy	Avenue Emile Max 175, 1040 Brussels, Belgium. Tel: Brussels 732 9659
British Embassy	Moscow, Russia
Trouble spots	Secession by ethnic Ukrainians and Russians, who declared the Transdniester republic in 1991. War between government and Transdniester forces in 1992; cease-fire since August 1992 but no political solution and state of armed truce remains

Defence

Military expenditure	2.1% of GDP (1996)
Military personnel	14,430: Army 9,300, Air Force 1,730, Paramilitaries 3,400
Conscription duration	Up to 18 months

Economy

GNP	US$2,542 million (1996)
	US$590 per capita (1996)
GDP	US$7,396 million (1994)
	US$322 per capita (1994)
Unemployment	1% (1995)
Total external debt	US$834 million (1996)

Education

Enrolment (percentage of age group)	tertiary 25% (1995)
Illiteracy rate	1.1%

MONACO

Area	0.4 sq. miles (1 sq. km)
Population	32,000 (1994 UN estimate)
Main language	French
Capital	Monaco (population 27,063, 1982)
Currency	French franc of 100 centimes
Exchange rate (at 29 May)	Francs 9.7561
Public holidays	January 1, 27; February 24; March 17; April 13; May 1, 8, 21; June 1, 11; July 14; September 3; November 1, 2, 11, 19; December 8, 24, 25
Usual business hours	Mon.–Fri. 9–12, 14–17
Electrical rating	220v AC, 50Hz

Demography

Population growth rate	1.3% (1995)
Population density	21,477 per sq. km (1995)

Government and diplomacy

Political system	Constitutional monarchy
Head of state	Prince Rainier III
Head of government	Michel Lévêque
Consulate-General in UK	4 Cromwell Place, London SW7 2JE. Tel: 0171-225 2679
British Consulate-General	Marseilles, France

Economy

GDP	US$668 million (1994)
	US$24,693 per capita (1994)

MONGOLIA

Area	604,829 sq. miles (1,566,500 sq. km)
Population	2,410,000 (1994 UN estimate)
Main languages	Mongolian (many dialects), Kazakh
Capital	Ulan Bator (population 515,100, 1987 estimate)
Currency	Tugrik of 100 möngö
Exchange rate (at 29 May)	Tugriks 1279.71
Public holidays	January 1, 28–30; June 1; July 10; November 26
Usual business hours	Mon.–Fri. 9–18; Sat. 9–15
Electrical rating	220v AC, 50Hz

Demography

Life expectancy (years)	male 62.32; female 65
Population growth rate	2% (1995)
Population density	2 per sq. km (1995)
Urban population	57.1% (1989)

Government and diplomacy

Political system	Republic
Head of state	President Natsagiin Bagabandi
Head of government	Tsahiagiyn Elbegdorj
Embassy in UK	7 Kensington Court, London W8 5DL. Tel: 0171-937 0150
British Embassy in Ulan Bator	30 Enkh Taivny Gudamzh (PO Box 703), Ulan Bator 13. Tel: Ulan Bator 358133

Defence

Military expenditure	1.5% of GDP (1996)
Military personnel	14,900: Army 8,500, Air Defence 500, Paramilitaries 5,900
Conscription duration	12 months

Economy

GNP	US$902 million (1996)
	US$360 per capita (1996)
GDP	US$609 million (1994)
	US$290 per capita (1994)
Annual average growth of GDP	-11.6% (1992)
Inflation rate	45.8% (1996)
Total external debt	US$524 million (1996)

Education

Enrolment (percentage of age group)	primary 80% (1995); secondary 57% (1995); tertiary 15.2% (1995)
Illiteracy rate	17.1%

MONTSERRAT

Area	39 sq. miles (102 sq. km)
Population	3,500 (1994 UN estimate)
Main language	English
Capital	Plymouth (largely destroyed by volcanic activity)
Currency	East Caribbean dollar (EC$) of 100 cents
Exchange rate (at 29 May)	EC$ 4.4029
Public holidays	January 1; March 17; April 10, 13; May 4; June 1; August 3; December 25, 26, 31
Usual business hours	Mon.–Fri. 8–16
Electrical rating	110/220v AC, 60Hz

Demography

Population growth rate	0% (1995)
Population density	108 per sq. km (1995)

Government and diplomacy

Political system	UK Overseas Territory
Governor	Anthony Abbott
Trouble spots	Two-thirds of island affected by volcanic eruption and lava flow; mass evacuation to neighbouring islands

Economy

GDP	US$68 million (1994)
	US$6,795 per capita (1994)

MOROCCO

Area	172,414 sq. miles (446,550 sq. km)
Population	27,111,000 (1994 UN estimate)
Main languages	Arabic, Berber. French and Spanish also spoken
Capital	Rabat (population 1,220,000, 1993 estimate)
Currency	Dirham (DH) of 100 centimes
Exchange rate (at 29 May)	DH 15.8326
Public holidays	January 1, 11, 30; March 3; April 7 (2 days), 28; May 1, 23; July 6, 9; August 14, 20; November 6, 18
Usual business hours	Sept–July 8.30–12, 14.30–18.30; July–Sept 8–16; Ramadan 9–16
Electrical rating	110/220v AC, 50Hz

Demography

Life expectancy (years)	male 61.58; female 65
Population growth rate	2% (1995)
Population density	61 per sq. km (1995)
Urban population	51.6% (1995)

Government and diplomacy

Political system	Constitutional monarchy (though the King exercises most political power)
Head of state	King Hassan II
Head of government	Abderrahmane El Youssoufi
Embassy in UK	49 Queen's Gate Gardens, London SW7 5NE. Tel: 0171-581 5001/4
British Embassy in Rabat	17 Boulevard de la Tour Hassan (BP 45), Rabat. Tel: Rabat 7209 05/6
Trouble spots	Separatist movement (Polisario) in Western Sahara and the government agreed a UN peace plan in 1988 but impasse over voter eligibility has prevented implementation; situation unstable

Defence

Military expenditure	4.3% of GDP (1996)
Military personnel	238,300: Army 175,000, Navy 7,800, Air Force 13,500, Paramilitaries 42,000
Conscription duration	18 months

Economy

GNP	US$34,936 million (1996) US$1,290 per capita (1996)
GDP	US$26,925 million (1994) US$1,098 per capita (1994)
Annual average growth of GDP	12% (1996)

Inflation rate	3% (1996)
Unemployment	16% (1992)
Total external debt	US$21,767 million (1996)

Education

Enrolment (percentage of age group)	primary 72% (1995); secondary 20% (1980); tertiary 11.3% (1994)
Illiteracy rate	56.3%

MOZAMBIQUE

Area	309,496 sq. miles (801,590 sq. km)
Population	17,423,000 (1995 estimate)
Main language	Portuguese
Capital	Maputo (population 882,601, 1986 estimate)
Currency	Metical (MT) of 100 centavos
Exchange rate (at 29 May)	MT 18744.9
Public holidays	January 1; February 3; April 7; May 1; June 25; September 7, 25; November 10; December 25
Usual business hours	Mon.–Fri. 7.30–12.30, 14–17.30
Electrical rating	220v AC, 50Hz

Demography

Life expectancy (years)	male 44.88; female 48.01
Population growth rate	4.2% (1995)
Population density	22 per sq. km (1995)

Government and diplomacy

Political system	Republic
Head of state and of government	President Joaquim Chissano High Commission in UK21 Fitzroy Square, London W1P 5HJ. Tel: 0171-383 3800
British High Commission in Maputo	Av. Vladimir I Lenine 310, CP 55, Maputo. Tel: Maputo 420111/2/5/6/7

Defence

Military expenditure	3.6% of GDP (1996)
Military personnel	6,100: Army 5,000, Navy 100, Air Force 1,000

Economy

GNP	US$1,472 million (1996) US$80 per capita (1996)
GDP	US$1,676 million (1994) US$92 per capita (1994)
Annual average growth of GDP	5.7% (1994)
Inflation rate	45% (1996)
Total external debt	US$5,842 million (1996)

Education

Enrolment (percentage of age group)	primary 40% (1995); secondary 6% (1995); tertiary 0.5% (1995)
Illiteracy rate	59.9%

MYANMAR

Area	261,228 sq. miles (676,578 sq. km)
Population	46,527,000 (1994 UN estimate)
Main languages	Burmese, English and Shan, Karen, Chin, Kayah, Kachin dialects
Capital	Yangon (Rangoon) (population 2,513,023, 1983)
Currency	Kyat (K) of 100 pyas
Exchange rate (at 29 May)	K 10.1947
Public holidays	February 12; March 2, 12, 27; April 13 (4 days), 17; May 1, 10; July 4, 8, 19; October 1, 5; November 3, 13; December 18, 25
Usual business hours	Mon.–Fri. 9.30–16.30
Electrical rating	220/230v AC, 50Hz

Demography

Life expectancy (years)	male 57.89; female 63.14
Population growth rate	2.1 per cent (1995)
Population density	69 per sq. km (1995)

Government and diplomacy

Political system	Republic; one-party (SLORC) military regime
Head of state and of government	Gen. Than Shwe
Embassy in UK	19A Charles Street, Berkeley Square, London W1X 8ER. Tel: 0171-499 8841
British Embassy in Yangon	80 Strand Road (Box No. 638), Yangon. Tel: Yangon 95300
Trouble spots	Various armed insurgencies by Kachin, Karen, Karenni, Wa, Shan, Mon, Arakan and Chin ethnic groups since independence; most now ended by cease-fire agreements or government offensives

Defence

Military expenditure	3.2 per cent of GDP (1996)
Military personnel	429,000: Army 400,000, Navy 20,000, Air Force 9,000

Economy

GDP	US$29,769 million (1994) US$1,485 per capita (1994)
Annual average growth of GDP	5.7 per cent (1996)

Inflation rate	16.3 per cent (1996)
Total external debt	US$5,184 million (1996)

Education

Enrolment (percentage of age group)	tertiary 5.4 per cent (1994)
Illiteracy rate	16.9 per cent

NAMIBIA

Area	318,261 sq. miles (824,292 sq. km)
Population	1,540,000 (1994 UN estimate)
Main languages	English, Afrikaans, German, local languages
Capital	Windhoek (population 147,056, 1990)
Currency	Namibian dollar of 100 cents
Exchange rate (at 29 May)	at parity with SA Rand
Public holidays	January 1; March 21; April 10, 13; May 1, 4, 21, 25; August 26; December 10, 25, 26
Usual business hours	Mon.–Fri. 8–17
Electrical rating	220/240v AC

Demography

Life expectancy (years)	male 57.50; female 60
Population growth rate	2.6% (1995)
Population density	2 per sq. km (1995)
Urban population	27.1% (1991)

Government and diplomacy

Political system	Republic
Head of state and of government	President Dr Sam Nujoma
High Commission in UK	6 Chandos Street, London W1M 0LQ. Tel: 0171-636 6244
British High Commission in Windhoek	116 Robert Mugabe Avenue, Windhoek 9000. Tel: Windhoek 223022

Defence

Military expenditure	2.6% of GDP (1996)
Military personnel	5,800: Army 5,700, Coast Guard 100

Economy

GNP	US$3,569 million (1996)
	US$2,250 per capita (1996)
GDP	US$2,773 million (1994)
	US$1,924 per capita (1994)
Annual average growth of GDP	2.6% (1995)
Inflation rate	10% (1995)

Education

Enrolment (percentage of age group)	primary 92% (1995); secondary 36% (1995); tertiary 8.1% (1995)

NAURU

Area	8 sq. miles (21 sq. km)
Population	11,000 (1994 UN estimate)
Main languages	Nauruan, English
Capital	Nauru
Currency	Australian dollar ($A) of 100 cents
Exchange rate (at 29 May)	$A 2.6035
Public holidays	January 1, 31; April 10, 13, 14; May 17; October 26; December 25, 26
Electrical rating	110/240v AC, 50Hz

Demography

Population growth rate	1.5% (1995)
Population density	514 per sq. km (1995)

Government and diplomacy

Political system	Republic
Head of state and of government	President Kinza Clodumar
Honorary Consulate in UK	Romshed, Underriver, Nr Sevenoaks, Kent TN15 0SD. Tel: 01732-746061
British High Commission	Suva, Fiji

Economy

GDP	US$213 million (1994) US$25,094 per capita (1994)

NEPAL

Area	56,827 sq. miles (147,181 sq. km)
Population	21,918,000 (1994 UN estimate)
Main language	Nepali
Capital	Kathmandu (population 419,073, 1991)
Currency	Nepalese rupee of 100 paisa
Exchange rate (at 29 May)	Rs 103.386
Public holidays	January 11, 29; February 12, 18; March 7–9, 24; April 7, 13, 16, 17; May 15; September 8; November 8; December 29
Usual business hours	Sun.–Thurs. 10–17; Fri. 10–15 (summer); Sun.–Fri. 10–16 (winter)
Electrical rating	220v AC, 50Hz; frequent power cuts

Demography

Life expectancy (years)	male 50.88; female 48.10
Population growth rate	3.8% (1995)
Population density	149 per sq. km (1995)

Government and diplomacy

Political system	Constitutional monarchy
Head of state	King Birendra Bir Bikram Shah Dev
Head of government	Girija Prasad Koirala
Embassy in UK	12A Kensington Palace Gardens, London W8 4QU. Tel: 0171-229 1594/6231
British Embassy in Kathmandu	Lainchaur Kathmandu, PO Box 106. Tel: Kathmandu 410583

Defence

Military expenditure	0.9% of GDP (1996)
Military personnel	46,215: Army 46,000, Air Force 215

Economy

GNP	US$4,710 million (1996)
	US$210 per capita (1996)
GDP	US$3,637 million (1994)
	US$158 per capita (1994)
Annual average growth of GDP	6.1% (1996)
Inflation rate	9.2% (1996)
Total external debt	US$2,413 million (1996)

Education

Enrolment (percentage of age group)	tertiary 5.2% (1993)
Illiteracy rate	72.5%

THE NETHERLANDS

Area	15,770 sq. miles (40,844 sq. km)
Population	15,451,000 (1996)
Main language	Dutch
Capital	Amsterdam (population 1,100,764, 1993 estimate). The seat of government is The Hague
Currency	Gulden (guilder) or florin of 100 cents
Exchange rate (at 29 May)	Guilders 3.2762
Public holidays	January 1; April 10, 13, 30; May 21; June 1; December 25, 26
Usual business hours	Mon.–Fri. 8.30–17
Electrical rating	220v AC, 50Hz

Demography

Life expectancy (years)	male 74.21; female 80.20
Population growth rate	0.7% (1995)
Population density	378 per sq. km (1995)
Urban population	60.6% (1994)

Government and diplomacy

Political system	Constitutional monarchy
Head of state	Queen Beatrix
Head of government	Wim Kok
Embassy in UK	38 Hyde Park Gate, London SW7 5DP. Tel: 0171-584 5040
British Embassy in The Hague	Lange Voorhout 10, The Hague, 2514 ED. Tel: The Hague 427 0427

Defence

Military expenditure	2.1% of GDP (1996)
Military personnel	56,380: Army 27,000, Navy 13,800, Air Force 11,980, Paramilitaries 3,600

Economy

GNP	US$402,565 million (1996) US$25,940 per capita (1996)
GDP	US$302,313 million (1994) US$21,536 per capita (1994)
Annual average growth of GDP	3.5% (1996)
Inflation rate	2.1% (1996)
Unemployment	7.1% (1995)

Education

Enrolment (percentage of age group)	primary 99% (1993); secondary 84% (1990); tertiary 48.9% (1993)

OVERSEAS TERRITORIES

ARUBA

Area	75 sq. miles (193 sq. km)
Population	70,000 (1996)
Main language	Dutch
Capitals	Oranjestad (population 25,000, 1993 estimate) and Sint Nicolaas (population 17,000)
Currency	Aruban florin
Exchange rate (at 29 May)	Florins 2.9190
Public holidays	January 1, 25; February 23; March 18; April 10, 13, 30; May 1, 21; December 25, 26
Usual business hours	Mon.–Fri. 8–12, 13–16.30
Electrical rating	110v AC, 60Hz

Demography

Life expectancy (years)	male 68.30; female 75.40
Population growth rate	0.9% (1995)
Population density	363 per sq. km (1995)

Government

Political system	Self-government
Governor	O. L. Koolman

NETHERLANDS ANTILLES

Area	309 sq. miles (800 sq. km)
Population	199,000 (1996)
Main language	Dutch
Capital	Willemstad (population 50,000, 1993 estimate), on Curaçao
Currency	Netherlands Antilles guilder of 100 cents
Exchange rate (at 29 May)	Guilders 2.9190
Public holidays	January 1; February 23; April 10, 13, 30; May 1, 21; December 25, 26

Demography

Life expectancy (years)	male 72.28; female 77.87
Population growth rate	1.2% (1995)
Population density	249 per sq. km (1995)

Government

Political system	Self-government
Governor	Dr Jaime Saleh

Economy

GNP	US$51,655 million (1995)
GDP	US$1,588 million (1994)
	US$8,679 per capita (1994)
Inflation rate	3.6% (1996)

NEW CALEDONIA, see FRANCE

NEW ZEALAND

Area	104,454 sq. miles (270,534 sq. km)
Population	3,542,000 (1995)
Main language	English
Capital	Wellington (population 326,900, 1992 estimate)
Currency	New Zealand dollar (NZ$) of 100 cents
Exchange rate (at 29 May)	NZ$ 3.0461
Public holidays	January 1, 2; February 6; April 10, 13, 25; June 1; October 26; December 25, 26
Usual business hours	Mon.–Fri. 9–17
Electrical rating	230v AC, 50Hz

Demography

Life expectancy (years)	male 72.86; female 78.74
Population growth rate	1% (1995)
Population density	13 per sq. km (1995)
Urban population	84.9% (1991)

Government and diplomacy

Political system	Constitutional monarchy
Head of state	Queen Elizabeth II
Governor-General	Sir Michael Hardie Boys
Head of government	Jenny Shipley
High Commission in UK	New Zealand House, Haymarket, London SW1Y 4TQ. Tel: 0171-930 8422
British High Commission in Wellington	44 Hill Street (PO Box 1812), Wellington 1. Tel: Wellington 472 6049

Defence

Military expenditure	1.2% of GDP (1996)
Military personnel	9,550: Army 4,400, Navy 2,100, Air Force 3,050

Economy

GNP	US$57,135 million (1996)
	US$15,720 per capita (1996)
GDP	US$48,132 million (1994)
	US$14,649 per capita (1994)
Annual average growth of GDP	4.3% (1995)
Inflation rate	2.3% (1996)
Unemployment	6.3% (1995)

Education

Enrolment (percentage of age group)	primary 100% (1995); secondary 93% (1995); tertiary 58.2% (1995)

TERRITORY

TOKELAU

Area	5 sq. miles (12 sq. km)
Population	2,000
Main language	English
Currency	Currency is that of New Zealand

Demography

Population growth rate	0% (1995)
Population density	167 per sq. km (1995)

Government

Political system	New Zealand Territory
Administrator	Lindsay Watt
Head of government	Rotates annually; Kuresa Nasau (1998)

ASSOCIATED STATES

COOK ISLANDS

Area	91 sq. miles (236 sq. km)
Population	19,000
Capital	Rarotonga
Main language	English
Currency	Currency is that of New Zealand
Public holidays	January 1; April 10, 13; June 1; July 25, 27; August 4; October 26; December 25, 26, 28
Usual business hours	Mon.–Fri. 8–16
Electrical rating	230v AC, 50Hz

Demography

Life expectancy (years)	male 63.17; female 67.09
Population growth rate	0.9% (1995)
Population density	81 per sq. km (1995)

Government

Political system	Self-governing in free association with New Zealand
Queen's representative	Apenera Short
Head of government	Sir Geoffrey Henry
New Zealand representative	James Kember

Economy

GDP	US$58 million (1994)
	US$3,717 per capita (1994)

NIUE

Area	100 sq. miles (260 sq. km)
Population	2,000
Main language	English

Capital	Alofi
Currency	Currency is that of New Zealand
Usual business hours	Mon.–Fri. 7.30–15.30
Electrical rating	240v AC, 50Hz

Demography

Population growth rate	0% (1995)
Population density	8 per sq. km (1995)

Government

Political system	Self-governing in free association with New Zealand
High Commissioner	W. Searall

NICARAGUA

Area	50,193 sq. miles (130,000 sq. km)
Population	4,539,000 (1994 UN estimate)
Main languages	Spanish, English
Capital	Managua (population 608,020, 1979 estimate)
Currency	Córdoba (C$) of 100 centavos
Exchange rate (at 29 May)	C$ 17.0636
Public holidays	January 1; April 9, 10; May 1, 30; July 19; August 1, 10; September 14, 15; November 2; December 7, 8, 25
Usual business hours	Mon.–Fri. 8–17
Electrical rating	110v AC, 60Hz

Demography

Life expectancy (years)	male 64.80; female 67.71
Population growth rate	3.2% (1995)
Population density	35 per sq. km (1995)
Urban population	63.3% (1995)

Government and diplomacy

Political system	Republic
Head of state and of government	President Arnoldo Alemán Lacayo
Diplomatic representation in UK	Embassy closed 1997; a consulate-general is to open
British Embassy in Managua	PO Box A-169, Plaza Churchill, Reparto 'Los Robles', Managua. Tel: Managua 780014

Defence

Military expenditure	1.4% of GDP (1996)
Military personnel	17,000: Army 15,000, Navy 800, Air Force 1,200
Conscription duration	18–36 months

Economy

GNP	US$1,705 million (1996) US$380 per capita (1996)

GDP	US$2,285 million (1994)
	US$433 per capita (1994)
Annual average growth of GDP	5.8% (1996)
Inflation rate	11.6% (1996)
Unemployment	14% (1991)
Total external debt	US$5,929 million (1996)

Education

Enrolment (percentage of age group)	primary 83% (1995); secondary 27% (1993); tertiary 9.4% (1993)
Illiteracy rate	34.3%

NIGER

Area	489,191 sq. miles (1,267,000 sq. km)
Population	9,151,000 (1994 UN estimate)
Main languages	French. Hausa, Djerma and Fulani also spoken
Capital	Niamey (population 392,169, 1988)
Currency	Franc CFA of 100 centimes
Exchange rate (at 29 May)	Francs 975.610
Public holidays	January 1, 30; April 7, 13, 24; May 1; July 6; August 3; December 18, 25
Usual business hours	Mon.–Fri. 7.30–12.30, 15–18; Sat. 7.30–12.30
Electrical rating	220/380v AC, 50Hz

Demography

Life expectancy (years)	male 44.90; female 48.14
Population growth rate	3.4% (1995)
Population density	7 per sq. km (1995)
Urban population	15.3% (1988)

Government and diplomacy

Political system	Republic
Head of state and of government	President Brig.-Gen. Ibrahim Barre Mainassara
Embassy	154 rue de Longchamp, 75116, Paris, France. Tel: Paris 4504 8060
British Embassy	Abidjan, Côte d'Ivoire

Defence

Military expenditure	1.1% of GDP (1996)
Military personnel	10,700: Army 5,200, Air Force 100, Paramilitaries 5,400
Conscription duration	Two years

Economy

GNP	US$1,879 million (1996)
	US$200 per capita (1996)

GDP	US$2,769 million (1994)
	US$211 per capita (1994)
Annual average growth of GDP	-6.3% (1981)
Inflation rate	5.3% (1996)
Total external debt	US$1,557 million (1996)

Education

Enrolment (percentage of age group)	primary 25% (1990); secondary 6% (1990); tertiary 0.3% (1980)
Illiteracy rate	86.4%

NIGERIA

Area	356,669 sq. miles (923,768 sq. km)
Population	111,721,000 (1994 UN estimate)
Main languages	English, Hausa, Yoruba, Ibo
Capital	Abuja (population 378,671)
Currency	Naira (N) of 100 kobo
Exchange rate (at 29 May)	N 35.6895★
Public holidays	January 1, 30 (2 days); April 7 (2 days), 10, 13; May 1; July 6; October 1; December 25, 26
Usual business hours	Mon.–Fri. 7.30–15.30
Electrical rating	220/250v AC, 50Hz, single phase

Demography

Life expectancy (years)	male 48.81; female 52.01
Population growth rate	3% (1995)
Population density	121 per sq. km (1995)
Urban population	16.1% (1988)

Government and diplomacy

Political system	Republic; military regime, though democratic elections promised for August 1998; federal state
Head of state and of government	Gen. Abdulsalam Abubakar
High Commission in UK	9 Northumberland Avenue, London WC2N 5BX. Tel: 0171-839 1244
British High Commissions in Abuja and Lagos	Shehu Shangari Way (North), Maitama. Tel: Abuja 5232011 11 Eleke Crescent, Victoria Island, Lagos. Tel: Lagos 261 9531

Defence

Military expenditure	2.8% of GDP (1996)
Military personnel	77,000: Army 62,000, Navy 5,500, Air Force 9,500

Economy

GNP	US$27,599 million (1996)
	US$240 per capita (1996)

GDP	US$36,269 million (1994)
	US$376 per capita (1994)
Annual average growth of GDP	1.3% (1994)
Inflation rate	29.3% (1996)
Total external debt	US$31,407 million (1996)

Education

Enrolment (percentage of age group)	tertiary 4.1% (1993)
Illiteracy rate	42.9%

NORTHERN MARIANA ISLANDS, see USA

NORWAY

Area	125,050 sq. miles (323,877 sq. km), including Svalbard and Jan Mayen
Population	4,360,000 (1996)
Main languages	Norwegian (bokmål), 'new Norwegian' (based on dialects)
Capital	Oslo (population 758,949, 1993 estimate)
Currency	Krone of 100 øre
Exchange rate (at 29 May)	Kroner 12.2830
Public holidays	January 1; April 8–10, 13; May 1, 17, 21; June 1; December 24–26, 31
Usual business hours	Mon.–Fri. 8–16
Electrical rating	220v AC, 50Hz (European plugs)

Demography

Life expectancy (years)	male 74.24; female 80.25
Population growth rate	0.6% (1995)
Population density	13 per sq. km (1995)
Urban population	72% (1990)

Government and diplomacy

Political system	Constitutional monarchy
Head of state	King Harald V
Head of government	Kjell Magne Bondevik
Embassy in UK	25 Belgrave Square, London SW1X 8QD. Tel: 0171-591 5500
British Embassy in Oslo	Thomas Heftyesgate 8, 0244 Oslo. Tel: Oslo 552400

Defence

Military expenditure	2.4% of GDP (1996)
Military personnel	32,700: Army 15,800, Navy 9,000, Air Force 7,900
Conscription duration	12 months

Economy

GNP	US$151,198 million (1996)
	US$34,510 per capita (1996)

GDP	US$120,358 million (1994)
	US$25,378 per capita (1994)
Annual average growth of GDP	5.3% (1996)
Inflation rate	1.3% (1996)
Unemployment	4.9% (1995)

Education

Enrolment (percentage of age group)	primary 99% (1994); secondary 94% (1994); tertiary 54.5% (1994)

OMAN

Area	82,030 sq. miles (212,457 sq. km)
Population	2,163,000 (1994 UN estimate)
Main languages	Arabic, Qarra and Mahra dialects
Capital	Muscat (population 400,000)
Currency	Rial Omani (OR) of 1,000 baiza
Exchange rate (at 29 May)	OR 0.6278
Public holidays	January 30 (3 days); April 7 (3 days), 28; July 6; November 17–19; December 31
Usual business hours	Sat.–Wed. 8.30–13, 16–19; Thurs. 8–13
Electrical rating	220/240v AC, 50Hz

Demography

Life expectancy (years)	male 67.70; female 71.80
Population growth rate	1.6% (1995)
Population density	10 per sq. km (1995)

Government and diplomacy

Political system	Absolute monarchy
Head of state and of government	Sultan Qaboos Bin-Said
Embassy in UK	167 Queen's Gate, London SW7 5HE. Tel: 0171-225 0001
British Embassy in Muscat	PO Box 300, Muscat. Tel: Muscat 69377

Defence

Military expenditure	15.7% of GDP (1996)
Military personnel	44,200: Army 25,000, Navy 4,200, Air Force 4,100, Royal Household 6,500, Paramilitaries 4,400

Economy

GNP	US$10,578 million (1995)
	US$4,820 per capita (1995)
GDP	US$12,646 million (1994)
	US$5,698 per capita (1994)

Annual average growth of GDP	3.5% (1994)
Total external debt	US$3,415 million (1996)

Education

Enrolment (percentage of group)	primary 71% (1995); secondary *age* 56% (1995); tertiary 4.7% (1993)

PAKISTAN

Area	307,374 sq. miles (796,095 sq. km)
Population	129,808,000 (1994 UN estimate)
Main languages	Punjabi, Urdu, Sindi, Pushto, English
Capital	Islamabad (population 350,000)
Currency	Pakistan rupee of 100 paisa
Exchange rate (at 29 May)	Rs 72.5254
Public holidays	January 11, 30 (3 days); February 7; March 23; April 7 (3 days), 28 (2 days); May 1; July 1, 6; August 14; September 6, 11; November 9; December 25, 31
Usual business hours	Mon.–Thurs., Sat. 9–17; Fri. 9–12, 14.30–17
Electrical rating	220v AC, 50Hz

Demography

Life expectancy (years)	male 59.04; female 59.20
Population growth rate	2.9% (1995)
Population density	163 per sq. km (1995)
Urban population	28.2% (1991)

Government and diplomacy

Political system	Republic; federal state
Head of state	President Muhammad Rafiq Tarar
Head of government	Mian Muhammad Nawaz Sharif
High Commission in UK	35–36 Lowndes Square, London SW1X 9JN. Tel: 0171-235 2044
British High Commission in Islamabad	Diplomatic Enclave, Ramna 5, PO Box 1122, Islamabad. Tel: Islamabad 822131/5
Trouble spots	Civil disorder in Sind province, especially in Karachi, in two conflicts: the Mohajir Qaumi Movement (MQM) Party, which represents Urdu-speaking Indian Muslims, fighting for an autonomous Karachi province; and armed conflict between Shia and Sunni fundamentalists

Defence

Military expenditure	5.8% of GDP (1996)
Military personnel	834,000: Army 520,000, Navy 22,000, Air Force 45,000, Paramilitaries 247,000

Economy

GNP	US$63,567 million (1996)
	US$480 per capita (1996)
GDP	US$55,535 million (1994)
	US$434 per capita (1994)
Annual average growth of GDP	5.9% (1996)
Inflation rate	10.4% (1996)
Unemployment	4.8% (1994)
Total external debt	US$29,901 million (1996)

Education

Enrolment (percentage of age group)	tertiary 3% (1991)
Illiteracy rate	62.2%

PALAU

Area	177 sq. miles (459 sq. km)
Population	17,000 (1994 UN estimate)
Main languages	Palauan, English
Capital	Koror (population 10,493, 1994)
Currency	Currency is that of the USA
Exchange rate (at 29 May)	US$ 1.6307
Usual business hours	Mon.–Fri. 8–17
Electrical rating	110/120v AC, 60Hz (US plugs)

Demography

Population growth rate	2.5% (1995)
Population density	37 per sq. km (1995)

Government

Political system	Republic
Head of state and of government	President Kuniwo Nakamura

Economy

GDP	US$85 million (1994)
	US$5,833 per capita (1994)

PALESTINIAN AUTONOMOUS AREAS, see ISRAEL

PANAMA

Area	29,157 sq. miles (75,517 sq. km)
Population	2,631,000 (1995 estimate)
Main language	Spanish
Capital	Panama City (population 445,902, 1994)
Currency	Balboa of 100 centésimos (US notes are also in circulation)
Exchange rate (at 29 May)	Balboa 1.6307
Public holidays	January 1, 9; February 23–25; April 9–11; May 1; August 15; November 3, 4, 10, 28; December 8, 24, 25, 31
Usual business hours	Mon.–Fri. 8–12, 14–17
Electrical rating	120v AC, 60Hz (US plugs)

Demography

Life expectancy (years)	male 70.85; female 75
Population growth rate	1.9% (1995)
Population density	35 per sq. km (1995)
Urban population	54.9% (1995)

Government and diplomacy

Political system	Republic
Head of state and of government	President Ernesto Pérez Balladares
Embassy in UK	48 Park Street, London W1Y 3PD. Tel: 0171-493 4646
British Embassy in Panama City	Torre Swiss Bank, Calle 53 (Apartado 889) Zona 1, Panama City, Panama 1. Tel: Panama City 269 0866

Defence

Military expenditure	1.4% of GDP (1996)
Military personnel	11,800 Paramilitaries

Economy

GNP	US$8,249 million (1996) US$3,080 per capita (1996)
GDP	US$6,571 million (1994) US$2,550 per capita (1994)
Annual average growth of GDP	2.5% (1996)
Inflation rate	1.3% (1996)
Unemployment	13.7% (1995)
Total external debt	US$6,990 million (1996)

Education

Enrolment (percentage of age group)	primary 91% (1990); secondary 51% (1990); tertiary 30% (1995)
Illiteracy rate	9.2%

PAPUA NEW GUINEA

Area	178,704 sq. miles (462,840 sq. km)
Population	4,074,000 (1994 UN estimate)
Main languages	English, Pidgin English, Hiri Motu
Capital	Port Moresby (population 173,500, 1980)
Currency	Kina (K) of 100 toea
Exchange rate (at 29 May)	K 3.3520
Public holidays	January 1; April 10, 11, 13; June 15; July 18, 23; September 16; December 25, 26
Usual business hours	Mon.–Fri. 8–16.30
Electrical rating	240v AC, 50Hz (Australian plugs)

Demography

Life expectancy (years)	male 55.16; female 56.68
Population growth rate	1.9% (1995)
Population density	9 per sq. km (1995)

Government and diplomacy

Political system	Constitutional monarchy
Head of state	Queen Elizabeth II
Governor-General	Silas Atopare
Head of government	Bill Skate
High Commission in UK	3rd Floor, 14 Waterloo Place, London SW1R 4AR. Tel: 0171-930 0922/7
British High Commission in Port Moresby	PO Box 212, Waigani NCD 131, Port Moresby. Tel: Port Moresby 325 1677
Trouble spots	Insurrection on Bougainville Island; Bougainville Revolutionary Army (BRA) declared an independent republic in 1990; cease-fire from April 1998 but situation tense Volcanic activity in East New Britain Province and on Manam Island

Defence

Military expenditure	1.4% of GDP (1996)
Military personnel	4,300: Army 3,800, Navy 400, Air Force 100

Economy

GNP	US$5,049 million (1996)
	US$1,150 per capita (1996)
GDP	US$4,804 million (1994)
	US$1,267 per capita (1994)
Annual average growth of GDP	13.3% (1993)
Inflation rate	11.6% (1996)
Total external debt	US$2,359 million (1996)

Education

Enrolment (percentage of age group)	tertiary 3.2% (1995)
Illiteracy rate	27.8%

PARAGUAY

Area	157,048 sq. miles (406,752 sq. km)
Population	4,828,000 (1994 UN estimate)
Main languages	Spanish, Guaraní
Capital	Asunción (population 718,690)
Currency	Guaraní (Gs) of 100 céntimos
Exchange rate (at 29 May)	Gs 4402.89
Public holidays	January 1; March 1; April 9, 10; May 1, 15; June 12; August 15; September 29; December 8, 25
Usual business hours	Mon.–Fri. 8–12, 15–19
Electrical rating	220v AC, 50Hz

Demography

Life expectancy (years)	male 66.30; female 70.83
Population growth rate	2.7% (1995)
Population density	12 per sq. km (1995)
Urban population	50.3% (1992)

Government and diplomacy

Political system	Republic
Head of state and of government	President Raul Cubas
Embassy in UK	Braemar Lodge, Cornwall Gardens, London SW7 4AQ. Tel: 0171-937 1253
British Embassy in Asunción	Calle Presidente Franco 706 (PO Box 404), Asunción. Tel: Asunción 444472

Defence

Military expenditure	1.2% of GDP (1996)
Military personnel	35,000: Army 14,900, Navy 3,600, Air Force 1,700, Paramilitaries 14,800
Conscription duration	One to two years

Economy

GNP	US$9,179 million (1996) US$1,850 per capita (1996)
GDP	US$6,098 million (1994) US$1,593 per capita (1992)
Annual average growth of GDP	1.3% (1996)
Inflation rate	9.8% (1996)
Unemployment	4.4% (1994)
Total external debt	US$2,141 million (1996)

Education

Enrolment (percentage of age group)	primary 89% (1994); secondary 33% (1994); tertiary 10.3% (1993)
Illiteracy rate	7.9%

PERU

Area	496,225 sq. miles (1,285,216 sq. km)
Population	23,532,000 (1994 UN estimate)
Main languages	Spanish, Quechua, Aymará
Capital	Lima (including Callao, population 6,483,901, 1993)
Currency	New Sol of 100 cénts
Exchange rate (at 29 May)	New Sol 4.6667
Public holidays	January 1; April 9, 10; May 1; June 29; July 28, 29; August 30; October 8; November 1; December 8, 25
Usual business hours	Mon.–Fri. 9–17
Electrical rating	220v AC, 60Hz

Demography

Life expectancy (years)	male 62.74; female 66.55
Population growth rate	1.7% (1995)
Population density	18 per sq. km (1995)
Urban population	71.2% (1995)

Government and diplomacy

Political system	Republic
Head of state and of government	President Alberto Fujimori
Embassy in UK	52 Sloane Street, London SW1X 9SP. Tel: 0171-235 1917/2545/3802
British Embassy in Lima	Edificio El Pacifico Washington, Piso 12, Plaza Washington (PO Box 854), Lima 100. Tel: Lima 334738
Trouble spots	Some areas under states of emergency because of insurgencies by Maoist Sendero Luminoso (Shining Path) and the Movimiento Revolucionario Tapac Amaru (MRTA) Violence by drug cartels

Defence

Military expenditure	1.7% of GDP (1996)
Military personnel	203,000: Army 85,000, Navy 25,000, Air Force 15,000, Paramilitaries 78,000
Conscription duration	Two years

Economy

GNP	US$58,671 million (1996) US$2,420 per capita (1996)

GDP	US$42,436 million (1994)
	US$2,128 per capita (1994)
Annual average growth of GDP	2.6% (1996)
Inflation rate	11.5% (1996)
Unemployment	7.1% (1995)
Total external debt	US$29,176 million (1996)

Education

Enrolment (percentage of age group)	primary 91% (1994); secondary 53% (1994); tertiary 31.1% (1994)
Illiteracy rate	11.3%

THE PHILIPPINES

Area	115,831 sq. miles (300,000 sq. km)
Population	70,267,000 (1994 UN estimate)
Main languages	Filipino, English
Capital	Manila (population 8,594,150, 1994)
Currency	Philippine peso (P) of 100 centavos
Exchange rate (at 29 May)	P 63.5159
Public holidays	January 1; April 9, 10; May 1; June 12; August 30; November 1, 30; December 25, 30, 31
Usual business hours	Vary; usually Mon.–Fri. 8–12, 13–17
Electrical rating	220v AC, 60Hz; Baguio 110/220v AC, 60Hz

Demography

Life expectancy (years)	male 63.10; female 66.70
Population growth rate	2.7% (1995)
Population density	234 per sq. km (1995)
Urban population	42.7% (1990)

Government and diplomacy

Political system	Republic
Head of state and of government	President Joseph Estrada
Embassy in UK	9A Palace Green, London W8 4QE. Tel: 0171-937 1600
British Embassy in Manila	Locsin Building, 6752 Ayala Avenue, Corner Makati Avenue, 1226 Makati, Metro Manila (PO Box 2927 MCPO). Tel: Manila 816 7116
Trouble spots	Insurgency of Moro National Liberation Front (MNLF) ended 1996 with agreement to create autonomous Muslim region in Mindanao, Palawan, Sulu and Basilan, but splinter group, Moro Islamic Liberation Front

(MILF) continues to fight
The Communist New People's
Army (NPA) maintains a presence
in eastern Mindanao, Negros,
Samar, Bicol, the mountains of
northern Luzon and Bataan; peace
talks are continuing

Defence

Military expenditure	1.8% of GDP (1996)
Military personnel	153,000: Army 70,000, Navy 24,000, Air Force 16,500, Paramilitaries 42,500

Economy

GNP	US$83,298 million (1996)
	US$1,160 per capita (1996)
GDP	US$47,082 million (1994)
	US$965 per capita (1994)
Annual average growth of GDP	5.5% (1996)
Inflation rate	8.4% (1996)
Unemployment	8.4% (1995)
Total external debt	US$41,214 million (1996)

Education

Enrolment (percentage of age group)	primary 100% (1995); secondary 60% (1995); tertiary 27.4% (1994)
Illiteracy rate	5.4%

PITCAIRN ISLANDS

Area	2 sq. miles (5 sq. km)
Population	42 (1994 UN estimate)
Main language	English
Currency	Currency is that of New Zealand
Exchange rate (at 29 May)	NZ$ 3.0461

Government

Political system	UK Overseas Territory
Governor	Robert J. Alston (British High Commissioner to New Zealand)

POLAND

Area	124,808 sq. miles (323,250 sq. km)
Population	38,588,000 (1995)
Main language	Polish
Capital	Warsaw (population 1,643,203)
Currency	Złoty of 100 groszy
Exchange rate (at 29 May)	Złotys 5.6928
Public holidays	January 1; April 13; May 1, 3; June 11; August 15; November 1, 11; December 25, 26
Usual business hours	Mon.–Fri. 8–16
Electrical rating	220v AC, 50Hz (European plugs)

Demography

Life expectancy (years)	male 67.37; female 76
Population growth rate	0.2% (1995)
Population density	119 per sq. km (1995)
Urban population	61.9% (1995)

Government and diplomacy

Political system	Republic
Head of state	President Aleksander Kwaœniewski
Head of government	Jerzy Buzek
Embassy in UK	47 Portland Place, London W1N 4JH. Tel: 0171-580 4324/9
British Embassy in Warsaw	No. 1 Aleja Róz, 00-556 Warsaw. Tel: Warsaw 628 1001/5

Defence

Military expenditure	2.3% of GDP (1996)
Military personnel	265,150: Army 168,650, Navy 17,000, Air Force 56,100, Paramilitaries 23,400
Conscription duration	18 months

Economy

GNP	US$124,682 million (1996)
	US$3,230 per capita (1996)
GDP	US$61,360 million (1994)
	US$2,503 per capita (1994)
Annual average growth of GDP	5.7% (1996)
Inflation rate	20.2% (1996)
Unemployment	13.1% (1995)
Total external debt	US$40,895 million (1996)

Education

Enrolment (percentage of age group)	primary 97% (1994); secondary 83% (1994); tertiary 27.4% (1993)

PORTUGAL

Area	35,514 sq. miles (91,982 sq. km)
Population	10,797,000 (1994 UN estimate)
Main language	Portuguese
Capital	Lisbon (population 2,561,225, 1991)
Currency	Escudo (Esc) of 100 centavos
Exchange rate (at 29 May)	Esc 297.521
Public holidays	January 1; February 24; April 9, 10, 25; May 1, 21; June 10, 11; August 15; October 5; November 1; December 1, 8, 24–26
Usual business hours	Mon.–Fri. 9–13, 15–19
Electrical rating	220v AC, 50Hz; 110v AC in places; 200v DC in parts of the south (European plugs)

Demography

Life expectancy (years)	male 71.18; female 78.23
Population growth rate	1.7% (1995)
Population density	117 per sq. km (1995)
Urban population	48.2% (1991)

Government and diplomacy

Political system	Republic
Head of state	President Jorge Sampaio
Head of government	António Guterres
Embassy in UK	11 Belgrave Square, London SW1X 8PP. Tel: 0171-235 5331
British Embassy in Lisbon	Rua de S. Bernardo 33, 1200 Lisbon. Tel: Lisbon 392 4000

Defence

Military expenditure	2.8% of GDP (1996)
Military personnel	95,500: Army 32,100, Navy 14,800, Air Force 7,700, Paramilitaries 40,900
Conscription duration	Four to 18 months

Economy

GNP	US$100,934 million (1996) US$10,160 per capita (1996)
GDP	US$69,276 million (1994) US$8,822 per capita (1994)
Annual average growth of GDP	1.9% (1995)
Inflation rate	3.1% (1996)
Unemployment	5.5% (1993)

Education

Enrolment (percentage of age group)	primary 100% (1993); secondary 78% (1993); tertiary 34% (1993)
Illiteracy rate	10.4%

MACAO

Area	7 sq. miles (18 sq. km)
Population	418,000 (1994 UN estimate)
Main language	Portuguese
Capital	Macao
Currency	Pataca of 100 avos
Exchange rate (at 29 May)	Pataca 13.0525
Public holidays	January 1, 28–30; April 6, 10, 11, 13, 25; May 1, 30; June 10; July 1; August 17; October 1, 2, 5, 6, 28; November 2; December 1, 8, 24–26
Usual business hours	Banking hours: Mon.–Fri. 9.30–16; Sat. 9.30–12
Electrical rating	Mainly 220v AC, 50Hz

Demography

Life expectancy (years)	male 75.01; female 80.26
Population growth rate	4.4% (1995)
Population density	23,194 per sq. km (1995)

Government and diplomacy

Political system	Autonomous overseas territory; becomes a Special Administrative Region of China in December 1999
Governor	Gen. Vasco Rocha Vieira

Education

Enrolment (percentage of age group)	primary 81% (1991); secondary 53% (1991); tertiary 26.4% (1992)

PUERTO RICO, see USA

QATAR

Area	4,247 sq. miles (11,000 sq. km)
Population	551,000 (1994 UN estimate)
Main languages	Arabic, English
Capital	Doha (population 217,294, 1986)
Currency	Qatar riyal of 100 dirhams
Exchange rate (at 29 May)	Riyals 5.9366
Public holidays	January 30 (4 days); April 7 (5 days); September 3; December 31
Usual business hours	Sat.–Thurs. 7.30–12.30, 14.30–18
Electrical rating	240/415v AC, 50Hz

Demography
Life expectancy (years)	male 68.75; female 74.20
Population growth rate	2.5% (1995)
Population density	50 per sq. km (1995)

Government and diplomacy
Political system	Absolute monarchy
Head of state and of government	Sheikh Hamad bin Khalifa Al-Thani (Amir)
Embassy in UK	1 South Audley Street, London W1Y 5DQ. Tel: 0171-493 2200
British Embassy in Doha	PO Box 3, Doha. Tel: Doha 421991

Defence
Military expenditure	10.4% of GDP (1996)
Military personnel	11,800: Army 8,500, Navy 1,800, Air Force 1,500

Economy
GNP	US$7,448 million (1995)
	US$11,600 per capita (1995)
GDP	US$8,074 million (1994)
	US$13,020 per capita (1994)
Inflation rate	4.4% (1991)

Education
Enrolment (percentage of age group)	primary 80% (1993); secondary 70% (1993); tertiary 27.4% (1994)
Illiteracy rate	20.6%

RÉUNION, see FRANCE

ROMANIA

Area	92,043 sq. miles (238,391 sq. km)
Population	22,680,000 (1997 estimate)
Main language	Romanian
Capital	Bucharest (population 2,060,551, 1996)
Currency	Leu (Lei) of 100 bani
Exchange rate (at 29 May)	Lei 13877.3
Public holidays	January 1; April 19, 20; December 1, 25, 26
Usual business hours	Mon.–Fri. 7–15.30
Electrical rating	220v AC, 50Hz

Demography

Life expectancy (years)	male 65.88; female 73.32
Population growth rate	-0.5% (1995)
Population density	95 per sq. km (1995)
Urban population	54.7% (1994)

Government and diplomacy

Political system	Republic
Head of state	President Prof. Emil Constantinescu
Head of government	Radu Vasile
Embassy in UK	Arundel House, 4 Palace Green, London W8 4QD. Tel: 0171-937 9666
British Embassy in Bucharest	24 Strada Jules Michelet, 70154 Bucharest. Tel: Bucharest 312 0303

Defence

Military expenditure	2.3% of GDP (1996)
Military personnel	273,550: Army 129,350, Navy 17,500, Air Force 47,600, Paramilitaries 79,100
Conscription duration	12–18 months

Economy

GNP	US$36,191 million (1996) US$1,600 per capita (1996)
GDP	US$30,023 million (1994) US$1,274 per capita (1994)
Annual average growth of GDP	4% (1994)
Inflation rate	32.2% (1995)
Unemployment	8% (1995)
Total external debt	US$8,291 million (1996)

Education

Enrolment (percentage of age group)	primary 92% (1995); secondary 73% (1995); tertiary 18.3% (1995)
Illiteracy rate	2.1%

RUSSIA

Area	6,592,850 sq. miles (17,075,400 sq. km)
Population	147,855,000 (1997 estimate)
Main language	Russian
Capital	Moscow (population 8,663,142, 1993 estimate)
Currency	Rouble of 100 kopeks
Exchange rate (at 29 May)	Roubles 10.0606
Public holidays	January 1, 2, 7; March 8, 9; May 1, 2, 4, 9; June 12; November 7, 9; December 12, 14
Usual business hours	Mon.–Fri. 9–18
Electrical rating	220v AC, 50Hz

Demography

Life expectancy (years)	male 57.59; female 71.18
Population growth rate	0% (1995)
Population density	9 per sq. km (1995)
Urban population	72.9% (1995)

Government and diplomacy

Political system	Republic; federal state
Head of state	President Boris Yeltsin
Head of government	Sergei Kiriyenko
Embassy in UK	13 Kensington Palace Gardens, London W8 4QX. Tel: 0171-229 3628
British Embassy in Moscow	Sofiiskaya Naberezhnaya 14, Moscow 109072. Tel: Moscow 956 7200
Trouble spots	Secession in Chechenia in 1991. Government forces' attempts to retake republic ended with cease-fire in 1996 and withdrawal by 1997; decision about Chechenia's status postponed to 2001 State of emergency in Ingushetia and North Ossetia since 1993 Ethnic tension in Dagestan

Defence

Military expenditure	6.5% of GDP (1996)
Military personnel	1,672,000: Missile Forces 149,000, Army 420,000, Navy 220,000, Air Force 130,000, Air Defence Troops 170,000, Paramilitaries 583,000
Conscription duration	18–24 months. Due to be ended by 2000

Economy

GNP	US$356,030 million (1996) US$2,410 per capita (1996)

GDP	US$626,929 million (1994)
	US$1,951 per capita (1994)
Inflation rate	47.6% (1996)
Unemployment	8.3% (1995)
Total external debt	US$124,785 million (1996)

Education

Enrolment (percentage of age group)	primary 100% (1994); tertiary 42.9% (1994)
Illiteracy rate	0.5%

RWANDA

Area	10,169 sq. miles (26,338 sq. km)
Population	7,952,000 (1994 UN estimate)
Main languages	Kinyarwanda, French, English, Swahili
Capital	Kigali (population 156,000)
Currency	Rwanda franc of 100 centimes
Exchange rate (at 29 May)	Francs 501.636
Public holidays	January 1, 30; April 7; May 1; July 1, 4; August 15; September 25; October 1; November 1; December 25
Usual business hours	Mon.–Fri. 8–12.30, 13.30–17
Electrical rating	220v AC, 50Hz

Demography

Life expectancy (years)	male 45.10; female 47.70
Population growth rate	2% (1995)
Population density	302 per sq. km (1995)
Urban population	5.4% (1991)

Government and diplomacy

Political system	Republic
Head of state	President Pasteur Bizimungu
Head of government	Pierre Celestin Rwigyema
Embassy in UK	Uganda House, 58–59 Trafalgar Square, London WC2N 5DX. Tel: 0171-930 2570
British Embassy in Kigali	Parcelle No. 1071, Kimihurura, Kigali. Tel: Kigali 84098
Trouble spots	Ethnic tension between Hutus and Tutsis
	Violence frequent in north-west and mid-west
	Rebel activity to south of Kigali

Defence

Military expenditure	6.3% of GDP (1996)
Military personnel	62,000: Army 55,000, Paramilitaries 7,000

Economy

GNP	US$1,268 million (1996)
	US$190 per capita (1996)
GDP	US$995 million (1994)
	US$65 per capita (1994)
Annual average growth of GDP	-15.9% (1993)
Inflation rate	7.4% (1996)
Total external debt	US$1,034 million (1996)

Education

Enrolment (percentage of age group)	primary 76% (1991); secondary 8% (1991); tertiary 0.6% (1990)
Illiteracy rate	39.5%

ST CHRISTOPHER AND NEVIS

Area	101 sq. miles (261 sq. km)
Population	41,000 (1994 UN estimate)
Main language	English
Capital	Basseterre (population 14,161, 1980)
Currency	East Caribbean dollar (EC$) of 100 cents
Exchange rate (at 29 May)	EC$ 4.4029
Public holidays	January 1, 2; April 10, 13; May 4; June 1; August 3; September 19; December 25, 26
Usual business hours	Mon.–Fri. 8–12, 13–16
Electrical rating	220v AC, 60Hz; 110v AC available in some hotels

Demography

Life expectancy (years)	male 65.10; female 70.08
Population growth rate	-0.5% (1995)
Population density	157 per sq. km (1995)

Government and diplomacy

Political system	Constitutional monarchy
Head of state	Queen Elizabeth II
Governor-General	Sir Cuthbert Sebastian
Head of government	Dr Denzil Douglas
High Commission in UK	10 Kensington Court, London W8 5DL. Tel: 0171-937 9522
British High Commission	Bridgetown, Barbados

Economy

GNP	US$240 million (1996)
	US$5,870 per capita (1996)
GDP	US$146 million (1994)
	US$4,217 per capita (1994)
Annual average growth of GDP	4% (1993)
Inflation rate	2.5% (1996)
Total external debt	US$58 million (1996)

ST HELENA

Area	47 sq. miles (122 sq. km)
Population	7,000 (1994 UN estimate)
Main language	English
Capital	Jamestown (population 1,332, 1994)
Currency	St Helena pound (£) of 100 pence
Exchange rate (at 29 May)	at parity with £ sterling

Demography

Population growth rate	0.6% (1995)
Population density	54 per sq. km (1995)
Urban population	42.8% (1987)

Government

Political system	UK Overseas Territory
Governor	David L. Smallman

ASCENSION ISLAND

Area	34 sq. miles (88 sq. km)
Population	1,051 (1994 UN estimate)
Capital	Georgetown
Currency	Currency is that of St Helena

Government

Political system	Dependency of St Helena
Administrator	Roger Huxley

TRISTAN DA CUNHA

Area	38 sq. miles (98 sq. km)
Population	288 (1994 UN estimate)
Capital	Edinburgh of the Seven Seas
Currency	Currency is that of the UK

Government

Political system	Dependency of St Helena
Administrator	Brian Baldwin

ST LUCIA

Area	240 sq. miles (622 sq. km)
Population	145,000 (1994 UN estimate)
Main language	English
Capital	Castries (population 56,000, 1989)
Currency	East Caribbean dollar (EC$) of 100 cents
Exchange rate (at 29 May)	EC$ 4.4029
Public holidays	January 1, 2; February 23, 24; April 10, 13; May 1; June 1, 11; August 3; October 5; December 13, 25, 26
Usual business hours	Mon.–Fri. 8–16
Electrical rating	220v AC, 50Hz

Demography

Life expectancy (years)	male 68; female 74.80
Population growth rate	1.8% (1995)
Population density	234 per sq. km (1995)

Government and diplomacy

Political system	Constitutional monarchy
Head of state	Queen Elizabeth II
Governor-General	Perlette Louisy
Head of government	Kenny Anthony
High Commission in UK	10 Kensington Court, London W8 5DL. Tel: 0171-937 9522
British High Commission in Castries	Derek Walcott Square, PO Box 227, Castries. Tel: Castries 452 2484

Economy

GNP	US$553 million (1996) US$3,500 per capita (1996)
GDP	US$381 million (1994) US$3,014 per capita (1994)
Annual average growth of GDP	6.6% (1992)
Inflation rate	2.7% (1995)
Total external debt	US$142 million (1996)

ST PIERRE AND MIQUELON, see FRANCE

ST VINCENT AND THE GRENADINES

Area	150 sq. miles (388 sq. km)
Population	111,000 (1994 UN estimate)
Main language	English
Capital	Kingstown (population 33,694)
Currency	East Caribbean dollar (EC$) of 100 cents
Exchange rate (at 29 May)	EC$ 4.4029
Public holidays	January 1, 22; April 10, 13; May 1; June 1; July 7, 8; August 3; October 27; December 25, 26
Usual business hours	Banking hours: Mon.–Thurs. 8–15; Fri. 8–17
Electrical rating	220/240v AC, 50z

Demography

Population growth rate	0.7% (1995)
Population density	285 per sq. km (1995)

Government and diplomacy

Political system	Constitutional monarchy
Head of state	Queen Elizabeth II
Governor-General	Sir David Jack
Head of government	Sir James Mitchell
High Commission in UK	10 Kensington Court, London W8 5DL. Tel: 0171-937 9522
British High Commission in Kingstown	Granby Street (PO Box 132), Kingstown. Tel: St Vincent 457 1701/2

Economy

GNP	US$264 million (1996)
	US$2,370 per capita (1996)
GDP	US$217 million (1994)
	US$2,248 per capita (1994)
Annual average growth of GDP	7.4% (1995)
Inflation rate	4.4% (1996)
Total external debt	US$213 million (1996)

EL SALVADOR

Area	8,124 sq. miles (21,041 sq. km)
Population	5,768,000 (1994 UN estimate)
Main language	Spanish
Capital	San Salvador (population 422,570, 1992)
Currency	El Salvador colón (¢) of 100 centavos
Exchange rate (at 29 May)	¢ 14.2768
Public holidays	January 1; April 8, 9, 10; May 1; June 30; August 5, 6; September 15; November 2; December 25, 30, 31
Usual business hours	Mon.–Fri. 8–12.30, 14.30–17.30
Electrical rating	110v AC, 60Hz

Demography

Life expectancy (years)	male 50.74; female 63.89
Population growth rate	2.2% (1995)
Population density	274 per sq. km (1995)
Urban population	50.4% (1992)

Government and diplomacy

Political system	Republic
Head of state and of government	President Armando Calderón Sol
Embassy in UK	Tennyson House, 159 Great Portland Street, London W1N 5FD. Tel: 0171-436 8282
British Embassy in San Salvador	PO Box 1591, San Salvador. Tel: San Salvador 263 6527

Defence

Military expenditure	1.4% of GDP (1996)
Military personnel	40,400: Army 25,700, Navy 1,100, Air Force 1,600, Paramilitaries 12,000
Conscription duration	12 months

Economy

GNP	US$9,868 million (1996) US$1,700 per capita (1996)
GDP	US$6,335 million (1994) US$1,584 per capita (1994)
Annual average growth of GDP	25.4% (1996)
Inflation rate	9.8% (1996)
Unemployment	7.7% (1995)
Total external debt	US$2,894 million (1996)

Education

Enrolment (percentage of age group)	primary 79% (1995); secondary 21% (1995); tertiary 17.7% (1995)
Illiteracy rate	28.5%

SAMOA

Area	1,093 sq. miles (2,831 sq. km)
Population	171,000 (1994 UN estimate)
Main languages	Samoan, English
Capital	Apia (population 36,000, 1989)
Currency	Tala (S$) of 100 sene
Exchange rate (at 29 May)	S$ 4.8546
Public holidays	January 1, 2; April 10, 11, 13, 25; May 11; June 1, 2; August 3; October 12; November 6; December 25, 26
Usual business hours	Mon.–Fri. 8–12, 13–16.30
Electrical rating	240v AC, 50Hz

Demography

Life expectancy (years)	male 61; female 64.30
Population growth rate	0.9% (1995)
Population density	60 per sq. km (1995)

Government and diplomacy

Political system	Constitutional monarchy
Head of state	Malietoa Tanumafili II
Head of government	Tofilau Eti Alesana
High Commission	Avenue Franklin D.Roosevelt 123, 1050 Brussels, Belgium. Tel: Brussels 660 8454
British High Commission	Wellington, New Zealand

Economy

GNP	US$200 million (1996) US$1,170 per capita (1996)
GDP	US$101 million (1994) US$700 per capita (1994)
Annual average growth of GDP	0.5% (1983)
Inflation rate	7.6% (1996)
Total external debt	US$167 million (1996)

Education

Enrolment (percentage of age group)	primary 99% (1995); secondary 45% (1995)

SAN MARINO

Area	24 sq. miles (61 sq. km)
Population	25,000 (1996)
Main language	Italian
City	San Marino (population 4,251, 1994)
Currency	San Marino and Italian currencies are in circulation
Exchange rate (at 29 May)	Lire 2864.81
Public holidays	January 1, 6; February 5; March 25; April 1, 13; May 1; June 11; July 28; August 15; September 3; October 1; November 1, 2; December 8, 24–26, 31
Electrical rating	220v AC, 50Hz

Demography

Life expectancy (years)	male 73.16; female 79.12
Population growth rate	1.5% (1995)
Population density	410 per sq. km (1995)
Urban population	90.4% (1994)

Government and diplomacy

Political system	Republic
Heads of state and of government	Two 'Capitani Reggenti' (regents), elected every six months
Consulate-General in UK	166 High Holborn, London WC1V 6TT. Tel: 0171-836 7744
British Consulate-General	Florence, Italy

Economy

GDP	US$471 million (1994) US$17,213 per capita (1994)
Unemployment	39% (1995)

SÃO TOMÉ AND PRINCÍPE

Area	372 sq. miles (964 sq. km)
Population	127,000 (1994 UN estimate)
Main language	Portuguese
Capital	São Tomé (population 43,420, 1991)
Currency	Dobra of 100 centavos
Exchange rate (at 29 May)	Dobra 3897.37
Public holidays	January 1; February 3; May 1; July 12; September 6, 30; December 21, 25
Usual business hours	Banking hours: Mon.–Fri. 7.30–11.30
Electrical rating	220v AC, 50Hz

Demography

Population growth rate	2% (1995)
Population density	132 per sq. km (1995)

Government and diplomacy

Political system	Republic
Head of state	President Miguel Trovoada
Head of government	Raul Bragança Neto
Embassy	Square Montgomery, 174 avenue de Tervuren, 1150 Brussels, Belgium. Tel: Brussels 734 8966
Honorary consulate in UK	42 North Audley Street, London W1A 4PY. Tel: 0171-499 1995
British Consulate in São Tomé	Residencial Avenida, Av. Da Independencia CP 257, São Tomé

Economy

GNP	US$45 million (1996)
	US$330 per capita (1996)
GDP	US$60 million (1994)
	US$120 per capita (1994)
Total external debt	US$261 million (1996)

SAUDI ARABIA

Area	830,000 sq. miles (2,149,690 sq. km)
Population	17,880,000 (1994 UN estimate)
Main languages	Arabic, English
Capital	Riyadh (population 1,800,000, 1991)
Currency	Saudi riyal (SR) of 20 qursh or 100 halala
Exchange rate (at 29 May)	SR 6.1167
Public holidays	January 30 (4 days); April 7 (5 days)
Usual business hours	Sat.–Thurs. 9–13, 16.30–20 (different hours during Ramadan)
Electrical rating	125/215v AC, 50/60Hz

Demography

Life expectancy (years)	male 68.39; female 71.41
Population growth rate	3.7% (1995)
Population density	8 per sq. km (1995)

Government and diplomacy

Political system	Absolute monarchy
Head of state and of government	King Fahd bin Abdul Aziz Al Saud
Embassy in UK	30 Charles Street, London W1X 7PM. Tel: 0171-917 3000
British Embassy in Riyadh	PO Box 94351, Riyadh 11693. Tel: Riyadh 488 0077
Trouble spots	Opposition to the Al-Saud regime has led to attacks on government and US targets

Defence

Military expenditure	12.7% of GDP (1996)
Military personnel	198,000: Army 70,000, Navy 13,500, Air Force 18,000, Air Defence Force 4,000, National Guard 77,000, Paramilitaries 15,500

Economy

GNP	US$133,540 million (1995) US$7,040 per capita (1995)
GDP	US$108,923 million (1994) US$6,977 per capita (1994)
Annual average growth of GDP	0.5% (1995)
Inflation rate	1.2% (1996)

Education

Enrolment (percentage of age group)	primary 62% (1995); secondary 48% (1995); tertiary 15.3% (1994)
Illiteracy rate	37.2%

SENEGAL

Area	75,955 sq. miles (196,722 sq. km)
Population	8,312,000 (1994 UN estimate)
Main languages	French, Wollof, Sengalo-Guinean and Mandé dialects
Capital	Dakar (population 1,641,358, 1994)
Currency	Franc CFA of 100 centimes
Exchange rate (at 29 May)	Francs 975.610
Public holidays	January 1, 30; April 4, 7, 12, 13; May 1, 11, 21; June 1; July 6; August 15; November 1; December 25
Usual business hours	Mon.–Fri. 8–12.30, 13–16
Electrical rating	220v AC, 50Hz

Demography

Life expectancy (years)	male 48.30; female 50.30
Population growth rate	2% (1995)
Population density	42 per sq. km (1995)
Urban population	42.9% (1993)

Government and diplomacy

Political system	Republic
Head of state and of government	President Abdou Diouf Embassy in UK 39 Marloes Road, London W8 6LA. Tel: 0171-930 7606
British Embassy in Dakar	BP 6025, Dakar. Tel: Dakar 237392
Trouble spots	Insurgency by Movement of Democratic Forces of Casamance (MFDC) in southern Casamance region

Defence

Military expenditure	1.5% of GDP (1996)
Military personnel	17,350: Army 12,000, Navy 700, Air Force 650, Paramilitaries 4,000
Conscription duration	Two years

Economy

GNP	US$4,856 million (1996) US$570 per capita (1996)
GDP	US$5,955 million (1994) US$493 per capita (1994)
Annual average growth of GDP	-1.5% (1989)
Inflation rate	2.8% (1996)
Total external debt	US$3,663 million (1996)

Education

Enrolment (percentage of age group)	primary 54% (1995); tertiary 3.4% (1995)
Illiteracy rate	66.9%

SEYCHELLES

Area	176 sq. miles (455 sq. km)
Population	75,000 (1994 UN estimate)
Main languages	French, English, Creole
Capital	Victoria (population 24,324, 1987)
Currency	Seychelles rupee of 100 cents
Exchange rate (at 29 May)	Rs 8.4332
Public holidays	January 1, 2; April 10; May 1; June 5, 11; June 18, 29; August 15; November 2; December 8, 25
Usual business hours	Mon.–Fri. 8–12, 13–16
Electrical rating	240v AC, 50Hz (UK plugs)

Demography

Life expectancy (years)	male 65.26; female 74.05
Population growth rate	1.6% (1995)
Population density	165 per sq. km (1995)

Government and diplomacy

Political system	Republic
Head of state and of government	President France Albert René
	High Commission in UK Box No. 4PE, 2nd Floor, Eros House, 111 Baker Street, London W1M 1FE. Tel: 0171-224 1660
British High Commission in Victoria	Victoria House, PO Box 161 Victoria, Mahé. Tel: Victoria 225225

Defence

Military expenditure	2.1% of GDP (1996)
Military personnel	450: Army 200, Paramilitaries 250

Economy

GNP	US$526 million (1996)
	US$6,850 per capita (1996)
GDP	US$425 million (1994)
	US$6,798 per capita (1994)
Annual average growth of GDP	2.2% (1991)
Inflation rate	-1.2% (1996)
Total external debt	US$148 million (1996)

SIERRA LEONE

Area	27,699 sq. miles (71,740 sq. km)
Population	4,509,000 (1994 UN estimate)
Main languages	English, French, Krio dialects
Capital	Freetown (population 469,776, 1985)
Currency	Leone (Le) of 100 cents
Exchange rate (at 29 May)	Le 1475.78
Public holidays	January 1, 30; April 7, 10, 13, 27; July 6; December 25, 26
Usual business hours	Mon.–Fri. 8–12, 14–16.45
Electrical rating	220/240v AC, 50Hz

Demography

Life expectancy (years)	male 37.47; female 40.58
Population growth rate	2.4% (1995)
Population density	63 per sq. km (1995)

Government and diplomacy

Political system	Republic
Head of state and of government	President Ahmad Tejan Kabbah
High Commission in UK	33 Portland Place, London W1N 3AG. Tel: 0171-636 6483/4/5/6
British High Commission in Freetown	Spur Road, Freetown. Tel: Freetown 223961
Trouble spots	Civil war since 1991 between government and Revolutionary United Front (RUF)

Defence

Military expenditure	4.9% of GDP (1996)
Military personnel	13,200: Army 13,000, Navy 200

Economy

GNP	US$925 million (1996)
	US$200 per capita (1996)
GDP	US$598 million (1994)
	US$184 per capita (1994)
Annual average growth of GDP	–2.8% (1995)
Inflation rate	23.2% (1996)
Total external debt	US$1,167 million (1996)

Education

Enrolment (percentage of age group)	tertiary 1.3% (1990)
Illiteracy rate	68.6%

SINGAPORE

Area	239 sq. miles (618 sq. km)
Population	2,987,000 (1996)
Main languages	Malay, Mandarin, Tamil, English
Currency	Singapore dollar (S$) of 100 cents
Exchange rate (at 29 May)	S$ 2.7298
Public holidays	January 1, 28, 30; April 7, 10; May 1, 10, 11; August 9, 10; October 19; December 25
Usual business hours	Mon.–Fri. 9–13, 14–17
Electrical rating	220/240v AC, 50Hz

Demography
Life expectancy (years)	male 74.20; female 78.50
Population growth rate	2% (1995)
Population density	4,833 per sq. km (1995)

Government and diplomacy
Political system	Republic
Head of state	President Ong Teng Cheong
Head of government	Goh Chok Tong
High Commission in UK	9 Wilton Crescent, London SW1X 8RW. Tel: 0171-235 8315
British High Commission in Singapore	Tanglin Road, Singapore 247919. Tel: Singapore 473 9333

Defence
Military expenditure	4.4% of GDP (1996)
Military personnel	178,000: Army 55,000, Navy 9,000, Air Force 6,000, Paramilitaries 108,000
Conscription duration	24–30 months

Economy
GNP	US$92,987 million (1996) US$30,550 per capita (1996)
GDP	US$49,979 million (1994) US$23,556 per capita (1994)
Annual average growth of GDP	7.3% (1996)
Inflation rate	1.4% (1996)
Unemployment	2.7% (1995)

Education
Enrolment (percentage of age group)	primary 99% (1980); tertiary 33.7% (1995)
Illiteracy rate	8.9%

SLOVAKIA

Area	18,924 sq. miles (49,012 sq. km)
Population	5,364,000 (1994 UN estimate)
Main languages	Slovak, Hungarian, Czech
Capital	Bratislava (population 451,272, 1993)
Currency	Koruna (Kčs) of 100 haléřu
Exchange rate (at 29 May)	Kčs 56.2510
Public holidays	January 1, 6; April 10, 13; May 1, 8; July 5; August 29; September 1, 15; November 1; December 24–26
Usual business hours	Mon.–Fri. 8–16
Electrical rating	Mainly 220v AC, 50Hz

Demography

Life expectancy (years)	male 68.34; female 76.48
Population growth rate	0.2% (1995)
Population density	109 per sq. km (1995)
Urban population	57% (1994)

Government and diplomacy

Political system	Republic
Head of state	Vacant
Head of government	Vladimír Mečiar
Embassy in UK	25 Kensington Palace Gardens, London W8 4QY. Tel: 0171-243 0803
British Embassy in Bratislava	Panska 16, 81101 Bratislava. Tel: Bratislava 531 9632

Defence

Military expenditure	2.3% of GDP (1996)
Military personnel	39,750: Army 23,800, Air Force 12,000, Paramilitaries 3,950
Conscription duration	12 months

Economy

GNP	US$18,206 million (1996) US$3,410 per capita (1996)
GDP	US$11,190 million (1994) US$2,331 per capita (1994)
Annual average growth of GDP	6.9% (1996)
Inflation rate	5.8% (1996)
Unemployment	13.1% (1995)
Total external debt	US$7,704 million (1996)

Education

Enrolment (percentage of age group)	tertiary 20.2% (1995)

SLOVENIA

Area	7,821 sq. miles (20,256 sq. km)
Population	1,984,000 (1994 UN estimate)
Main languages	Slovene, Hungarian, Italian
Capital	Ljubljana (population 330,000)
Currency	Tolar (SIT) of 100 stotin
Exchange rate (at 29 May)	Tolars 272.085
Public holidays	January 1, 2; February 8; April 13, 27; May 1, 2; June 25; August 15; October 31; November 1; December 25, 26
Usual business hours	Mon.–Fri. 8–16
Electrical rating	220v AC, 50Hz

Demography

Life expectancy (years)	male 69.58; female 77.38
Population growth rate	-0.1% (1995)
Population density	98 per sq. km (1995)
Urban population	50% (1995)

Government and diplomacy

Political system	Republic
Head of state	President Milan Kučan
Head of government	Janez Drnovšek
Embassy in UK	11–15 Wigmore Street, London W1H 9LA. Tel: 0171-495 7775
British Embassy in Ljubljana	4th Floor, Trg Republike 3, 61-000. Tel: Ljubljana 125 7191

Defence

Military expenditure	1.4% of GDP (1996)
Military personnel	14,050: Army 9,550, Paramilitaries 4,500
Conscription duration	Seven months

Economy

GNP	US$18,390 million (1996) US$9,240 per capita (1996)
GDP	US$15,789 million (1994) US$7,206 per capita (1994)
Annual average growth of GDP	4.9% (1995)
Inflation rate	9.7% (1996)
Unemployment	7.4% (1995)
Total external debt	US$4,031 million (1996)

Education

Enrolment (percentage of age group)	primary 100% (1995); tertiary 31.9% (1995)

SOLOMON ISLANDS

Area	11,157 sq. miles (28,896 sq. km)
Population	378,000 (1994 UN estimate)
Main language	English
Capital	Honiara (population 40,000, 1991)
Currency	Solomon Islands dollar (SI$) of 100 cents
Exchange rate (at 29 May)	SI$ 7.8222
Public holidays	January 1; April 10, 11, 13; June 1, 12, 13; July 6, 7; December 25, 26
Usual business hours	Mon.–Fri. 8–12, 13–16.30
Electrical rating	240v AC, 50Hz (Australian plugs)

Demography

Life expectancy (years)	male 59.90; female 61.40
Population growth rate	3.3% (1995)
Population density	13 per sq. km (1995)

Government and diplomacy

Political system	Constitutional monarchy
Head of state	Queen Elizabeth II
Governor-General	Sir Moses Pitakaka
Head of government	Bartholomew Ulufa'alu
High Commission	Boulevard Saint Michel 28, Box 23, 1040 Brussels, Belgium. Tel: Brussels 2732 7085
Honorary Consulate in UK	19 Springfield Road, London SW19 7AL. Tel: 0181-296 0232
British High Commission in Honiara	Telekon House, Mendana Avenue (PO Box 676), Honiara. Tel: Honiara 21705/6

Economy

GNP	US$349 million (1996) US$900 per capita (1996)
GDP	US$216 million (1994) US$669 per capita (1994)
Annual average growth of GDP	-5.1% (1987)
Inflation rate	11.8% (1996)
Total external debt	US$145 million (1996)

SOMALIA

Area	246,201 sq. miles (637,657 sq. km)
Population	9,250,000 (1994 UN estimate)
Main languages	Somali, Arabic, English
Capital	Mogadishu (population 1,000,000, 1987 estimate)
Currency	Somali shilling of 100 cents
Exchange rate (at 29 May)	Shillings 4272.43
Public holidays	January 1, 30 (2 days); April 7 (2 days); May 1; July 6; October 21 (2 days)
Usual business hours	Sat.–Thurs. 8–14
Electrical rating	220v AC, 50Hz

Demography

Life expectancy (years)	male 45.41; female 48.60
Population growth rate	1.3% (1995)
Population density	15 per sq. km (1995)
Urban population	23.5% (1987)

Government and diplomacy

Political system	Republic; no constitution currently in place
Head of state	None
Head of government	None
Embassy in UK	Closed 1992
British Embassy in Mogadishu	Closed 1991
Trouble spots	Civil war in north from 1988; Somali National Movement (SNM) seceded in 1991 Civil war in rest of country since downfall of longstanding dictator Siad Barre in 1991; situation now calmer but volatile

Defence

Military expenditure	4.8% of GDP (1996)

Economy

GDP	US$731 million (1994) US$124 per capita (1994)
Annual average growth of GDP	10.1% (1987)
Inflation rate	81.9% (1988)
Total external debt	US$2,643 million (1996)

Education

Enrolment (percentage of age group)	primary 8% (1985); secondary 3% (1985); tertiary 2.1% (1985)

SOUTH AFRICA

Area	471,445 sq. miles (1,221,037 sq. km)
Population	37,900,000 (1996)
Main languages	English, Afrikaans, Zulu, Xhosa, Ndebele, Sesotho, Tswana
Capital	The seat of government is Pretoria (population 525,583, 1991); the seat of the legislature is Cape Town (population 1,911,521, 1991)
Currency	Rand (R) of 100 cents
Exchange rate (at 29 May)	R 8.4079
Public holidays	January 1; March 21; April 10, 13, 27; May 1; June 16; August 9, 10; September 24; December 16, 25, 26
Usual business hours	Mon.–Fri. 8.30–16.30
Electrical rating	220/230v AC, 50Hz; Pretoria 250v AC, 50 Hz

Demography
Life expectancy (years)	male 60.01; female 66
Population growth rate	2.1% (1995)
Population density	34 per sq. km (1995)
Urban population	56.6% (1991)

Government and diplomacy
Political system	Republic
Head of state and of government	Nelson Mandela
High Commission in UK	South Africa House, Trafalgar Square, London WC2N 5DP. Tel: 0171-451 7299
British High Commission in Pretoria	255 Hill Street, Pretoria 0002. Tel: Pretoria 433121

Defence
Military expenditure	2% of GDP (1996)
Military personnel	211,440: Army 54,300, Navy 8,000, Air Force 11,140, Paramilitaries 138,000
Conscription duration	Three categories (full career; up to ten years; up to six years)

Economy
GNP	US$132,455 million (1996) US$3,520 per capita (1996)
GDP	US$102,812 million (1994) US$2,835 per capita (1994)
Annual average growth of GDP	3.1% (1996)
Inflation rate	7.4% (1996)
Unemployment	4.5% (1995)
Total external debt	US$23,590 million (1996)

Education

Enrolment (percentage of age group)	primary 96% (1994); secondary 52% (1994); tertiary 17.3% (1995)
Illiteracy rate	18.2%

SPAIN

Area	195,365 sq. miles (505,992 sq. km)
Population	39,210,000 (1996 census)
Main languages	Spanish, Basque
Capital	Madrid (population 3,084,673, 1996)
Currency	Peseta of 100 céntimos
Exchange rate (at 29 May)	Pesetas 246.749
Public holidays	January 1, 6; April 9–11; May 1; August 15; October 12; November 1, 2; December 6, 8, 25
Usual business hours	Vary; banking hours: Mon.–Fri. 9–14; Sat. 9–13
Electrical rating	220v AC, 50Hz

Demography

Life expectancy (years)	male 73.40; female 80.49
Population growth rate	0.1% (1995)
Population density	77 per sq. km (1995)
Urban population	64.1% (1991)

Government and diplomacy

Political system	Constitutional monarchy
Head of state	King Juan Carlos I de Borbón y Borbón
Head of government	José María Aznar López
Embassy in UK	39 Chesham Place, London SW1X 8SB. Tel: 0171-235 5555
British Embassy in Madrid	Calle de Fernando el Santo 16, 28010 Madrid. Tel: Madrid 319 0200
Trouble spots	Basque separatist guerrillas (ETA) carried out terrorist acts to gain independence for the Basque country; vigorous government action has left it greatly weakened

Defence

Military expenditure	1.5% of GDP (1996)
Military personnel	273,250: Army 128,500, Navy 39,000, Air Force 30,000, Paramilitaries 75,750
Conscription duration	Nine months

Economy

GNP	US$563,249 million (1996) US$14,350 per capita (1996)

GDP	US$510,763 million (1994)
	US$12,201 per capita (1994)
Annual average growth of GDP	2.2% (1996)
Inflation rate	3.6% (1996)
Unemployment	22.9% (1995)

Education

Enrolment (percentage of age group)	primary 100% (1994); secondary 94% (1994); tertiary 46.1% (1994)
Illiteracy rate	2.9%

SRI LANKA

Area	25,332 sq. miles (65,610 sq. km)
Population	18,354,000 (1994 UN estimate)
Main languages	Sinhala, Tamil, English
Capital	Colombo (population 615,000)
Currency	Sri Lankan rupee of 100 cents
Exchange rate (at 29 May)	Rs 105.881
Public holidays	January 12, 14, 30; February 4, 10, 25; March 12; April 7, 10, 11, 13, 14; May 1, 11, 12; June 9; July 6, 9; August 7; September 8; October 5, 19; November 3; December 3, 25
Usual business hours	Mon.–Fri. 8–16.30
Electrical rating	230/240v AC, 50Hz

Demography

Life expectancy (years)	male 67.78; female 71.66
Population growth rate	1.5% (1995)
Population density	280 per sq. km (1995)

Government and diplomacy

Political system	Republic
Head of state and of government	President Chandrika Bandaranaike Kumaratunga
High Commission in UK	13 Hyde Park Gardens, London W2 2LU. Tel: 0171-262 1841
British High Commission in Colombo	Galle Road 190, Kollupitiya (PO Box 1433), Colombo 3. Tel: Colombo 437336
Trouble spots	Conflict in north and east since 1983 between government and Tamil guerrillas fighting for control of the Tamil majority areas; occasional bombings in Colombo

Defence

Military expenditure	6.5% of GDP (1996)
Military personnel	227,200: Army 95,000, Navy 12,000, Air Force 10,000, Paramilitaries 110,200

Economy

GNP	US$13,475 million (1996)
	US$740 per capita (1996)
GDP	US$9,811 million (1994)
	US$649 per capita (1994)
Annual average growth of GDP	4.8% (1991)
Inflation rate	15.9% (1996)
Unemployment	12.5% (1995)
Total external debt	US$7,995 million (1996)

Education

Enrolment (percentage of age group)	tertiary 5.1% (1995)
Illiteracy rate	9.8%

SUDAN

Area	967,500 sq. miles (2,505,813 sq. km)
Population	28,098,000 (1994 UN estimate)
Main languages	Arabic, English
Capital	Khartoum (population 924,505, 1994)
Currency	Sudanese dinar (SD) of 10 pounds
Exchange rate (at 29 May)	SD 263.015
Public holidays	January 1, 7, 30 (3 days); February 12; April 7 (4 days), 20, 28; June 30; July 6; November 17; December 25
Usual business hours	Sat.–Thurs. 8–14.30
Electrical rating	240v AC, 50Hz

Demography

Life expectancy (years)	male 51.58; female 54.37
Population growth rate	1.7% (1995)
Population density	11 per sq. km (1995)
Urban population	27.1% (1994)

Government and diplomacy

Political system	Republic
Head of state and of government	President Lt.-Gen. Omar Hassan Ahmad al-Bashir
Embassy in UK	3 Cleveland Row, London SW1A 1DD. Tel: 0171-839 8080
British Embassy in Khartoum	PO Box 801, Khartoum. Tel: Khartoum 777105
Trouble spots	Insurrection in predominantly non-Muslim southern provinces; Sudan People's Liberation Army (SPLA) attacks on government-controlled areas
	War-induced famine and refugee problems

Defence

Military expenditure	4.2% of GDP (1996)
Military personnel	94,700: Army 75,000, Navy 1,700, Air Force 3,000, Paramilitaries 15,000
Conscription duration	Three years

Economy

GDP	US$26,328 million (1994) US$62 per capita (1994)
Inflation rate	101.4% (1993)
Total external debt	US$16,972 million (1996)

Education

Enrolment (percentage of age group)	tertiary 3% (1990)
Illiteracy rate	53.9%

SURINAME

Area	63,037 sq. miles (163,265 sq. km)
Population	423,000 (1994 UN estimate)
Main languages	Dutch, Sranang Tongo, Hindustani, Javanese
Capital	Paramaribo (population 200,970, 1993)
Currency	Suriname guilder of 100 cents
Exchange rate (at 29 May)	Guilders 653.910
Public holidays	January 1, 30; April 10, 11, 13; May 1; July 1; November 25; December 25
Usual business hours	Mon.–Fri. 7–15; Sat. 7–14.30
Electrical rating	110/220v AC, 60Hz (European plugs)

Demography

Life expectancy (years)	male 67.80; female 72.78
Population growth rate	0.9% (1995)
Population density	3 per sq. km (1995)

Government and diplomacy

Political system	Republic
Head of state and of government	President Jules Wijdenbosch
Embassy	2 Alexander Gogelweg, The Hague, The Netherlands. Tel: The Hague 365 0844
British Consulate in Paramaribo	c/o VSH United Buildings, Van't Hogerhuystraat, PO Box 1300, Paramaribo

Defence

Military expenditure	3.5% of GDP (1996)

Military personnel	1,800: Army 1,400, Navy 240, Air Force 160

Economy

GNP	US$433 million (1996)
	US$1,000 per capita (1996)
GDP	US$1,811 million (1994)
	US$858 per capita (1994)
Annual average growth of GDP	-4.5% (1993)
Inflation rate	-0.7% (1996)
Unemployment	12.7% (1994)

Education

Illiteracy rate	7%

SWAZILAND

Area	6,704 sq. miles (17,364 sq. km)
Population	908,000 (1994 UN estimate)
Main languages	SiSwati, English
Capital	Mbabane (population 38,290, 1986)
Currency	Lilangeni (E) of 100 cents (South African currency is also in circulation)
Exchange rate (at 29 May)	E 8.4079
Public holidays	January 1; April 10, 13, 19, 20, 25; May 1, 21; July 22; September 6; December 25, 26
Usual business hours	Mon.–Fri. 8–13, 14–16.45
Electrical rating	220v AC, 50Hz

Demography

Life expectancy (years)	male 42.90; female 49.50
Population growth rate	3.3% (1995)
Population density	52 per sq. km (1995)
Urban population	24.8% (1995)

Government and diplomacy

Political system	Absolute monarchy; no political parties permitted
Head of state and of government	King Mswati III
High Commission in UK	20 Buckingham Gate, London SW1E 6LB. Tel: 0171-630 6611
British High Commission in Mbabane	Allister Miller Street, Mbabane. Tel: Mbabane 42581/4

Economy

GNP	US$1,122 million (1996)
	US$1,210 per capita (1996)
GDP	US$949 million (1994)
	US$1,311 per capita (1994)
Annual average growth of GDP	2.5% (1995)

Inflation rate	12.5% (1996)
Total external debt	US$220 million (1996)

Education

Enrolment (percentage of age group)	primary 95% (1994); secondary 37% (1994); tertiary 5.1% (1993)
Illiteracy rate	23.3%

SWEDEN

Area	173,732 sq. miles (449,964 sq. km)
Population	8,831,000 (1994 UN estimate)
Main language	Swedish
Capital	Stockholm (population 1,532,803, 1993)
Currency	Swedish krona of 100 öre
Exchange rate (at 29 May)	Kronor 12.7699
Public holidays	January 1, 6; April 10, 13; May 1, 21; June 1, 19; October 31; November 1; December 24–26, 31
Usual business hours	Flexible; banking hours: Mon.–Wed., Fri. 9.30–15; Thurs. 9.30–17.30
Electrical rating	220v AC, 50Hz (European plugs)

Demography

Life expectancy (years)	male 76.08; female 81.38
Population growth rate	0.6% (1995)
Population density	20 per sq. km (1995)
Urban population	83.4% (1990)

Government and diplomacy

Political system	Constitutional monarchy
Head of state	King Carl XVI Gustaf
Head of government	Göran Persson
Embassy in UK	11 Montagu Place, London W1H 2AL. Tel: 0171-917 6400
British Embassy in Stockholm	Skarpögatan 6–8, S115 93 Stockholm. Tel: Stockholm 671 9000

Defence

Military expenditure	2.5% of GDP (1996)
Military personnel	53,950: Army 35,100, Navy 9,500, Air Force 8,750, Paramilitaries 600
Conscription duration	Seven to 15 months

Economy

GNP	US$227,315 million (1996) US$25,710 per capita (1996)
GDP	US$222,951 million (1994) US$22,499 per capita (1994)

Annual average growth of GDP	3% (1995)
Inflation rate	0.5% (1996)
Unemployment	7.7% (1995)

Education

| Enrolment (percentage of age group) | primary 100% (1994); secondary 96% (1994); tertiary 42.5% (1994) |

SWITZERLAND

Area	15,940 sq. miles (41,284 sq. km)
Population	7,040,000 (1994 UN estimate)
Main languages	German, French, Italian
Capital	Berne (population 321,932, 1993)
Currency	Swiss franc of 100 rappen (or centimes)
Exchange rate (at 29 May)	Francs 2.4112
Public holidays	January 1, 2; April 10, 13; May 21; August 1; December 24–26
Usual business hours	Mon.–Fri. 8–12, 14–17
Electrical rating	220v AC, 50Hz

Demography

Life expectancy (years)	male 75.10; female 81.60
Population growth rate	1% (1995)
Population density	171 per sq. km (1995)
Urban population	67.8% (1994)

Government and diplomacy

Political system	Republic; federal state
Head of state and of government	President of the Swiss Confederation, elected annually; Flavio Cotti, 1998
Embassy in UK	16–18 Montagu Place, London W1H 2BQ. Tel: 0171-616 6000
British Embassy in Berne	Thunstrasse 50, 3005 Berne. Tel: Berne 352 5021/6

Defence

Military expenditure	1.6% of GDP (1996)
Military personnel	3,300 active (390,060 reserves: Army 357,460, Air Force 32,600)
Conscription duration	15 weeks, then ten refresher courses

Economy

GNP	US$313,729 million (1996) US$44,350 per capita (1996)
GDP	US$226,007 million (1994) US$36,096 per capita (1994)
Annual average growth of GDP	-0.7% (1996)
Inflation rate	0.8% (1996)
Unemployment	3.3% (1995)

Education

Enrolment (percentage of age group)	primary 100% (1993); secondary 79% (1990); tertiary 31.8% (1994)

SYRIA

Area	71,498 sq. miles (185,180 sq. km)
Population	14,315,000 (1994 UN estimate)
Main languages	Arabic, Kurdish, Turkish, Armenian
Capital	Damascus (population 1,549,000, 1994)
Currency	Syrian pound (S£) of 100 piastres
Exchange rate (at 29 May)	S£ 65.2280
Public holidays	January 1, 30 (3 days); March 8, 21; April 7 (4 days), 12, 17, 19, 28; May 6; July 6; October 6; December 25
Usual business hours	Sat.–Thurs. 8.30–14.30
Electrical rating	220v AC, 50Hz (European plugs)

Demography

Life expectancy (years)	male 64.42; female 68.05
Population growth rate	3.3% (1995)
Population density	77 per sq. km (1995)
Urban population	51.7% (1995)

Government and diplomacy

Political system	Republic; *de facto* one-party (Ba'ath) state
Head of state and of government	President Hafez Al-Assad
Embassy in UK	8 Belgrave Square, London SW1X 8PH. Tel: 0171-245 9012
British Embassy in Damascus	Kotob Building, 11 rue Mohammad Kurd Ali, Malki, Damascus (PO Box 37). Tel: Damascus 371 2561

Defence

Military expenditure	5.8% of GDP (1996)
Military personnel	328,000: Army 215,000, Navy 5,000, Air Force 40,000, Air Defence Command 60,000, Paramilitaries 8,000
Conscription duration	30 months

Economy

GNP	US$16,808 million (1996) US$1,160 per capita (1996)
GDP	US$30,408 million (1994) US$2,827 per capita (1994)
Annual average growth of GDP	3.6% (1995)
Inflation rate	8.2% (1996)
Unemployment	6.8% (1991)
Total external debt	US$21,420 million (1996)

Education

Enrolment (percentage of age group)	primary 91% (1995); secondary 39% (1995); tertiary 17.9% (1993)
Illiteracy rate	29.2%

TAIWAN

Area	13,800 sq. miles (35,742 sq. km)
Population	21,450,183 (1996)
Main languages	Mandarin Chinese, Taiwanese
Capital	Taipei (population 2,607,010, 1996)
Currency	New Taiwan dollar (NT$) of 100 cents
Exchange rate (at 29 May)	NT$ 55.4031
Public holidays	January 1, 3, 27–30; April 5, 6; May 30; July 1; October 5, 10; November 12
Usual business hours	Banking hours: Mon.–Fri. 9–15.30; Sat. 9–12
Electrical rating	110v AC, 60Hz

Government and diplomacy

Political system	Republic
Head of state	President Lee Teng-hui
Head of government	Vincent Siew
Representation in UK	50 Grosvenor Gardens, London, SW1W 0EB

Defence

Military expenditure	4.7% of GDP (1996)
Military personnel	402,650: Army 240,000, Navy 68,000, Air Force 68,000, Paramilitaries 26,650
Conscription duration	Two years

TAJIKISTAN

Area	55,251 sq. miles (143,100 sq. km)
Population	5,836,000 (1997)
Main languages	Tajik, Uzbek, Russian
Capital	Dushanbe (population 602,000, 1990)
Currency	Tajik rouble (TJR) of 100 tanga
Public holidays	January 1, 30; March 21 (2 days); September 9; November 6
Usual business hours	Mon.–Fri. 9–18
Electrical rating	220v AC, 50Hz (European plugs)

Demography

Life expectancy (years)	male 65.40; female 71.70
Population growth rate	1.9% (1995)
Population density	41 per sq. km (1995)
Urban population	29.1% (1993)

Government and diplomacy

Political system	Republic
Head of state and of government	President Imamali Rakhmonov
Honorary Consulate in UK	33 Ovington Square, London SW3 1LJ. Tel: 0171-584 5111
British Embassy	Tashkent, Uzbekistan
Trouble spots	Conflict between government and Islamic and democratic groups along Afghan border

Defence

Military expenditure	10.5% of GDP (1996)
Military personnel	8,200: Army 7,000, Paramilitaries 1,200
Conscription duration	Two years

Economy

GNP	US$1,976 million (1995)
	US$340 per capita (1995)
GDP	US$5,074 million (1994)
	US$131 per capita (1994)
Total external debt	US$707 million (1996)

Education

Enrolment (percentage of age group)	tertiary 20.3% (1994)
Illiteracy rate	0.3%

TANZANIA

Area	341,217 sq. miles (883,749 sq. km)
Population	30,337,000 (1994 UN estimate)
Main languages	Swahili, English
Capital	Dodoma (population 88,474, 1988)
Currency	Tanzanian shilling of 100 cents
Exchange rate (at 29 May)	Shillings 1056.86
Public holidays	January 1, 12, 30 (2 days); April 7, 10, 13, 26; May 1; July 6, 7; August 8; December 9, 25, 26
Usual business hours	Mon.–Fri. 8.30–16.30
Electrical rating	240v AC, 50Hz

Demography

Life expectancy (years)	male 47; female 50
Population growth rate	3.4% (1995)
Population density	34 per sq. km (1995)
Urban population	20.8% (1990)

Government and diplomacy

Political system	Republic
Head of state and of government	President Benjamin Mkapa
High Commission in UK	43 Hertford Street, London W1Y 8DB. Tel: 0171-499 8951/4
British High Commission in Dar es Salaam	Hifadhi House, Samora Avenue (PO Box 9200), Dar es Salaam. Tel: Dar es Salaam 117659/64

Defence

Military expenditure	1.8% of GDP (1996)
Military personnel	36,000: Army 30,000, Navy 1,000, Air Force 3,600, Paramilitaries 1,400
Conscription duration	Two years

Economy

GNP	US$5,174 million (1996)
	US$170 per capita (1996)
GDP	US$2,737 million (1994)
	US$119 per capita (1994)
Annual average growth of GDP	3% (1994)
Inflation rate	19.7% (1996)
Total external debt	US$7,412 million (1996)

Education

Enrolment (percentage of age group)	primary 48% (1995); tertiary 0.5% (1995)
Illiteracy rate	32.2%

THAILAND

Area	198,115 sq. miles (513,115 sq. km)
Population	60,206,000 (1997)
Main languages	Thai, Chinese, Khmer, Malay
Capital	Bangkok (population 5,876,000, 1993)
Currency	Baht of 100 satang
Exchange rate (at 29 May)	Baht 65.8640
Public holidays	January 1, 30; February 11; April 6, 13; May 1, 5, 11; July 1, 9; August 12; October 23; December 7, 10, 31
Usual business hours	Mon.–Fri. 8–17
Electrical rating	220v AC, 50Hz (US and European plugs)

Demography

Life expectancy (years)	male 63.82; female 68.85
Population growth rate	1.4% (1995)
Population density	117 per sq. km (1995)
Urban population	18.7% (1990)

Government and diplomacy

Political system	Constitutional monarchy
Head of state	King Bhumibol Adulyadej
Head of government	Chuan Leekpai
Embassy in UK	29–30 Queen's Gate, London SW7 5JB. Tel: 0171-589 0173
British Embassy in Bangkok	Thanon Witthayu, Bangkok 10330. Tel: Bangkok 2530 1919

Defence

Military expenditure	2.5% of GDP (1996)
Military personnel	266,000: Army 150,000, Navy 73,000, Air Force 43,000

Economy

GNP	US$177,476 million (1996)
	US$2,960 per capita (1996)
GDP	US$117,649 million (1994)
	US$2,454 per capita (1994)
Annual average growth of GDP	8.6% (1995)
Inflation rate	5.8% (1996)
Unemployment	1.5% (1993)
Total external debt	US$90,824 million (1996)

Education

Enrolment (percentage of age group)	tertiary 20.1% (1995)
Illiteracy rate	6.2%

TOGO

Area	21,925 sq. miles (56,785 sq. km)
Population	4,138,000 (1994 UN estimate)
Main languages	French, Ewe
Capital	Lomé (population 366,476, 1983)
Currency	Franc CFA of 100 centimes
Exchange rate (at 29 May)	Francs 975.610
Public holidays	January 1, 13, 30; April 7, 13, 27; May 1, 21; June 1, 21; August 15; November 1; December 25
Usual business hours	Mon.–Fri. 7–17.30
Electrical rating	220v AC, 50Hz, single phase

Demography

Life expectancy (years)	male 53.23; female 56.82
Population growth rate	3.2% (1995)
Population density	73 per sq. km (1995)

Government and diplomacy

Political system	Republic
Head of state and of government	President Gen. Gnassingbé Eyadéma
Embassy in UK	Closed 1991
British Consulate	BP 20050, Lomé
Trouble spots	Tension between government and pro-democracy groups following irregularities in presidential election in June 1998

Defence

Military expenditure	2.1% of GDP (1996)
Military personnel	7,700: Army 6,500, Navy 200, Air Force 250, Paramilitaries 750
Conscription duration	Two years

Economy

GNP	US$1,278 million (1996) US$300 per capita (1996)
GDP	US$2,023 million (1994) US$419 per capita (1994)
Annual average growth of GDP	0.1% (1990)
Inflation rate	15.7% (1995)
Total external debt	US$1,463 million (1996)

Education

Enrolment (percentage of age group)	primary 85% (1995); secondary 18% (1990); tertiary 3.2% (1994)
Illiteracy rate	48.3%

TONGA

Area	288 sq. miles (747 sq. km)
Population	98,000 (1994 UN estimate)
Main languages	Tongan, English
Capital	Nuku'alofa (population 29,018)
Currency	Pa'anga (T$) of 100 seniti
Exchange rate (at 29 May)	T$ 2.6035
Public holidays	January 1; April 10, 13, 25; May 4; June 4; July 4; November 4; December 4, 25, 26
Usual business hours	Mon.–Fri. 8.30–16.30
Electrical rating	240v AC, 50Hz

Demography

Population growth rate	0.3% (1995)
Population density	131 per sq. km (1995)
Urban population	30.7% (1986)

Government and diplomacy

Political system	Constitutional monarchy
Head of state	King Taufa'ahau Tupou IV
Head of government	Baron Vaea of Houma
High Commission in UK	36 Molyneux Street, London W1H 6AB. Tel: 0171-724 5828
British High Commission in Nuku'alofa	PO Box 56, Nuku'alofa. Tel: Nuku'alofa 21020

Economy

GNP	US$175 million (1996) US$1,790 per capita (1996)
GDP	US$134 million (1994) US$1,482 per capita (1994)
Annual average growth of GDP	4.8% (1994)
Inflation rate	3% (1996)
Total external debt	US$70 million (1996)

TRINIDAD AND TOBAGO

Area	1,981 sq. miles (5,130 sq. km)
Population	1,306,000 (1994 UN estimate)
Main language	English
Capital	Port of Spain (population 50,878, 1990)
Currency	Trinidad and Tobago dollar (TT$) of 100 cents
Exchange rate (at 29 May)	TT$ 10.1479
Public holidays	January 1; February 23 (2 days); March 30; April 10, 13; May 30; June 11, 19; August 1, 31; December 25, 26
Usual business hours	Mon.–Fri. 8–16
Electrical rating	110/220v AC, 60Hz (European plugs)

Demography
Life expectancy (years)	male 68.39; female 73.20
Population growth rate	1.4% (1995)
Population density	255 per sq. km (1995)

Government and diplomacy
Political system	Republic
Head of state	President Arthur Robinson
Head of government	Basdeo Panday
High Commission in UK	42 Belgrave Square, London SW1X 8NT. Tel: 0171-245 9351
British High Commission in Port of Spain	19 St Clair Avenue, St Clair, Port of Spain. Tel: Port of Spain 622 2748

Defence
Military expenditure	1% of GDP (1996)
Military personnel	6,900: Army 1,400, Coast Guard 700, Paramilitaries 4,800

Economy
GNP	US$5,017 million (1996) US$3,870 per capita (1996)
GDP	US$5,356 million (1994) US$3,709 per capita (1994)
Annual average growth of GDP	2.3% (1995)
Inflation rate	3.4% (1996)
Unemployment	17.2% (1995)
Total external debt	US$2,242 million (1996)

Education
Enrolment (percentage of age group)	primary 88% (1995); secondary 64% (1992); tertiary 7.7% (1995)
Illiteracy rate	2.1%

TRISTAN DA CUNHA, see ST HELENA

TUNISIA

Area	63,170 sq. miles (163,610 sq. km)
Population	8,896,000 (1994 UN estimate)
Main languages	Arabic, French, English
Capital	Tunis (population, 1,394,749, 1984)
Currency	Tunisian dinar of 1,000 millimes
Exchange rate (at 29 May)	Dinars 1.8787
Public holidays	January 1, 30; March 20, 21; April 7–9; May 1; July 6, 25; August 13; November 7
Usual business hours	Mon.–Fri. 8–12.30, 14.30–18
Electrical rating	220v AC, 50Hz

Demography

Life expectancy (years)	male 66.85; female 68.68
Population growth rate	1.9% (1995)
Population density	54 per sq. km (1995)
Urban population	58% (1990)

Government and diplomacy

Political system	Republic
Head of state and of government	President Zine el-Abidine
Embassy in UK	29 Prince's Gate, London SW7 1QG. Tel: 0171-584 8117
British Embassy in Tunis	5 Place de la Victoire, Tunis 1015 R.P. Tel: Tunis 134 1444

Defence

Military expenditure	2% of GDP (1996)
Military personnel	47,000: Army 27,000, Navy 4,500, Air Force 3,500, Paramilitaries 12,000
Conscription duration	12 months

Economy

GNP	US$17,581 million (1996) US$1,930 per capita (1996)
GDP	US$14,069 million (1994) US$1,541 per capita (1994)
Annual average growth of GDP	6.9% (1996)
Inflation rate	3.7% (1996)
Total external debt	US$9,887 million (1996)

Education

Enrolment (percentage of age group)	primary 97% (1995); secondary 23% (1980); tertiary 12.9% (1995)
Illiteracy rate	33.3%

TURKEY

Area	299,158 sq. miles (774,815 sq. km)
Population	61,644,000 (1994 UN estimate)
Main language	Turkish
Capital	Ankara (population 3,103,000, 1994)
Currency	Turkish lira (TL) of 100 kurus
Exchange rate (at 29 May)	TL 421242.5
Public holidays	January 1, 30 (3 days); April 7 (4 days), 23; May 19; August 30; October 29
Usual business hours	Mon.–Fri. 8.30–12, 13.30–17.30
Electrical rating	220v AC, 50Hz

Demography

Life expectancy (years)	male 63.26; female 66.01
Population growth rate	1.9% (1995)
Population density	80 per sq. km (1995)
Urban population	62.6% (1995)

Government and diplomacy

Political system	Republic
Head of state	President Süleyman Demirel
Head of government	Mesut Yilmaz
Embassy in UK	43 Belgrave Square, London SW1X 8PA. Tel: 0171-393 0202
British Embassy in Ankara	Sehit Ersan Caddesi 46/A, Cankaya, Ankara. Tel: Ankara 468 6230/42
Trouble spots	South-east under martial law because of Kurdish insurgency; government troops have attacked Kurdish bases in Syria and northern Iraq

Defence

Military expenditure	3.9% of GDP (1996)
Military personnel	821,200: Army 525,000, Navy 51,000, Air Force 63,000, Paramilitaries 182,200
Conscription duration	18 months

Economy

GNP	US$177,530 million (1996) US$2,830 per capita (1996)
GDP	US$163,441 million (1994) US$2,227 per capita (1994)
Annual average growth of GDP	-3% (1994)
Inflation rate	80.3% (1996)
Unemployment	6.6% (1995)
Total external debt	US$79,789 million (1996)

Education

Enrolment (percentage of age group)	primary 96% (1994); secondary 50% (1994); tertiary 18.2% (1994)
Illiteracy rate	17.7%

TURKMENISTAN

Area	188,456 sq. miles (488,100 sq. km)
Population	4,099,000 (1997 estimate)
Main languages	Turkmenian, Russian, Uzbek
Capital	Ashkhabad (population 407,000, 1990)
Currency	Manat
Public holidays	January 1, 12, 30; February 16; March 8, 21; April 7; May 9; October 18
Usual business hours	Mon.–Fri. 9–18
Electrical rating	220v AC, 50Hz (European plugs)

Demography

Life expectancy (years)	male 61.80; female 68.40
Population growth rate	2.2% (1995)
Population density	8 per sq. km (1995)
Urban population	45.2% (1989)

Government and diplomacy

Political system	Republic; *de facto* presidential autocracy
Head of state and of government	President Saparmurad Niyazov
Embassy in UK	2nd Floor South, St George's House, 14/17 Wells Street, London W1P 3FP. Tel: 0171-255 1071
British Embassy in Ashkhabad	3rd Floor, Office Building, Ak Altin Plaza Hotel, Ashkhabad

Defence

Military expenditure	2.8% of GDP (1996)
Military personnel	21,000: Army 18,000, Air Force 3,000
Conscription duration	Two years

Economy

GNP	US$4,319 million (1996) US$940 per capita (1996)
GDP	US$7,415 million (1994) US$2,023 per capita (1994)
Total external debt	US$825 million (1996)

Education

Enrolment (percentage of age group)	tertiary 21.8% (1990)
Illiteracy rate	0.3%

TURKS AND CAICOS ISLANDS

Area	166 sq. miles (430 sq. km)
Population	19,000 (1994 UN estimate)
Main language	English
Capital	Grand Turk (population 3,691, 1994)
Currency	US dollar (US$)
Exchange rate (at 29 May)	US$ 1.6307
Public holidays	January 1; March 10; April 10, 13; May 25; June 13, 14; August 1, 3; September 28; October 12, 24, 26; December 25, 26
Usual business hours	Mon.–Fri. 8–13, 14–16.30
Electrical rating	110v AC

Demography
Population growth rate	3.1% (1995)
Population density	33 per sq. km (1995)

Government
Political system	UK Overseas Territory
Governor	John P. Kelly

TUVALU

Area	10 sq. miles (26 sq. km)
Population	10,000 (1994 UN estimate)
Main languages	Tuvaluan, English
Capital	Funafuti (population 2,856)
Currency	Australian dollar ($A) of 100 cents is legal tender. In addition there are Tuvalu dollar and cent coins in circulation
Exchange rate (at 29 May)	$A 2.6035
Usual business hours	Mon.–Thurs. 7.30–16.15; Fri. 7.30–12.45
Electrical rating	Funafuti 240v AC, 60Hz

Demography
Population growth rate	2.1% (1995)
Population density	385 per sq. km (1995)

Government and diplomacy
Political system	Constitutional monarchy
Head of state	Queen Elizabeth II
Governor-General	Sir Tulaga Manuella
Head of government	Bikenibeu Paeniu
Honorary Consulate in UK	Tuvalu House, 230 Worple Road, London SW20 8RH. Tel: 0181-879 0985
British High Commission	Suva, Fiji

Economy

GDP   US$7 million (1994)
                                   US$924 per capita (1994)

UGANDA

Area	93,065 sq. miles (241,038 sq. km)
Population	21,297,000 (1994 UN estimate)
Main languages	English, Swahili
Capital	Kampala (population 750,000, 1990)
Currency	Uganda shilling of 100 cents
Exchange rate (at 29 May)	Shillings 1989.45
Public holidays	January 1, 26, 30 (2 days); March 8; April 7, 10, 13; May 1; June 3, 9; October 9; December 25, 26
Usual business hours	Mon.–Fri. 8–12.45, 14–17
Electrical rating	240v AC, 50Hz

Demography

Life expectancy (years)	male 43.57; female 46.19
Population growth rate	3.4% (1995)
Population density	88 per sq. km (1995)
Urban population	11.3% (1991)

Government and diplomacy

Political system	Republic; non-party political system
Head of state and of government	President Yoweri Museveni
High Commission in UK	Uganda House, 58–59 Trafalgar Square, London WC2N 5DX. Tel: 0171-839 5783
British High Commission in Kampala	10–12 Parliament Avenue, PO Box 7070, Kampala. Tel: Kampala 257054/9

Defence

Military expenditure	2.1% of GDP (1996)
Military personnel	50,600: Ugandan People's Defence Force 50,000, Paramilitaries 600

Economy

GNP	US$5,826 million (1996)
	US$300 per capita (1996)
GDP	US$4,930 million (1994)
	US$255 per capita (1994)
Annual average growth of GDP	10% (1995)
Inflation rate	7.2% (1996)
Total external debt	US$3,674 million (1996)

Education

Enrolment (percentage of age group)	tertiary 1.5% (1994)
Illiteracy rate	38.2%

UKRAINE

Area	233,090 sq. miles (603,700 sq. km)
Population	51,639,000 (1996 estimate)
Main languages	Ukrainian, Russian
Capital	Kiev (population 2,646,100, 1992)
Currency	Hryvna of 100 kopiykas
Exchange rate (at 29 May)	Hryvnas 3.3568
Public holidays	January 1, 7; March 9; April 19, 20; May 1–3, 9, 11; June 1, 8, 29; August 24; November 9 (2 days)
Usual business hours	Mon.–Fri. 9–18
Electrical rating	220v AC, 50Hz

Demography

Life expectancy (years)	male 63.50; female 73.70
Population growth rate	–0.1% (1995)
Population density	86 per sq. km (1995)
Urban population	67.9% (1993)

Government and diplomacy

Political system	Republic
Head of state	President Leonid Kuchma
Head of government	Valery Pustovoytenko
Embassy in UK	78 Kensington Park Road, London W11 2PL. Tel: 0171-727 6312
British Embassy in Kiev	252025 Kiev Desyatinna 9. Tel: Kiev 462 0011

Defence

Military expenditure	3% of GDP (1996)
Military personnel	337,900: Army 161,500, Navy 16,000, Air Force 124,400, Paramilitaries 36,000
Conscription duration	18 months to two years

Economy

GNP	US$60,904 million (1996)
	US$1,200 per capita (1996)
GDP	US$131,195 million (1994)
	US$339 per capita (1994)
Inflation rate	80.3% (1996)
Total external debt	US$9,335 million (1996)

Education

Enrolment (percentage of age group)	tertiary 40.6% (1993)
Illiteracy rate	1.2%

UNITED ARAB EMIRATES

Area	32,278 sq. miles (83,600 sq. km)
Population	2,314,000 (1995)
Main languages	English, Arabic
Capital	Abu Dhabi (population 450,000)
Currency	UAE dirham of 100 fils
Exchange rate (at 29 May)	Dirham 5.9897
Public holidays	January 1, 30 (3 days); April 7 (3 days), 16, 28; July 6; August 6; November 17; December 2, 3
Usual business hours	Sat.–Wed. 8–13, 16–19; Thurs. 8–12
Electrical rating	220/240v AC, 50Hz

Demography

Life expectancy (years)	male 72.95; female 75.27
Population growth rate	6.5% (1995)
Population density	28 per sq. km (1995)

Government and diplomacy

Political system	Federation of seven absolute monarchies
Head of state	President Sheikh Zayed bin Sultan al-Nahyan
Head of government	Sheikh Maktoun bin Rashid al-Maktoum
Embassy in UK	30 Princes Gate, London SW7 1PT. Tel: 0171-581 1281
British Embassies in UAE	PO Box 248, Abu Dhabi. Tel: Abu Dhabi 326600; PO Box 65, Dubai. Tel: Dubai 521070

Defence

Military expenditure	4.8% of GDP (1996)
Military personnel	64,500: Army 59,000, Navy 1,500, Air Force 4,000

Economy

GNP	US$42,806 million (1995) US$17,400 per capita (1995)
GDP	US$34,461 million (1994) US$20,654 per capita (1994)
Annual average growth of GDP	2.7% (1992)

Education

Enrolment (percentage of age group)	primary 83% (1994); secondary 71% (1994); tertiary 8.8% (1993)
Illiteracy rate	20.8%

UNITED KINGDOM

Area	94,248 sq. miles (244,101 sq. km)
Population	58,258,000 (1994 UN estimate)
Main languages	English
Capital	London (population 6,962,319, 1992)
Currency	Pound sterling (£) of 100 pence
Public holidays	January 1; April 10, 13; May 4, 25; August 31; December 25, 26, 28; also January 2 in Scotland and March 17, July 12 in Northern Ireland
Usual business hours	Mon.–Fri. 9–17 or 9.30–17.30
Electrical rating	240v AC, 50Hz

Demography

Life expectancy (years)	male 74.17; female 79.44
Population growth rate	0.2% (1995)
Population density	239 per sq. km (1995)

Government

Political system	Constitutional monarchy
Head of state	Queen Elizabeth II
Head of government	Anthony Blair
Trouble spots	Inter-communal violence by Irish nationalists and Ulster loyalists in Northern Ireland, and occasional nationalist bombings in Britain since 1969; peace accord 1998

Defence

Military expenditure	2.9% of GDP (1996)
Military personnel	215,700: Strategic Forces 1,900, Army 112,200, Navy 44,900, Air Force 56,700

Economy

GNP	US$1,152,136 million (1996) US$19,600 per capita (1996)
GDP	US$1,007,945 million (1994) US$17,471 per capita (1994)
Annual average growth of GDP	2.1% (1996)
Inflation rate	2.4% (1996)
Unemployment	5.9% (1997)

Education

Enrolment (percentage of age group)	primary 100% (1994); secondary 92% (1994); tertiary 48.3% (1994)

UK OVERSEAS TERRITORIES, see under individual entries

UNITED STATES OF AMERICA

Area	3,615,276 sq. miles (9,363,520 sq. km)
Population	263,034,000 (1996 estimate)
Main languages	English, Spanish
Capital	Washington DC (population 7,051,495, 1992)
Currency	US dollar (US$) of 100 cents
Exchange rate (at 29 May)	US$ 1.6307
Public holidays	January 1, 19; February 16; May 25; July 4; September 7; October 12; November 11, 26; December 25
Usual business hours	Mon.–Fri. 9–17.30
Electrical rating	110/120v AC, 60Hz

Demography

Life expectancy (years)	male 72.20; female 78.80
Population growth rate	1% (1995)
Population density	28 per sq. km (1995)
Urban population	75.2% (1990)

Government and diplomacy

Political system	Republic; federal state
Head of state and of government	President William Clinton
Embassy in UK	24 Grosvenor Square, London W1A 1AE. Tel: 0171-499 9000
British Embassy in Washington DC	3100 Massachusetts Avenue NW, Washington DC 20008. Tel: Washington DC 462 1340

Defence

Military expenditure	3.5% of GDP (1996)
Military personnel	1,447,600: Army 495,000, Navy 395,500, Marine Corps 174,900, Air Force 382,200

Economy

GNP	US$7,433,517 million (1996) US$28,020 per capita (1996)
GDP	US$6,027,216 million (1994) US$25,514 per capita (1994)
Annual average growth of GDP	2.4% (1996)
Inflation rate	2.9% (1996)
Unemployment	5.6% (1995)

Education

Enrolment (percentage of age group)	primary 96% (1993); secondary 89% (1993); tertiary 81.1% (1994)

TERRITORIES

AMERICAN SAMOA

Area	77 sq. miles (199 sq. km)
Population	56,000 (1996 estimate)
Main language	English
Capital	Pago Pago (population 3,519, 1992)
Currency	Currency is that of USA
Usual business hours	Banking hours: Mon.–Fri. 9–15
Electrical rating	110v AC, 60Hz (US plugs)

Demography

Population growth rate	3.5% (1995)
Population density	283 per sq. km (1995)
Urban population	33.4% (1990)

Government

Political system	Self-government
Governor	Tauese Sunia

GUAM

Area	212 sq. miles (549 sq. km)
Population	149,000 (1996 estimate)
Main languages	Chamorro, English
Capital	Agaña (population 1,139, 1992)
Currency	Currency is that of USA
Public holidays	January 1, 19; February 16; March 4; April 10; May 25; July 4, 21; September 7; October 12; November 2, 11, 26; December 8, 25
Usual business hours	Banking hours: Mon.–Thurs. 9–15; Fri. 9–18
Electrical rating	120v AC, 60Hz

Demography

Life expectancy (years)	male 69.53; female 75.59
Population growth rate	2.3% (1995)
Population density	272 per sq. km (1995)
Urban population	38.2% (1995)

Government

Political system	Self-government
Governor	Carl Gutierrez

NORTHERN MARIANA ISLANDS

Area	179 sq. miles (464 sq. km)
Population	47,000 (1996 estimate)
Population density	101 per sq. km (1995)
Main languages	English, Spanish
Capital	Saipan (population 52,706, 1992)
Currency	Currency is that of USA

Usual business hours	Mon.–Fri. 8–17
Electrical rating	110/120v AC, 60Hz (US plugs)

Government

Political system	Self-government
Governor	Froilan Tenorio

PUERTO RICO

Area	3,427 sq. miles (8,875 sq. km)
Population	3,674,000 (1996 estimate)
Main languages	Spanish, English
Capital	San Juan (population 1,222,316, 1992)
Currency	Currency is that of USA
Public holidays	January 1, 6, 13, 19; February 16; March 22; April 10, 21; May 25; July 4, 21, 25, 28; September 7; October 12; November 11, 19, 26; December 25
Usual business hours	Mon.–Fri. 9–18
Electrical rating	120v AC, 60Hz

Demography

Life expectancy (years)	male 69.60; female 78.50
Population growth rate	0.8% (1995)
Population density	414 per sq. km (1995)
Urban population	71.2% (1990)

Government

Political system	Self-government
Governor	Dr Pedro Rossello

Economy

GDP	US$37,271 million (1994) US$11,469 per capita (1994)

US VIRGIN ISLANDS

Area	134 sq. miles (347 sq. km)
Population	105,000 (1996 estimate)
Main language	English
Capital	Charlotte Amalie (population 11,842, 1992)
Currency	Currency is that of USA
Public holidays	January 1, 6, 19; February 16; March 31; April 9, 10, 13, 24 (2 days); May 25; June 15; July 3, 4, 27; September 7; October 12, 19; November 1–3, 11, 26; December 25, 26
Usual business hours	Banking hours: Mon.–Thurs. 9–14.30; Fri. 9–14, 15.30–17
Electrical rating	120v AC, 60Hz

Demography

Population growth rate	0.6% (1995)
Population density	303 per sq. km (1995)
Urban population	38.5% (1985)

Government

Political system	Self-government
Governor	Roy Schneider

URUGUAY

Area	68,500 sq. miles (177,414 sq. km)
Population	3,186,000 (1994 UN estimate)
Main language	Spanish
Capital	Montevideo (population 1,383,660, 1992)
Currency	New Uruguayan peso of 100 centésimos
Exchange rate (at 29 May)	Pesos 16.9022
Public holidays	January 1, 6; February 24, 25; April 9, 10, 19; May 1, 18; June 19; July 18; August 25; October 12; November 2; December 25
Usual business hours	Mon.–Fri. 8.30–12, 14.30–18.30
Electrical rating	220v AC, 50Hz

Demography

Life expectancy (years)	male 68.43; female 74.88
Population growth rate	0.6% (1995)
Population density	18 per sq. km (1995)
Urban population	90.1% (1995)

Government and diplomacy

Political system	Republic
Head of state and of government	President Julio Maria Sanguinetti
Embassy in UK	2nd Floor, 140 Brompton Road, London SW3 1HY. Tel: 0171-584 8192
British Embassy in Montevideo	Calle Marco Bruto 1073, Montevideo 11300 (PO Box 16024). Tel: Montevideo 623650

Defence

Military expenditure	1.5% of GDP (1996)
Military personnel	26,520: Army 17,600, Navy 5,000, Air Force 3,000, Paramilitaries 920

Economy

GNP	US$18,464 million (1996) US$5,760 per capita (1996)
GDP	US$8,496 million (1994) US$4,199 per capita (1994)

Annual average growth of GDP	4.9% (1996)
Inflation rate	28.3% (1996)
Unemployment	10.2% (1995)
Total external debt	US$5,899 million (1996)

Education

Enrolment (percentage of age group)	primary 95% (1995); tertiary 27.3% (1993)
Illiteracy rate	2.7%

UZBEKISTAN

Area	172,742 sq. miles (447,400 sq. km)
Population	22,843,000 (1995 estimate)
Main languages	Uzbek, Russian
Capital	Tashkent (population 2,094,000, 1990)
Currency	Sum (Som) of 100 tiyin
Usual business hours	Mon.–Fri. 9–18
Electrical rating	220v AC, 50Hz

Demography

Life expectancy (years)	male 66; female 72.10
Population growth rate	2.1% (1995)
Population density	51 per sq. km (1995)
Urban population	40.6% (1989)

Government and diplomacy

Political system	Republic; little political opposition tolerated
Head of state	President Islam Karimov
Head of government	Utkur Sultanov
Embassy in UK	41 Holland Park, London W11 2RP. Tel: 0171-229 7679
British Embassy in Tashkent	Ul. Gogolya 67, Tashkent 700000. Tel: Tashkent 406288

Defence

Military expenditure	3.8% of GDP (1996)
Military personnel	65,000: Army 45,000, Air Force 4,000, Paramilitaries 16,000
Conscription duration	18 months

Economy

GNP	US$23,490 million (1996) US$1,010 per capita (1996)
GDP	US$38,532 million (1994) US$187 per capita (1994)
Unemployment	0.4% (1995)
Total external debt	US$2,319 million (1996)

Education

Enrolment (percentage of age group)	tertiary 31.7% (1992)
Illiteracy rate	0.3%

VANUATU

Area	4,706 sq. miles (12,189 sq. km)
Population	165,000 (1994 UN estimate)
Main languages	Bislama, English, French
Capital	Port Vila (population 26,100, 1993)
Currency	Vatu of 100 centimes
Exchange rate (at 29 May)	Vatu 207.507
Public holidays	January 1; March 5; April 10, 13; May 1; July 24, 30; August 15; October 5; November 29; December 25, 26
Usual business hours	Mon.–Fri. 7.30–11.30, 13.30–16.30
Electrical rating	220/280v AC (Australian plugs)

Demography

Life expectancy (years)	male 63.48; female 67.34
Population growth rate	2.7% (1995)
Population density	14 per sq. km (1995)
Urban population	18.4% (1989)

Government and diplomacy

Political system	Republic
Head of state	President Jean-Marie Leye
Head of government	Donald Kalpokas
High Commission	Department for Foreign Affairs, Port Vila, Vanuatu
British High Commission in Port Vila	PO Box 567, Port Vila. Tel: Vila 23100

Economy

GNP	US$224 million (1996) US$1,290 per capita (1996)
GDP	US$159 million (1994) US$1,117 per capita (1994)
Annual average growth of GDP	3.2% (1995)
Inflation rate	0.9% (1996)
Total external debt	US$47 million (1996)

Education

Enrolment (percentage of age group)	primary 74% (1989); secondary 17% (1991)

VATICAN CITY STATE

Area	0.2 sq. miles (0.44 sq. km)
Population	1,000 (1994 UN estimate)
Main language	Italian
Capital	Vatican City (population 766, 1988)
Currency	Italian currency is legal tender
Exchange rate (at 29 May)	Lire 2864.81
Public holidays	January 1, 6, 31; February 11; March 19; April 9–11, 13, 14; May 1, 21; June 11, 29; August 14; October 16; November 1, 2, 4; December 8, 24, 25, 27
Electrical rating	220v AC, 50Hz

Demography

Population growth rate	0% (1995)
Population density	2,273 per sq. km (1995)

Government and diplomacy

Political system	Sovereign state of the Holy See in the city of the Vatican; absolute rule
Sovereign pontiff	Pope John Paul II
Secretary of state	Cardinal Angelo Sodano
Apostolic Nunciature in UK	54 Parkside, London SW19 5NE. Tel: 0181-946 1410
British Embassy to the Holy See	91 Via Condotti, I–00187 Rome. Tel: Rome 6992 3561

Economy

GDP	US$20 million (1994) US$17,930 per capita (1994)

VENEZUELA

Area	352,145 sq. miles (912,050 sq. km)
Population	21,644,000 (1994 UN estimate)
Main language	Spanish
Capital	Caracas (population 2,784,042, 1990)
Currency	Bolívar (Bs) of 100 céntimos
Exchange rate (at 29 May)	Bs 878.132
Public holidays	January 1; February 24, 25; March 19; April 9, 10, 19; May 1; June 24; July 5, 24; October 12; November 1; December 8, 25
Usual business hours	Mon.–Fri. 8–18
Electrical rating	110v AC, 60Hz (US plugs)

Demography

Life expectancy (years)	male 66.68; female 72.80
Population growth rate	2.3% (1995)
Population density	24 per sq. km (1995)
Urban population	84.1% (1990)

Government and diplomacy

Political system	Republic; federal state
Head of state and of government	President Rafael Caldera Rodríguez
Embassy in UK	1 Cromwell Road, London SW7 2HW. Tel: 0171-584 4206/7
British Embassy in Caracas	Apartado 1246, Caracas 1010–A. Tel: Caracas 993 4111

Defence

Military expenditure	1.2% of GDP (1996)
Military personnel	79,000: Army 34,000, Navy 15,000, Air Force 7,000, National Guard 23,000
Conscription duration	30 months

Economy

GNP	US$67,333 million (1996)
	US$3,020 per capita (1996)
GDP	US$54,488 million (1994)
	US$2,618 per capita (1994)
Annual average growth of GDP	-1.6% (1996)
Inflation rate	99.9% (1996)
Unemployment	10.3% (1995)
Total external debt	US$35,344 million (1996)

Education

Enrolment (percentage of age group)	primary 88% (1992); secondary 20% (1992); tertiary 28.5% (1991)
Illiteracy rate	8.9%

VIETNAM

Area	128,066 sq. miles (331,689 sq. km)
Population	74,545,000 (1994 UN estimate)
Main languages	Vietnamese, French, English
Capital	Hanoi (population 3,056,146, 1989)
Currency	Dông of 10 hào or 100 xu
Exchange rate (at 29 May)	Dông 21171.4
Public holidays	January 1, 27 (4 days); April 30; May 1; September 2
Usual business hours	Mon.–Sat. 7.30–12, 13–16.30
Electrical rating	220v AC, 50Hz

Demography

Life expectancy (years)	male 63.66; female 67.89
Population growth rate	2.4% (1995)
Population density	225 per sq. km (1995)
Urban population	19.5% (1994)

Government and diplomacy

Political system	Republic; one-party (Communist) military regime
Head of state	President Tran Duc Luong
Head of government	Phan Van Khai
Embassy in UK	12–14 Victoria Road, London W8 5RD. Tel: 0171-937 1912/8564
British Embassy in Hanoi	Central Building, 31 Hai Ba Trung, Hanoi. Tel: Hanoi 825 2510

Defence

Military expenditure	9.2% of GDP (1996)
Military personnel	557,000: Army 420,000, Navy 42,000, Air Force 15,000, Air Defence Force 15,000, Paramilitaries 65,000
Conscription duration	Two to three years

Economy

GNP	US$21,915 million (1996) US$290 per capita (1996)
GDP	US$8,764 million (1994) US$213 per capita (1994)
Total external debt	US$26,764 million (1996)

Education

Enrolment (percentage of age group)	primary 95% (1980); tertiary 4.1% (1995)
Illiteracy rate	6.3%

VIRGIN ISLANDS, see BRITISH VIRGIN ISLANDS or USA

WALLIS AND FORTUNA ISLANDS, see FRANCE

YEMEN

Area	203,850 sq. miles (527,968 sq. km)
Population	14,501,000 (1995)
Main language	Arabic
Capital	Sana'a (population 926,595, 1995)
Currency	Riyal of 100 fils
Exchange rate (at 29 May)	Riyals 213.605
Public holidays	January 30 (4 days); April 7 (5 days), 28; May 1, 22; July 6, 7; November 17
Usual business hours	Mon.–Wed. 8–12.30, 16–19; Thurs. 8–11
Electrical rating	220/230v AC, 50Hz

Demography

Life expectancy (years)	male 49.90; female 50.40
Population growth rate	2.9% (1994)
Population density	27 per sq. km (1995)
Urban population	26.4% (1994)

Government and diplomacy

Political system	Republic
Head of state	President Gen. Ali Abdullah Saleh
Head of government	Abdulkarim Al-Eryani
Embassy in UK	57 Cromwell Road, London SW7 2ED. Tel: 0171-584 6607
British Embassy in Sana'a	PO Box 1287, Sana'a. Tel: Sana'a 264081
Trouble spots	Territorial dispute with Eritrea over Hanish Islands can flare up unpredictably Some northern and eastern areas volatile Random kidnappings occur

Defence

Military expenditure	3.7% of GDP (1996)
Military personnel	146,300: Army 61,000, Navy 1,800, Air Force 3,500, Paramilitaries 80,000
Conscription duration	Three years

Economy

GNP	US$6,016 million (1996) US$380 per capita (1996)
GDP	US$9,183 million (1994) US$1,049 per capita (1994)
Total external debt	US$6,356 million (1996)

Education

Enrolment (percentage of age group)	tertiary 4.3% (1991)

FEDERAL REPUBLIC OF YUGOSLAVIA

Area	39,449 sq. miles (102,173 sq. km)
Population	10,544,000 (1994 UN estimate)
Main languages	Serbo-Croat, Albanian, Hungarian
Capital	Belgrade (population 1,136,786, 1991)
Currency	New dinar of 100 paras
Exchange rate (at 29 May)	New dinars 17.2888
Public holidays	January 1, 2, 7; April 20, 27; May 1; November 30; December 1
Usual business hours	Mon.–Fri. 7–15 or 8–16
Electrical rating	220v AC, 50Hz

Demography

Life expectancy (years)	male 69.50; female 74.49
Population growth rate	0% (1995)
Population density	103 per sq. km (1995)

Government and diplomacy

Political system	Republic; federal state
Head of state	President Slobodan Milosevic
Head of government	Radoje Kontic
Embassy in UK	5 Lexham Gardens, London W8 5JJ. Tel: 0171-370 6105
British Embassy in Belgrade	Generala Ždanova 46, 11000 Belgrade. Tel: Belgrade 645055
Trouble spots	Civilians in predominantly Albanian province of Kosovo under frequent attack by Serbian troops claiming to be eliminating support for the Kosovo Liberation Army, which fights for independence for Kosovo

Defence

Military expenditure	12.9% of GDP (1996)
Military personnel	114,200: Army 90,000, Navy 7,500, Air Force 16,700
Conscription duration	12–15 months

Economy

GDP	US$16,654 million (1994) US$1,171 per capita (1994)
Annual average growth of GDP	-2% (1988)
Inflation rate	117.4% (1991)
Total external debt	US$13,439 million (1996)

Education

Enrolment (percentage of age group)	primary 69% (1990); secondary 62% (1990); tertiary 21.1% (1995)
Illiteracy rate	2.1%

ZAMBIA

Area	290,587 sq. miles (752,618 sq. km)
Population	9,373,000
Main languages	English, Nyanja, Tonga, Beruba, tribal dialects
Capital	Lusaka (population 982,362)
Currency	Kwacha (K) of 100 ngwee
Exchange rate (at 29 May)	K 3118.73
Public holidays	January 1; March 12; April 10, 11, 13; May 1, 25; July 6, 7; August 3; October 24; December 25
Usual business hours	Mon.–Fri. 8–13, 14–17
Electrical rating	220/240v AC, 50Hz

Demography

Life expectancy (years)	male 50.70; female 53
Population growth rate	3% (1995)
Population density	12 per sq. km (1995)
Urban population	39.4% (1990)

Government and diplomacy

Political system	Republic
Head of state and of government	President Frederick J. Chiluba
High Commission in UK	2 Palace Gate, London W8 5NG. Tel: 0171-589 6655
British High Commission in Lusaka	Independence Avenue (PO Box 50050), 15 101 Ridgeway, Lusaka. Tel: Lusaka 251133

Defence

Military expenditure	1.1% of GDP (1996)
Military personnel	23,000: Army 20,000, Air Force 1,600, Paramilitaries 1,400

Economy

GNP	US$3,363 million (1996)
	US$360 per capita (1996)
GDP	US$4,114 million (1994)
	US$367 per capita (1994)
Annual average growth of GDP	6.4% (1996)
Inflation rate	43.9% (1996)
Total external debt	US$7,113 million (1996)

Education

Enrolment (percentage of age group)	primary 75% (1995); secondary 16% (1994); tertiary 2.5% (1994)
Illiteracy rate	21.8%

ZIMBABWE

Area	150,872 sq. miles (390,757 sq. km)
Population	11,526,000 (1994 UN estimate)
Main languages	English, Shona, Ndebele
Capital	Harare (population 1,189,103, 1992)
Currency	Zimbabwe dollar (Z$) of 100 cents
Exchange rate (at 29 May)	Z$ 29.2712
Public holidays	January 1; April 10, 11, 13, 18; May 1, 25; August 11, 12; December 22, 25, 26
Usual business hours	Mon.–Fri. 8–16.30
Electrical rating	220/240v AC, 50Hz

Demography

Life expectancy (years)	male 58; female 62
Population growth rate	4.1% (1995)
Population density	29 per sq. km (1995)

Government and diplomacy

Political system	Republic
Head of state and of government	President Robert Mugabe
High Commission in UK	Zimbabwe House, 429 Strand, London WC2R 0SA. Tel: 0171-836 7755
British High Commission in Harare	Corner House, Samora Machel Avenue (PO Box 4490), Harare. Tel: Harare 772990

Defence

Military expenditure	3.8% of GDP (1996)
Military personnel	60,800: Army 35,000, Air Force 4,000, Paramilitaries 21,800

Economy

GNP	US$6,815 million (1996) US$610 per capita (1996)
GDP	US$7,033 million (1994) US$568 per capita (1994)
Annual average growth of GDP	-2.8% (1991)
Inflation rate	21.4% (1996)
Total external debt	US$5,005 million (1996)

Education

Enrolment (percentage of age group)	tertiary 6.9% (1995)
Illiteracy rate	14.9%

WORLD RANKING TABLES

LIFE EXPECTANCY

MEN

HIGHEST

		Years
1	Iraq	77.43
2	Iceland	76.85
3	Japan	76.57
4	Sweden	76.08
5	Hong Kong	75.84
6	Israel	75.33
7	Switzerland	75.10
8	Australia	75.04
9	Macao	75.01
10	Malta	74.86
11	Cyprus	74.64
12	Greece	74.61
13	Norway	74.24
14	The Netherlands	74.21
15	Singapore	74.20
16	UK	74.17
17	Italy	73.79
18	Spain	73.40
19	Austria	73.34
20	Faröe Islands	73.30

LOWEST

1	Sierra Leone	37.47
2	Guinea-Bissau	41.92
3	Swaziland	42.90
4	Afghanistan	43.00
5	The Gambia	43.41
6	Malawi	43.51
7	Uganda	43.57
8	Guinea	44.00
9	Equatorial Guinea	44.86
10	Mozambique	44.88
11	Angola	44.90
	Niger	44.90
13	Rwanda	45.10
14	Somalia	45.41
15	Liberia	45.80
16	Burkina Faso	45.84
17	Benin	45.92
18	Chad	45.93
	Ethiopia	45.93
20	Djibouti	46.72

WOMEN

HIGHEST

		Years
1	Japan	82.98
2	Switzerland	81.60
3	Sweden	81.38
4	Hong Kong	81.16
5	France	81.15
6	Australia	80.94
7	Iceland	80.75
8	Spain	80.49
9	Italy	80.36
10	Macao	80.26
11	Norway	80.25
12	The Netherlands	80.20
13	Finland	80.15
14	Greece	79.96
15	Canada	79.79
16	Austria	79.73
17	Faröe Islands	79.60
18	UK	79.44
19	Germany	79.30
20	Belgium	79.13

LOWEST

1	Sierra Leone	40.58
2	Afghanistan	44.00
	Liberia	44.00
4	Guinea	45.00
5	Guinea-Bissau	45.12
6	Uganda	46.19
7	The Gambia	46.63
8	Malawi	46.75
9	Rwanda	47.70
10	Equatorial Guinea	47.78
11	Mozambique	48.01
12	Angola	48.10
	Nepal	48.10
14	Niger	48.14
15	Somalia	48.60
16	Burkina Faso	49.01
17	Ethiopia	49.06
18	Chad	49.12
19	Benin	49.29
20	Swaziland	49.50

POPULATION GROWTH RATE 1995

HIGHEST ANNUAL PERCENTAGE CHANGE

		%
1	United Arab Emirates	6.5
2	Andorra	5.1
3	Jordan	4.9
4	French Guiana	4.6
5	Macao	4.4
6	Democratic Republic of Congo	4.2
	Iran	4.2
	Mozambique	4.2
9	Western Sahara	4.1
	Zimbabwe	4.1
11	Côte d'Ivoire	3.9
12	The Gambia	3.8
	Nepal	3.8
14	The Comoros	3.7
	Marshall Islands	3.7
	Saudi Arabia	3.7
17	American Samoa	3.5
	Costa Rica	3.5
	Israel	3.5
20	British Virgin Islands	3.4
	Niger	3.4
	Tanzania	3.4
	Uganda	3.4

LOWEST ANNUAL PERCENTAGE CHANGE

1	Kuwait	-4.7
2	Gibraltar	-1.9
3	Bulgaria	-1.4
4	Croatia	-1.2
	Latvia	-1.2
6	Estonia	-0.5
	Romania	-0.5
	St Christopher and Nevis	-0.5
9	Hungary	-0.3
10	Belarus	-0.2
	Faröe Islands	-0.2
	Italy	-0.2
13	Czech Republic	-0.1
	Dominica	-0.1
	Kazakhstan	-0.1
	Slovenia	-0.1
	Ukraine	-0.1
18	Georgia	0
19	Lithuania	0

		%
20	Russia	0
	St Pierre and Miquelon	0
	Vatican City State	0
	Wallis and Futuna Islands	0
	Federal Republic of Yugoslavia	0

POPULATION DENSITY 1995

HIGHEST

		Per sq. km
1	Macao	23,194
2	Monaco	21,477
3	Hong Kong	5,758
4	Singapore	4,833
5	Gibraltar	4,667
6	Vatican City State	2,273
7	Bermuda	1,189
8	Malta	1,173
9	Maldives	852
10	Bahrain	844
11	Bangladesh	836
12	Barbados	614
13	Mauritius	550
14	Nauru	514
15	South Korea	452
16	Puerto Rico	414
17	San Marino	410
18	Tuvalu	385
19	The Netherlands	378
20	Aruba	363

LOWEST

1	Australia	2
	French Guiana	2
	Mauritania	2
	Mongolia	2
	Namibia	2
6	Botswana	3
	Canada	3
	Iceland	3
	Libya	3
	Suriname	3
11	Guyana	4
12	Central African Republic	5
	Chad	5
	Gabon	5
15	Kazakhstan	6
16	Bolivia	7
	Niger	7

		Per sq. km
18	Republic of Congo	8
	Niue	8
	Saudi Arabia	8
	Turkemenistan	8

URBAN POPULATION
AS A PERCENTAGE OF THE TOTAL POPULATION

HIGHEST

		%
1	Italy	96.6
2	Andorra	95.6
3	Hong Kong	93.1
4	Iceland	91.3
5	San Marino	90.4
6	Uruguay	90.1
7	Israel	89.7
8	Bahrain	88.4
9	Australia	85.4
10	New Zealand	84.9
11	Chile	84.5
12	Venezuela	84.1
13	The Bahamas	83.5
14	Sweden	83.4
15	Greenland	80.6
16	Japan	77.4
17	Canada	76.6
18	Germany	76.3
19	Falkland Islands	76.0
20	Brazil	75.6

LOWEST

1	Burundi	5.0
2	Rwanda	5.4
3	Uganda	11.3
4	Cambodia	12.6
5	Bangladesh	13.8
6	Burkina Faso	15.0
7	Ethiopia	15.3
	Niger	15.3
9	Nigeria	16.1
10	Vanuatu	18.4
11	Thailand	18.7
12	Malawi	18.9
13	Vietnam	19.5
14	Tanzania	20.8
15	Chad	21.7
16	Mali	22.0
17	Somalia	23.5
18	Swaziland	24.8
19	Maldives	25.9
20	China	26.2

MILITARY EXPENDITURE
AS A PERCENTAGE OF GDP 1996

HIGHEST

		%
1	North Korea	27.0
2	Oman	15.7
3	Afghanistan	15.4
4	Kuwait	14.5
5	Yugoslavia	12.9
6	Saudi Arabia	12.7
7	Tajikistan	10.5
8	Qatar	10.4
9	Israel	10.2
10	Vietnam	9.2
11	Iraq	8.7
12	Eritrea	8.4
13	Former Yugoslav Republic of Macedonia	7.5
14	Croatia	6.9
15	Brunei	6.5
	Russia	6.5
	Sri Lanka	6.5
18	Angola	6.4
19	Rwanda	6.3
20	Bosnia-Hercegovina	6.2

LOWEST

1	Iceland	0.1
2	The Bahamas	0.5
	Costa Rica	0.5
	Jamaica	0.5
5	Barbados	0.7
	Luxembourg	0.7
7	Antigua and Barbuda	0.8
	Madagascar	0.8
	Mexico	0.8
10	Austria	0.9
	Côte d'Ivoire	0.9
	Nepal	0.9
13	Guyana	1.0
	Japan	1.0
	Trinidad and Tobago	1.0
16	Dominican Republic	1.1
	Equatorial Guinea	1.1
	Honduras	1.1
	Republic of Ireland	1.1
	Malta	1.1
	Niger	1.1
	Zambia	1.1

GROSS DOMESTIC PRODUCT 1994

HIGHEST

		US$ million
1	USA	6,027,216
2	Japan	3,152,205
3	Germany	1,767,217
4	France	1,241,147
5	Italy	1,134,661
6	UK	1,007,945
7	Iran	656,589
8	Russia	626,929
9	China	613,617
10	Canada	599,578
11	Brazil	523,392
12	Spain	510,763
13	India	349,071
14	Australia	335,527
15	South Korea	317,891
16	The Netherlands	302,313
17	Mexico	270,699
18	Switzerland	226,007
19	Sweden	222,951
20	Belgium	201,125

LOWEST

1	Tuvalu	7
2	Vatican City State	20
3	Kiribati	41
4	Cook Islands	58
5	São Tomé and Princípe	60
6	Anguilla	67
7	Montserrat	68
8	Marshall Islands	72
9	Palau	85
10	Samoa	101
11	Tonga	134
12	St Christopher and Nevis	146
13	Vanuatu	159
14	British Virgin Islands	171
15	Equatorial Guinea	174
16	Maldives	180
17	Dominica	204
18	Grenada	208
19	Nauru	213
20	Solomon Islands	216

GDP PER CAPITA 1994

HIGHEST

		US$
1	Liechtenstein	49,368
2	Japan	36,782
3	Switzerland	36,096
4	Bermuda	29,859
5	Denmark	28,245
6	Luxembourg	27,611
7	USA	25,514
8	Norway	25,378
9	Germany	25,179
10	Nauru	25,094
11	Austria	24,823
12	Monaco	24,693
13	France	24,608
14	Singapore	23,556
15	Iceland	23,280
16	Hong Kong	22,590
17	French Guiana	22,516
18	Sweden	22,499
19	Belgium	21,765
20	The Netherlands	21,536

LOWEST

1	Sudan	62
2	Rwanda	65
3	Mozambique	92
4	Ethiopia	96
5	Eritrea	96
6	Armenia	117
7	Tanzania	119
8	Kazakhstan	120
	São Tomé and Princípe	120
10	Somalia	124
11	Malawi	130
12	Tajikistan	131
13	Nepal	158
14	Chad	162
15	Bhutan	163
16	Burundi	172
17	Azerbaijan	176
18	Guinea-Bissau	182
19	Mali	183
20	Sierra Leone	184

TOTAL EXTERNAL DEBT 1996

HIGHEST EXTERNAL DEBT

		US$ million
1	Brazil	179,047
2	Mexico	157,125
3	Indonesia	129,033
4	China	128,817
5	Russia	124,785
6	Argentina	93,841
7	Thailand	90,824
8	India	89,827
9	Turkey	79,789
10	The Philippines	41,214
11	Poland	40,895
12	Malaysia	39,777
13	Venezuela	35,344
14	Algeria	33,260
15	Egypt	31,407
	Nigeria	31,407
17	Pakistan	29,901
18	Peru	29,176
19	Colombia	28,859
20	Chile	27,411

LOWEST EXTERNAL DEBT

1	Eritrea	46
2	Vanuatu	47
3	St Christopher and Nevis	58
4	Tonga	70
5	Bhutan	87
6	Dominica	111
7	Grenada	120
8	St Lucia	142
9	Solomon Islands	145
10	Seychelles	148
11	Maldives	167
	Samoa	167
13	The Comoros	206
14	Cape Verde	211
15	St Vincent and the Grenadines	213
16	Fiji	217
17	Swaziland	220
18	Djibouti	241
19	São Tomé and Princípe	261
20	Equatorial Guinea	282

ILLITERACY RATE

HIGHEST ILLITERACY RATES

		%
1	Niger	86.4
2	Burkina Faso	80.8
3	Nepal	72.5
4	Mali	69.0
5	Sierra Leone	68.6
6	Afghanistan	68.5
7	Senegal	66.9
8	Burundi	64.7
9	Ethiopia	64.5
10	Guinea	64.1
11	Benin	63.0
12	Mauritania	62.3
13	Pakistan	62.2
14	Bangladesh	61.9
15	Liberia	61.7
16	The Gambia	61.4
17	Côte d'Ivoire	59.9
	Mozambique	59.9
19	Bhutan	57.8
20	Morocco	56.3

TRAVEL OVERSEAS

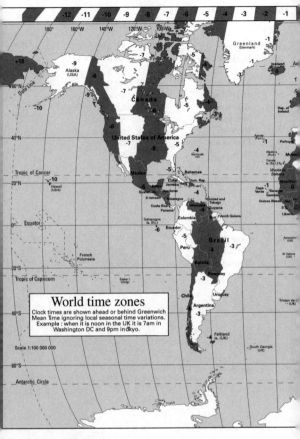

World time zones

Clock times are shown ahead or behind Greenwich Mean Time ignoring local seasonal time variations. Example : when it is noon in the UK it is 7am in Washington DC and 9pm in Tokyo.

Scale 1:100 000 000

TIME ZONES

Standard time differences from the Greenwich meridian
+   hours ahead of GMT
-     hours behind GMT
★   may vary from standard time at some part of the year
      (Summer Time or Daylight Saving Time)

	Hours	Min
Afghanistan	+ 4	30
Albania★	+ 1	
Algeria	+ 1	
Andorra★	+ 1	
Angola	+ 1	
Anguilla	- 4	

Alb. Albania	Es. Estonia	Sing. Singapore
Ar. Armenia	Gui. Guinea	Slov Slovakia
Azer. Azerbaijan	Isr. Israel	Slo. Slovenia
Ba. Bangladesh	Kyrg. Kyrgyzstan	Sur. Suriname
Belg. Belgium	La. Latvia	Sw. Switzerland
Bh. Bhutan	Leb. Lebanon	Taj. Tajikistan
Bos. Herc. Bosnia & Hercegovina	Li. Lithuania	Thai. Thailand
Ca. Cameroon	Lux. Luxembourg	T. Togo
Cam. Cambodia	Ma. FYR Macedonia	Turk. Turkmenistan
Cen. Af. Rep. Central African Republic	Mal. Malawi	UAE United Arab Emirates
Cr. Croatia	Mol. Moldova	UK United Kingdom
Cyp. Cyprus	Neth. Netherlands	Yugo. Federal Republic
Cz. Rep. Czech Republic	Q. Qatar	of Yugoslavia
Dom. Rep. Dominican Republic	Rus. Russia (Kaliningrad)	Zim. Zimbabwe
Eq. Gui. Equatorial Guinea	S.L. Sierra Leone	

A n t a r c t i c a

© Oxford Cartographers

	Hours	Min
Antigua and Barbuda	− 4	
Argentina	− 3	
Armenia★	+ 3	
Aruba	− 4	
Ascension Island	0	
Australia★	+10	
Broken Hill area (NSW)★	+ 9	30
Lord Howe Island★	+10 30	
Northern Territory	+ 9 30	
South Australia★	+ 9 30	
Western Australia	+ 8	
Austria★	+ 1	
Azerbaijan★	+ 4	
Azores★	− 1	

	Hours	Min
Bahamas★	– 5	
Bahrain	+ 3	
Bangladesh	+ 6	
Barbados	– 4	
Belarus★	+ 2	
Belgium★	+ 1	
Belize	– 6	
Benin	+ 1	
Bermuda★	– 4	
Bhutan	+ 6	
Bolivia	– 4	
Bosnia-Hercegovina★	+ 1	
Botswana	+ 2	
Brazil		
Acre	– 5	
eastern, including all coast and Brasilia★	– 3	
Fernando de Noronha Island	– 2	
southern★	– 4	
western	– 4	
British Antarctic Territory	– 3	
British Indian Ocean Territory	+ 5	
Diego Garcia	+ 6	
British Virgin Islands	– 4	
Brunei	+ 8	
Bulgaria★	+ 2	
Burkina Faso	0	
Burundi	+ 2	
Cambodia	+ 7	
Cameroon	+ 1	
Canada		
Alberta★	– 7	
British Columbia★	– 8	
Labrador★	– 4	
Manitoba★	– 6	
New Brunswick★	– 4	
Newfoundland★	– 3	30
Northwest Territories★		
east of 85°W.	– 5	
85°W.–102°W.	– 6	
west of 102°W.	– 7	
Nova Scotia★	– 4	
Ontario★		
east of 90° W.	– 5	
west of 90° W.	– 6	
Prince Edward Island★	– 4	
Quebec		
east of 63° W.	– 4	
west of 63° W.★	– 5	
Saskatchewan	– 6	
Yukon★	– 8	
Canary Islands★	0	
Cape Verde	– 1	

	Hours	Min
Cayman Islands	− 5	
Central African Republic	+ 1	
Chad	+ 1	
Chatham Islands*	+12	45
Chile*	− 4	
China	+ 8	
Christmas Island (Indian Ocean)	+ 7	
Cocos Keeling Islands	+ 6	30
Colombia	− 5	
Comoros	+ 3	
Congo (Dem. Rep.)		
east	+ 2	
west	+ 1	
Congo (Rep. of)	+ 1	
Cook Islands	−10	
Costa Rica	− 6	
Côte d'Ivoire	0	
Croatia*	+ 1	
Cuba*	− 5	
Cyprus*	+ 2	
Czech Republic*	+ 1	
Denmark*	+ 1	
Djibouti	+ 3	
Dominica	− 4	
Dominican Republic	− 4	
Ecuador	− 5	
Galápagos Islands	− 6	
Egypt*	+ 2	
Equatorial Guinea	+ 1	
Eritrea	+ 3	
Estonia*	+ 2	
Ethiopia	+ 3	
Falkland Islands*	− 4	
Faröe Islands*	0	
Fiji	+12	
Finland*	+ 2	
France*	+ 1	
French Guiana	− 3	
French Polynesia	−10	
Marquesas Islands	− 9	30
Gabon	+ 1	
The Gambia	0	
Georgia	+ 5	
Germany*	+ 1	
Ghana	0	
Gibraltar*	+ 1	
Greece*	+ 2	
Greenland*	− 3	
Danmarkshavn	0	
Mesters Vig	0	
Scoresby Sound*	− 1	
Thule area*	− 4	

	Hours	Min
Grenada	– 4	
Guadeloupe	– 4	
Guam	+10	
Guatemala	– 6	
Guinea	0	
Guinea–Bissau	0	
Guyana	– 4	
Haiti★	– 5	
Honduras	– 6	
Hungary★	+ 1	
Iceland	0	
India	+ 5	30
Indonesia		
Bali	+ 8	
Flores	+ 8	
Irian Jaya	+ 9	
Java	+ 7	
Kalimantan (south and east)	+ 8	
Kalimantan (west and central)	+ 7	
Molucca Islands	+ 9	
Sulawesi	+ 8	
Sumatra	+ 7	
Sumbawa	+ 8	
Tanimbar	+ 9	
Timor	+ 8	
Iran★	+ 3	30
Iraq★	+ 3	
Ireland, Republic of★	0	
Israel★	+ 2	
Italy★	+ 1	
Jamaica	– 5	
Japan	+ 9	
Jordan★	+ 2	
Kazakhstan★		
western (Aktau)	+ 4	
central (Atyrau)	+ 5	
eastern	+ 6	
Kenya	+ 3	
Kiribati	+12	
Line Islands	+14	
Phoenix Islands	+13	
Korea, North	+ 9	
Korea, South	+ 9	
Kuwait	+ 3	
Kyrgyzstan★	+ 5	
Laos	+ 7	
Latvia★	+ 2	
Lebanon★	+ 2	
Lesotho	+ 2	
Liberia	0	
Libya★	+ 1	
Liechtenstein★	+ 1	

	Hours	Min
Line Islands not part of Kiribati	-10	
Lithuania★	+ 2	
Luxembourg★	+ 1	
Macao	+ 8	
Macedonia (Former Yug. Rep. of)★	+ 1	
Madagascar	+ 3	
Madeira★	0	
Malawi	+ 2	
Malaysia	+ 8	
Maldives	+ 5	
Mali	0	
Malta★	+ 1	
Marshall Islands	+12	
Ebon Atoll	-12	
Martinique	- 4	
Mauritania	0	
Mauritius	+ 4	
Mexico★	- 6	
central	- 7	
Quintana Roo★	- 5	
western	- 8	
Micronesia		
Caroline Islands	+10	
Kosrae	+11	
Pingelap	+11	
Pohnpei	+11	
Moldova★	+ 2	
Monaco★	+ 1	
Mongolia★	+ 8	
Montserrat	- 4	
Morocco	0	
Mozambique	+ 2	
Myanmar	+ 6	30
Namibia★	+ 1	
Nauru	+12	
Nepal	+ 5	45
Netherlands★	+ 1	
Netherlands Antilles	- 4	
New Caledonia	+11	
New Zealand★	+12	
Nicaragua	- 6	
Niger	+ 1	
Nigeria	+ 1	
Niue	-11	
Norfolk Island	+11	30
Northern Mariana Islands	+10	
Norway★	+ 1	
Oman	+ 4	
Pakistan	+ 5	
Palau	+ 9	
Panama	- 5	
Papua New Guinea	+10	

	Hours	*Min*
Paraguay★	− 4	
Peru	− 5	
Philippines	+ 8	
Poland★	+ 1	
Portugal★	0	
Puerto Rico	− 4	
Qatar	+ 3	
Réunion	+ 4	
Romania★	+ 2	
Russia★		
Zone 1	+ 2	
Zone 2	+ 3	
Zone 3	+ 4	
Zone 4	+ 5	
Zone 5	+ 6	
Zone 6	+ 7	
Zone 7	+ 8	
Zone 8	+ 9	
Zone 9	+10	
Zone 10	+11	
Zone 11	+12	
Rwanda	+ 2	
St Helena	0	
St Christopher and Nevis	− 4	
St Lucia	− 4	
St Pierre and Miquelon★	− 3	
St Vincent and the Grenadines	− 4	
El Salvador	− 6	
Samoa	−11	
Samoa, American	−11	
San Marino★	+ 1	
São Tomé and Princípe	0	
Saudi Arabia	+ 3	
Senegal	0	
Seychelles	+ 4	
Sierra Leone	0	
Singapore	+ 8	
Slovakia★	+ 1	
Slovenia★	+ 1	
Solomon Islands	+11	
Somalia	+ 3	
South Africa	+ 2	
South Georgia	− 2	
Spain★	+ 1	
Sri Lanka	+ 6	
Sudan	+ 2	
Suriname	− 3	
Swaziland	+ 2	
Sweden★	+ 1	
Switzerland★	+ 1	
Syria★	+ 2	
Taiwan	+ 8	

	Hours	Min
Tajikistan	+ 5	
Tanzania	+ 3	
Thailand	+ 7	
Togo	0	
Tonga	+13	
Trinidad and Tobago	– 4	
Tristan da Cunha	0	
Tunisia	+ 1	
Turkey★	+ 2	
Turkmenistan	+ 5	
Turks and Caicos Islands★	– 5	
Tuvalu	+12	
Uganda	+ 3	
Ukraine★	+ 2	
United Arab Emirates	+ 4	
United Kingdom★	0	
United States of America★		
Alaska	– 9	
Aleutian Islands, east of 169°30′;W.	– 9	
Aleutian Islands, west of 169°30′;W.	–10	
eastern time	– 5	
central time	– 6	
Hawaii	–10	
mountain time	– 7	
Pacific time	– 8	
Uruguay	– 3	
Uzbekistan	+ 5	
Vanuatu	+11	
Vatican City State★	+ 1	
Venezuela	– 4	
Vietnam	+ 7	
Virgin Islands (US)	– 4	
Yemen	+ 3	
Yugoslavia (Fed. Rep. of)★	+ 1	
Zambia	+ 2	
Zimbabwe	+ 2	

AIRMAIL AND IDD CODES

AIRMAIL ZONES (AZ)

The table includes airmail letter zones for countries outside
Europe, and destinations to which European and European
Union airmail letter rates apply

1   airmail zone 1
2   airmail zone 2
e   Europe
eu European Union

INTERNATIONAL DIRECT DIALLING (IDD)

International dialling codes are composed of four elements
which are dialled in sequence:

1. the international code
2. the country code (see below)
3. the area code
4. the customer's telephone number

Calls to some countries must be made via the international operator.

† Calls must be made via the international operator
p A pause in dialling is necessary whilst waiting for a second tone
★ Varies in some areas
★★ Varies depending on carrier

Country	AZ	IDD from UK	IDD to UK
Afghanistan	1	00 93	†
Albania	e	00 355	00 44
Algeria	1	00 213	00p44
Andorra	eu	00 376	00 44
Angola	1	00 244	00 44
Anguilla	1	00 1 264	00 11 44
Antigua and Barbuda	1	00 1 268	011 44
Argentina	1	00 54	00 44
Armenia	e	00 374	810 44
Aruba	1	00 297	00 44
Ascension Island	1	00 247	01 44
Australia	2	00 61	00 11 44
Austria	eu	00 43	00 44
Azerbaijan	e	00 994	810 44
Azores	eu	00 351	00 44
Bahamas	1	00 1 242	011 44
Bahrain	1	00 973	0 44
Bangladesh	1	00 880	00 44
Barbados	1	00 1 246	011 44
Belarus	e	00 375	810 44
Belgium	eu	00 32	00 44
Belize	1	00 501	011 44
Benin	1	00 229	00p44
Bermuda	1	00 1 441	011 44
Bhutan	1	00 975	00 44
Bolivia	1	00 591	00 44
Bosnia-Hercegovina	e	00 396	99 44
Botswana	1	00 267	00 44
Brazil	1	00 55	00 44
British Virgin Islands	1	00 1 809	011 44
Brunei	1	00 673	01 44
Bulgaria	e	00 359	00 44
Burkina Faso	1	00 226	00 44
Burundi	1	00 257	90 44
Cambodia	1	00 855	00 44
Cameroon	1	00 237	00 44
Canada	1	00 1	011 44
Canary Islands	eu	00 34	07p44
Cape Verde	1	00 238	0 44

Country	AZ	IDD from UK	IDD to UK
Cayman Islands	1	00 1 345	011 44
Central African Republic	1	00 236	00p44
Chad	1	00 235	†
Chile	1	00 56	00 44
China	2	00 86	00 44
Hong Kong	1	00 852	001 44
Colombia	1	00 57	90 44
Comoros	1	00 269	10 44
Congo, Dem. Rep. of	1	00 243	00 44
Congo, Republic of	1	00 242	00 44
Cook Islands	2	00 682	00 44
Costa Rica	1	00 506	00 44
Côte d'Ivoire	1	00 225	00 44
Croatia	e	00 385	00 44
Cuba	1	00 53	119 44
Cyprus	e	00 357	00 44
Czech Republic	e	00 420	00 44
Denmark	eu	00 45	00 44
Djibouti	1	00 253	00 44
Dominica	1	00 1 809	011 44
Dominican Republic	1	00 1 809	011 44
Ecuador	1	00 593	01 44
Egypt	1	00 20	00 44
Equatorial Guinea	1	00 240	19 44
Eritrea	1	00 291	†
Estonia	e	00 372	800 44
Ethiopia	1	00 251	00 44
Falkland Islands	1	00 500	01 44
Faröe Islands	e	00 298	009 44
Fiji	2	00 679	05 44
Finland	eu	00 358	00 44★★
France	eu	00 33	00 44
French Guiana	1	00 594	†
French Polynesia	2	00 689	00 44
Gabon	1	00 241	00 44
The Gambia	1	00 220	00 44
Georgia	e	00 995	810 44
Germany	eu	00 49	00 44
Ghana	1	00 233	00 44
Gibraltar	eu	00 350	00 44
Greece	eu	00 30	00 44
Greenland	e	00 299	009 44
Grenada	1	00 1 809	011 44
Guadeloupe	1	00 590	19 44
Guam	2	00 671	001 44
Guatemala	1	00 502	00 44
Guinea	1	00 224	00 44
Guinea-Bissau	1	00 245	†
Guyana	1	00 592	001 44
Haiti	1	00 509	†
Honduras	1	00 504	00 44

Country	AZ	IDD from UK	IDD to UK
Hungary	e	00 36	00 44
Iceland	e	00 354	00 44
India	1	00 91	00 44
Indonesia	1	00 62	001 44★★
			00844★★
Iran	1	00 98	00 44
Iraq	1	00 964	00 44
Ireland, Republic of	eu	00 353	00 44
Israel	1	00 972	00 44
Italy	eu	00 39	00 44
Jamaica	1	00 1 809	011 44
Japan	2	00 81	001 44★★
			004144★★
			006144★★
Jordan	1	00 962	00 44★
Kazakhstan	e	00 7	810 44
Kenya	1	00 254	00 44
Kiribati	2	00 686	0 44
Korea, North	2	00 850	010 44
Korea, South	2	00 82	001 44★★
			00244★★
Kuwait	1	00 965	00 44
Kyrgystan	e	00 996	810 44
Laos	1	00 856	†
Latvia	e	00 371	810 44
Lebanon	1	00 961	00 44
Lesotho	1	00 266	00 44
Liberia	1	00 231	00 44
Libya	1	00 218	00 44
Liechtenstein	e	00 41	00 44
Lithuania	e	00 370	810 44
Luxembourg	eu	00 352	00 44
Macao	1	00 853	00 44
Macedonia	e	00 389	99 44
Madagascar	1	00 261	16p44
Madeira	eu	00 351 91	00 44★
Malawi	1	00 265	101 44
Malaysia	1	00 60	00 44
Maldives	1	00 960	00 44
Mali	1	00 223	00 44
Malta	e	00 356	00 44
Mariana Islands, Northern	2	00 1 670	011 44
Marshall Islands	2	00 692	012 44
Martinique	1	00 596	19p44
Mauritania	1	00 222	00 44
Mauritius	1	00 230	00 44
Mayotte	1	00 269	19p44
Mexico	1	00 52	98 44
Micronesia, Federated States of	2	00 691	011 44
Moldova	e	00 373	810 44

Country	AZ	IDD from UK	IDD to UK
Monaco	eu	00 377 93	00 44
Mongolia	2	00 976	†
Montenegro	e	00 381	99 44
Montserrat	1	00 1 664	†
Morocco	1	00 212	00p44
Mozambique	1	00 258	00 44
Myanmar	1	00 95	0 44
Namibia	1	00 264	09 44
Nauru	2	00 674	00 44
Nepal	1	00 977	00 44
Netherlands	eu	00 31	00 44
Netherlands Antilles	1	00 599	00 44
New Caledonia	2	00 687	00 44
New Zealand	2	00 64	00 44
Nicaragua	1	00 505	00 44
Niger	1	00 227	00 44
Nigeria	1	00 234	009 44
Niue	2	00 683	†
Norfolk Island	2	00 672	00 44
Norway	e	00 47	00 44
Oman	1	00 968	00 44
Pakistan	1	00 92	00 44
Palau	2	00 680	†
Panama	1	00 507	00 44
Papua New Guinea	2	00 675	05 44
Paraguay	1	00 595	002 44
			003 44
Peru	1	00 51	00 44
Philippines	2	00 63	00 44
Poland	e	00 48	0p044
Portugal	eu	00 351	00 44
Puerto Rico	1	00 1 787	011 44
Qatar	1	00 974	044
Réunion	1	00 262	19p44
Romania	e	00 40	00 44
Russia	e	00 7	810 44
Rwanda	1	00 250	00 44
St Helena	1	00 290	01 44
St Christopher and Nevis	1	00 1 869	†
St Lucia	1	00 1 758	011 44
St Pierre and Miquelon	1	00 508	19p44
St Vincent and the Grenadines	1	00 1 809	0 44
El Salvador	1	00 503	00 44
Samoa	2	00 685	0 44
Samoa, American	2	00 684	144
San Marino	eu	00 378	00 44
São Tomé and Princípe	1	00 239	00 44
Saudi Arabia	1	00 966	00 44
Senegal	1	00 221	00p44

Country	AZ	IDD from UK	IDD to UK
Serbia	e	00 381	99 44
Seychelles	1	00 248	0 44
Sierra Leone	1	00 232	0 44
Singapore	1	00 65	005 44
Slovak Republic	e	00 42	00 44
Slovenia	e	00 386	00 44
Solomon Islands	2	00 677	00 44
Somalia	1	00 252	†
South Africa	1	00 27	09 44
Spain	eu	00 34	07p44
Sri Lanka	1	00 94	00 44
Sudan	1	00 249	00 44
Suriname	1	00 597	001 44
Swaziland	1	00 268	00 44
Sweden	eu	00 46	009 44★★
			007 44★★
			0087 44★★
Switzerland	e	00 41	00 44
Syria	1	00 963	00 44
Taiwan	2	00 886	002 44
Tajikistan	e	00 7	810 44
Tanzania	1	00 255	00 44
Thailand	1	00 66	001 44
Tibet	1	00 86	00 44
Togo	1	00 228	00 44
Tonga	2	00 676	00 44
Trinidad and Tobago	1	00 1 868	011 44
Tristan da Cunha	1	00 2 897	†
Tunisia	1	00 216	00 44
Turkey	e	00 90	00 44
Turkmenistan	e	00 993	810 44
Turks and Caicos Islands	1	00 1 649	0 44
Tuvalu	2	00 688	00 44
Uganda	1	00 256	00 44
Ukraine	e	00 380	810 44
United Arab Emirates	1	00 971	00 44
Uruguay	1	00 598	00 44
USA	1	00 1	011 44
Alaska		00 1 907	011 44
Hawaii		00 1 808	011 44
Uzbekistan	e	00 7	810 44
Vanuatu	2	00 678	00 44
Vatican City State	eu	00 39 66982	00 44
Venezuela	1	00 58	00 44
Vietnam	1	00 84	00 44
Virgin Islands (US)	1	00 1 340	011 44
Yemen	1	00 967	00 44
Yugoslavia, Fed. Rep.	e	00 381	99 44
Zambia	1	00 260	00 44
Zimbabwe	1	00 263	110 44

DISTANCES FROM LONDON BY AIR

The list of the distances in statute miles from London, Heathrow, to various cities (airport) abroad has been supplied by the publishers of *IATA/Serco Aviation Services Air Distances Manual*, Southall, Middx.

To	Miles
Abidjan	3,197
Abu Dhabi (International)	3,425
Addis Ababa	3,675
Adelaide (International)	10,111
Aden	3,670
Algiers	1,035
Amman (Queen Alia)	2,287
Amsterdam	230
Ankara (Esenboga)	1,770
Athens	1,500
Atlanta	4,198
Auckland	11,404
Baghdad (Saddam)	2,551
Bahrain	3,163
Baku	2,485
Bangkok	5,928
Barbados	4,193
Barcelona (Muntadas)	712
Basle	447
Beijing (Capital)	5,063
Beirut	2,161
Belfast (Aldergrove)	325
Belgrade	1,056
Berlin (Tegel)	588
Bermuda	3,428
Berne	476
Bogotá	5,262
Bombay (Mumbai)	4,478
Boston	3,255
Brasilia	5,452
Bratislava	817
Brisbane (Eagle Farm)	10,273
Brussels	217
Bucharest (Otopeni)	1,307
Budapest	923
Buenos Aires	6,915
Cairo (International)	2,194
Calcutta	4,958
Calgary	4,357
Canberra	10,563
Cape Town	6,011
Caracas	4,639
Casablanca (Mohamed V)	1,300
Chicago (O'Hare)	3,941
Cologne	331
Colombo (Katunayake)	5,411

To	Miles
Copenhagen	608
Dakar	2,706
Dallas (Fort Worth)	4,736
Dallas (Lovefield)	4,732
Damascus (International)	2,223
Dar-es-Salaam	4,662
Darwin	8,613
Delhi	4,180
Denver	4,655
Detroit (Metropolitan)	3,754
Dhahran	3,143
Dhaka	4,976
Doha	3,253
Dubai	3,414
Dublin	279
Durban	5,937
Düsseldorf	310
Entebbe	4,033
Frankfurt (Main)	406
Freetown	3,046
Geneva	468
Gibraltar	1,084
Gothenburg (Landvetter)	664
Hamburg	463
Harare	5,156
Havana	4,647
Helsinki (Vantaa)	1,148
Hobart	10,826
Ho Chi Minh City	6,345
Hong Kong	5,990
Honolulu	7,220
Houston (Intercontinental)	4,821
Houston (William P. Hobby)	4,837
Islamabad	3,767
Istanbul	1,560
Jakarta (Halim Perdanakusuma)	7,295
Jeddah	2,947
Johannesburg	5,634
Kabul	3,558
Karachi	3,935
Kathmandu	4,570
Khartoum	3,071
Kiev (Borispol)	1,357
Kiev (Julyany)	1,337
Kingston, Jamaica	4,668
Kuala Lumpur (Subang)	6,557
Kuwait	2,903
Lagos	3,107
Larnaca	2,036
Lima	6,303
Lisbon	972
Lomé	3,129

To	*Miles*
Los Angeles (International)	5,439
Madras	5,113
Madrid	773
Malta	1,305
Manila	6,685
Marseille	614
Mauritius	6,075
Melbourne (Essendon)	10,504
Melbourne (Tullamarine)	10,499
Mexico City	5,529
Miami	4,414
Milan (Linate)	609
Minsk	1,176
Montego Bay	4,687
Montevideo	6,841
Montreal (Mirabel)	3,241
Moscow (Sheremetievo)	1,557
Munich (Franz Josef Strauss)	584
Muscat	3,621
Nairobi (Jomo Kenyatta)	4,248
Naples	1,011
Nassau	4,333
New York (J. F. Kennedy)	3,440
Nice	645
Oporto	806
Oslo (Fornebu)	722
Ottawa	3,321
Palma, Majorca (Son San Juan)	836
Paris (Charles de Gaulle)	215
Paris (Le Bourget)	215
Paris (Orly)	227
Perth, Australia	9,008
Port of Spain	4,404
Prague	649
Pretoria	5,602
Reykjavik (Domestic)	1,167
Reykjavik (Keflavik)	1,177
Rhodes	1,743
Rio de Janeiro	5,745
Riyadh (King Khaled) International	3,067
Rome (Fiumicino)	895
St John's, Newfoundland	2,308
St Petersburg	1,314
Salzburg	651
San Francisco	5,351
São Paulo	5,892
Sarajevo	1,017
Seoul (Kimpo)	5,507
Shanghai	5,725
Shannon	369
Singapore (Changi)	6,756
Sofia	1,266

To	Miles
Stockholm (Arlanda)	908
Suva	10,119
Sydney (Kingsford Smith)	10,568
Tangier	1,120
Tehran	2,741
Tel Aviv	2,227
Tokyo (Narita)	5,956
Toronto	3,544
Tripoli (International)	1,468
Tunis	1,137
Turin (Caselle)	570
Ulan Bator	4,340
Valencia	826
Vancouver	4,707
Venice (Tessera)	715
Vienna (Schwechat)	790
Vladivostok	5,298
Warsaw	912
Washington (Dulles)	3,665
Wellington	11,692
Yangon/Rangoon	5,582
Yokohama (Aomori)	5,647
Zagreb	848
Zürich	490

PASSPORTS

Applications for United Kingdom passports must be made on the forms obtainable from regional passport offices, main post offices, World Choice Travel Agents and Lloyds Bank.

London – Passport Office, Clive House, 70–78 Petty France, London SW1H 9HD
Liverpool – Passport Office, 5th Floor, India Buildings, Water Street, Liverpool L2 0QZ
Newport – Passport Office, Olympia House, Upper Dock Street, Newport, Gwent NP9 1XA
Peterborough – Passport Office, Aragon Court, Northminster Road, Peterborough PE1 1QG
Glasgow – Passport Office, 3 Northgate, 96 Milton Street, Cowcaddens, Glasgow G4 0BT
Belfast – Passport Office, Hampton House, 47–53 High Street, Belfast BT1 2QS

The above offices all use a single telephone number (0870-521 0410) to handle incoming calls, which are normally routed automatically to the nearest office unless all lines are busy, when the call will be rerouted to other offices. Recorded messages to deal with routine enquiries operate 24 hours a day. The central fax number is: 0171-271 8581, and the Passport Agency Web site address is: http://www.open.gov.ukpass/ukpass.htm

The passport offices are open Monday–Friday 9 a.m. to 4.30 p.m. (8.15 a.m. to 4 p.m. in London). The Passport Office in London is also open for cases of emergency (e.g. death or serious illness) arising outside normal office hours between 4 p.m. and 6 p.m. Monday to Friday, between 10 a.m. and 7 p.m. on Saturdays, and between 9.30 a.m. and 2.30 p.m. on Sundays and Bank Holidays.

Straightforward, properly completed applications are processed within 15 working days from April to August, the busiest period, and within ten working days for the rest of the year. Applying in person does not guarantee that an application will be given priority.

The completed application form should be posted, with the appropriate documents and fee, to the regional passport office indicated on the addressed envelope provided with each application form (an exception to this is the London office which is a calling-in office only). Accompanying cheques and postal orders should be crossed and made payable to 'The Passport Office'.

Completed application forms may also be handed in at main post offices, branches of Lloyds Bank and branches of World Choice travel agents. Staff will check the application is correct and has the correct accompanying documentation, fee, etc., before transmitting it to one of the passport offices.

A passport cannot be issued or extended on behalf of a person already abroad; such persons should apply to the nearest British High Commission or Consulate.

Passport eligibility

UK passports are granted to:

*   British citizens
*   British Dependent Territories citizens
*   British Nationals (Overseas)
*   British Overseas citizens
*   British Subjects
*   British Protected Persons

Passports are generally available for travel to all countries. The possession of a passport does not, however, exempt the holder from compliance with any immigration regulations in force in British or foreign countries, or from the necessity of obtaining a visa where required.

A new, machine readable application form is being introduced from July 1998. This replaces the five different application forms previously used, and takes into account the fact that all children will require their own passports (*see* below). The new form also covers amendments and extensions.

Adults

A passport granted to a person over 16 will normally be valid for ten years and will not be renewable. Thereafter, or if at any time the passport contains no further space for visas, a new passport must be obtained.

The issue of passports including details of the holder's spouse has been discontinued, but existing family passports may be used until expiry. A spouse who is included in a family passport cannot travel on the passport without the holder.

Children

From 5 October 1998 all children under the age of 16 and who are not already included on a parent's passport will be required to have their own passport, primarily to help prevent child abductions. The passports will normally be valid for five years, after which a new passport application must be made. This replaces the system whereby children under the age of 16 could either have their own document or be added to their parents' passports.

A passport granted to a child prior to this date is still valid for five years, although the five-year extension option no longer exists. Children included in their parents' passports when the new regulations come into force will not be affected and can continue to travel on them until they reach the age of 16 or until the passport expires or is amended.

Countersignatures
The completed application form should be countersigned by a
Member of Parliament, justice of the peace, minister of religion,
a professionally qualified person (e.g. doctor, engineer, lawyer,
teacher), local councillor, bank officer, established Civil Servant,
police officer or a person of similar standing who has known the
applicant personally for at least two years, and who is either a
British citizen, British Dependent Territories citizen, British
National (Overseas), British Overseas citizen, British subject or
citizen of a Commonwealth country. A relative must not
countersign the application.

If the application is for a child under the age of 16, the
countersignature should be by someone of relevant standing who
has known the parent or person with parental responsibility who
signs the declaration of consent, rather than the child.

Photographs
Two identical unmounted photographs of the applicant must be
sent. These photographs should be printed on normal thin
photographic paper. They should measure 45mm x 35mm (1.77
in x 1.38 in) and should be taken full face against a white
background. One photograph should be certified as a true
likeness of the applicant by the person who countersigns the
application form.

Documentation
The applicant's birth certificate or previous British passport, and
other documents in support of the statements made in the
application, must be produced at the time of applying. Details of
which documents are required are set out in the notes
accompanying the application form.

If the applicant for a passport is a British national by
naturalization or registration, the certificate proving this must be
produced with the application, unless the applicant holds a
previous UK passport issued after registration or naturalization.

48-page passports
The 48-page passport is intended to meet the needs of frequent
travellers who fill standard passports before the validity has
expired. It is valid for ten years.

Passport fees★ (from March 1998)

New adult passport	£21
New child passport	£11
Renewal of passport	£21
Amendment of passport	£11
48-page passport	£31

★Postal applications only. A £10 charge is added for applications
made in person at a passport office in the UK or made abroad

VISAS

British nationals planning to travel overseas should enquire about visa requirements at the Foreign and Commonwealth Office, or the high commission or consulate of their country of destination. Visa requirements may vary depending on the purpose or the length of the visit, and regulations are also liable to change, sometimes at short notice.

Overseas nationals who wish to enter the UK must satisfy the immigration officer at the port of arrival that they meet the requirements of the UK immigration rules. Separate rules apply to nationals of a member state of the European Economic Area (member states of the European Union and Iceland, Liechtenstein and Norway). Details are available from the nearest British mission.

Nationals from the following countries must have a valid visa issued prior to travel to the UK, unless they are either settled in the UK, or are in the UK for some long-term purpose (more than six months) and returning within the period of a permission to stay granted previously:

Afghanistan; Albania; Algeria; Angola; Armenia; Azerbaijan; Bahrain; Bangladesh; Belarus; Benin; Bhutan; Bosnia-Hercegovina; Bulgaria; Burkina Faso; Burundi; Cambodia; Cameroon; Cape Verde; Central African Republic; Chad; China; Colombia; Comoros; Democratic Republic of Congo; Republic of Congo; Côte d'Ivoire; Cuba; Northern Cyprus ('Turkish Republic of Northern Cyprus'); Djibouti; Dominican Republic; Ecuador; Egypt; Equatorial Guinea; Eritrea; Ethiopia; Fiji; Gabon; Gambia; Georgia; Ghana; Guinea; Guinea-Bissau; Guyana; Haiti; India; Indonesia; Iran; Iraq; Jordan; Kazakhstan; Kenya; Korea (North); Kuwait; Kyrgyzstan; Laos; Lebanon; Liberia; Libya; Macedonia (Former Yugoslav Republic of); Madagascar; Maldives; Mali; Mauritania; Mauritius; Moldova; Mongolia; Morocco; Mozambique; Myanmar (Burma); Nepal; Niger; Nigeria; Oman; Pakistan; Papua New Guinea; Peru; Philippines; Qatar; Romania; Russia; Rwanda; São Tomé and Princípe; Saudi Arabia; Senegal; Sierra Leone; Somalia; Sri Lanka; Sudan; Suriname; Syria; Taiwan; Tajikistan; Tanzania; Thailand; Togo; Tunisia; Turkey; Turkmenistan; Uganda; Ukraine; United Arab Emirates; Uzbekistan; Vietnam; Yemen; Yugoslavia (Federal Republic of); Zambia

A valid entry clearance is also required by people who are stateless or who hold a non-national travel document or passport issued by an authority not recognized by the UK.

Nationals of any country not listed above do not need an entry clearance to visit or study in the UK but must obtain entry clearance to settle, work or set up business. Entry clearances take the form of an entry certificate for non-visa nationals.

UK entry clearances can be obtained from British Embassies, *Consulates and High Commissions overseas.*

HEALTH ADVICE

Health Advice for Travellers (booklet T6), published by the Department of Health, contains information on health precautions, reciprocal health agreements with other countries, and immunization. It is available from some travel agents, local post offices or the Department of Health, PO Box 410, Wetherby, W. Yorks LS23 7LN. Tel: 0800-555777 (single copy orders).

Immunization

In very general terms immunization against typhoid, polio, and hepatitis A should be considered for all countries where standards of hygiene and sanitation may be less than ideal. Protection against malaria, in the form of tablets, as well as measures to avoid mosquito bites, is advised for visits to malarious areas.

Immunization against yellow fever is compulsory for entry into some countries, either for all travellers or for those arriving from a yellow fever-infected area, and is recommended for all travellers to infected areas.

A doctor should be consulted, preferably at least eight weeks before departure, and will advise travellers and arrange vaccinations. If children will be travelling outside Europe, North America, Australia and New Zealand, the doctor should be informed, especially if they have not completed their full course of childhood immunization.

Country-by-country guidance is set out in *Health Advice for Travellers*. Health care professionals can obtain up-to-date information about immunization recommendations from the Department of Health publication *Health Information for Overseas Travel* or from:

England – Communicable Disease Surveillance Centre, 61
    Colindale Avenue, London NW9 5EQ. Tel: 0181-200 6868
Wales – Welsh Office, Cathays Park, Cardiff CF1 3NQ. Tel:
    01222-825111
Scotland – Scottish Office Department of Health, St Andrew's
    House, Edinburgh EH1 3DG. Tel: 0131-556 8400: or The
    Scottish Centre for Infection and Environmental Health,
    Clifton House, Clifton Place, Glasgow G3 7LN.
    Tel: 0141-300 1130
Northern Ireland – DHSS, Dundonald House, Upper
    Newtownards Road, Belfast BT4 3SF. Tel: 01232-520000

Medical treatment abroad

Details of free or reduced cost emergency medical treatment when visiting European countries, and countries with which the UK has reciprocal health arrangements, are set out in *Health*

Advice for Travellers. It also contains Form E111, the certificate
that entitles people to urgent medical treatment in the European
Economic Area (EEA), as well as guidance on its completion.
For countries where the UK has no health care agreements,
including Canada, the USA, India, the Far East, and the whole of
Africa and Latin America, it is advisable to take out medical
insurance. A certain amount of insurance is also needed in
countries with which the UK has health care agreements.

TROUBLE SPOTS

At the time of going to press, the Foreign and Commonwealth
Office advised against all travel to the following countries or areas
of a country:

Afghanistan
Algeria
Burundi
Cameroon – north-west
Eritrea
Guinea-Bissau
India – Jammu and Kashmir
Iraq
Morocco – Western Sahara
Papua New Guinea – Bougainville Island
Russia – Chechen Republic
Somalia
Tajikistan

Unless on essential business, the FCO also advises against travel
to:

Albania
Angola
Central African Republic
Liberia
Montserrat
Rwanda
Sierra Leone
Sudan – south
Togo
Turkey – south-east

Detailed up-to-date information is available from the Travel
Advice Unit, part of the Consular Division of the Foreign and
Commonwealth Office (for contact details, *see* below).

The Consular Division can provide a range of material for British
citizens travelling abroad, including:
*   information about over 130 countries
*   practical tips about laws, customs, acceptable and
    unacceptable behaviour, etc.
*   British consular services

- details of British Embassies, High Commissions and
  Consulates, including contact details and opening hours

Travel Advice Unit, Consular Division, FCO, 1 Palace Street,
London SW1E 5HE. Tel: 0171-238 4503/4. Fax: 0171-238 4545.
Web site: http://www.fco.gov.uk/reference/travel_advice

BUSINESS ABROAD

Working abroad

A passport issued after 31 December 1982 showing the holder's
national status as British citizen will secure for the holder the
right to take employment or to establish himself/herself in
business or other self-employed activity in another member state
of the European Union. A passport bearing the endorsement
'holder has the right of abode in the United Kingdom' where the
holder so qualifies will also secure the same right.

In most other countries employment permits are required, even
for casual labour. The nearest representative of the country
concerned should be consulted. Local employment offices have
a booklet entitled Working Abroad.

Export business

Those planning to travel overseas on export business are advised
to contact Overseas Trade Services (OTS), the joint Department
of Trade and Industry (DTI) and Foreign and Commonwealth
Office export operation. The aim of the OTS is to encourage
potential exporters to consider selling overseas and existing
exporters to sell more, and its offices can offer advice and
information about the markets to be visited. OTS can be
contacted through the following:

England – London: Government Office for London, Riverwalk
  House, 157–161 Millbank, London SW1P 4RR.
  Tel: 0171-217 3199

Wales –Welsh Office Industry Department, Cathays Park,
  Cardiff CF1 3NQ. Tel: 01222-825097

Scotland – Scottish Trade International, 120 Bothwell Street,
  Glasgow G2 7PJ. Tel: 0141-228 2808

Northern Ireland – Export Development Branch, IDB House,
  64 Chichester Street, Belfast BT1 4JX. Tel: 01232-233233

Information about specific overseas markets is available from
the country desks at the DTI's headquarters: 1 Victoria Street,
London SW1H 0ET. Tel: 0171-215 5000

For details of the nearest Business Link, contact the Business
Links Network. Tel: 0345-567765

INTERNATIONAL ORGANIZATIONS

MAJOR COUNTRY GROUPINGS

THE COMMONWEALTH

A free association of sovereign independent states, all of whom acknowledge Queen Elizabeth II as the head of the Commonwealth. The organization has no formal charter; policy is defined at Commonwealth heads of government meetings, which are held every two years.

Members

Antigua and Barbuda, Australia, Bahamas, Bangladesh, Barbados, Belize, Botswana, Brunei, Cameroon, Canada, Cyprus, Dominica, Fiji, The Gambia, Ghana, Grenada, Guyana, India, Jamaica, Kenya, Kiribati, Lesotho, Malawi, Malaysia, Maldives, Malta, Mauritius, Mozambique, Namibia, Nauru (special status), New Zealand, Nigeria (suspended 1995), Pakistan, Papua New Guinea, St Christopher and Nevis, St Lucia, St Vincent and the Grenadines, Samoa, Seychelles, Sierra Leone, Singapore, Solomon Islands, South Africa, Sri Lanka, Swaziland, Tanzania, Trinidad and Tobago, Tonga, Tuvalu (special status), Uganda, UK, Vanuatu, Zambia, Zimbabwe

COMMONWEALTH OF INDEPENDENT STATES (CIS)

A community of independent states which proclaimed itself successor to the USSR in some aspects of inter-republic and international affairs. It provides a framework for military, foreign policy and economic co-ordination among former republics of the USSR.

Members

Armenia, Azerbaijan, Belarus, Georgia, Kazakhstan, Kyrgyzstan, Moldova, Russia, Tajikistan, Turkmenistan, Ukraine, Uzbekistan

NORTH ATLANTIC TREATY ORGANIZATION (NATO)

NATO was formed to provide security for its members through political, economic and military co-operation, and by linking the security of North America to that of Europe. Since the fall of Communism, NATO has sought to establish close security links with the states of central and eastern Europe, as well as the states of the former USSR, through programmes such as Partnership for Peace (see below).

Members

Belgium, Canada, Denmark, France, Germany, Greece, Iceland, Italy, Luxembourg, Netherlands, Norway, Portugal, Spain, Turkey, UK, USA

ORGANIZATION OF THE ISLAMIC CONFERENCE (OIC)

The OIC was established to generate solidarity and co-operation between Islamic countries. It has the specific aims of: co-ordinating efforts to safeguard the Muslim holy places; supporting the formation of a Palestinian state; assisting member states to maintain their independence; co-ordinating the views of member states in international forums; and improving co-operation in the economic, cultural and scientific fields.

Members

Afghanistan, Albania, Algeria, Azerbaijan, Bahrain, Bangladesh, Benin, Bosnia-Hercegovina, Brunei, Burkino Faso, Cameroon, Chad, Comoros, Djibouti, Egypt, Gabon, The Gambia, Guinea, Guinea-Bissau, Indonesia, Iran, Iraq, Jordan, Kazakhstan, Kuwait, Kyrgyzstan, Lebanon, Libya, Malaysia, Maldives, Mali, Mauritania, Morocco, Mozambique, Niger, Nigeria, Oman, Pakistan, Palestine, Qatar, Saudi Arabia, Senegal, Sierra Leone, Somalia, Sudan, Syria, Tajikistan, Tunisia, Turkey, Turkmenistan, Uganda, UAE, Uzbekistan, Yemen

PARTNERSHIP FOR PEACE (PFP)

A NATO programme involving the states of central and eastern Europe (*see* above).

Members

Albania, Armenia, Austria, Azerbaijan, Belarus, Bulgaria, Czech Republic, Estonia, Finland, Georgia, Hungary, Kazakhstan, Kyrgyzstan, Latvia, Lithuania, Macedonia, Malta, Moldova, Poland, Romania, Russia, Slovakia, Slovenia, Sweden, Switzerland, Turkmenistan, Ukraine, Uzbekistan

THE UNITED NATIONS (UN)

Founded in 1945 as a successor to the pre-war League of Nations, the UN is an intergovernmental organization dedicated to the maintenance of international peace and security and the solution of economic, social and political problems through international co-operation. The principal organs are the General Assembly, the Security Council, the Economic and Social Council, the Trusteeship Council, the Secretariat and the International Court of Justice. A list of the 185 members can be obtained from the UN.

MAJOR TRADE BLOCS

ASIA-PACIFIC ECONOMIC CO-OPERATION GROUP (APEC)

APEC was founded to promote co-operation between members and to hold annual meetings of foreign and trade ministers. It also seeks to establish a free-trade zone by 2020.

Members

Australia, Brunei, Canada, Chile, China, Hong Kong, Indonesia, Japan, South Korea, Malaysia, Mexico, New Zealand, Papua New Guinea, the Philippines, Singapore, Taiwan, Thailand, USA. New members from November 1998 will be: Peru, Russia, Vietnam

ASSOCIATION OF SOUTH-EAST ASIAN NATIONS (ASEAN)

ASEAN seeks to promote economic growth, social progress and cultural development among member states, as well as maintaining stability and encouraging mutual assistance in the region.

Members

Brunei, Cambodia, Indonesia, Laos, Malaysia, Myanmar, Papua New Guinea, the Philippines, Singapore, Thailand, Vietnam

COMMON MARKET FOR EASTERN AND SOUTHERN AFRICA (COMESA)

A free-trade zone and customs area comprising countries with a system of common external tariffs.

Members

Angola, Burundi, Comoros, Democratic Republic of Congo, Djibouti, Eritrea, Ethiopia, Kenya, Lesotho, Madagascar, Malawi, Mauritius, Mozambique, Namibia, Rwanda, Seychelles, Somalia, South Africa, Sudan, Swaziland, Tanzania, Uganda, Zambia, Zimbabwe

ECONOMIC COMMUNITY OF WEST AFRICAN STATES (ECOWAS)

ECOWAS's main aims are: the elimination of restrictions on trade and the movement of people and capital between member countries; the harmonizing of economic, industrial and infrastructure policies; and the establishment of a Fund for Co-operation, Compensation and Development.

Members

Benin, Burkina Faso, Cape Verde, Côte d'Ivoire, The Gambia, Ghana, Guinea, Guinea-Bissau, Liberia, Mali, Mauritania, Niger, Nigeria, Senegal, Sierra Leone, Togo

EUROPEAN FREE TRADE ASSOCIATION (EFTA)

EFTA aims to ensure free trade between member countries through the elimination of internal custom tariffs and quotas, but without the political and economic obligations of the EU.

Members
Iceland, Liechtenstein, Norway, Switzerland

EUROPEAN UNION (EU)
The EU aims to further regional integration by economic, political and legislative means. Of its 15 member states, 11 have agreed to adopt a single currency by 2002.

Members
Austria, Belgium, Denmark, Finland, France, Germany, Greece, Ireland, Italy, Luxembourg, Netherlands, Portugal, Spain, Sweden, UK

G8 (Group of Eight)
The group originally comprised the seven most powerful industrial nations, which met at heads of government level at least once a year to discuss matters of mutual interest and concern. Russia has been included in the group in recent years.

Members
Canada, France, Germany, Italy, Japan, Russia, UK, USA

MERCOSUR (Common Market of the Southern Cone)
MERCOSUR was set up to establish a common market in the southern cone of South America. This was achieved in 1995.

Members
Argentina, Brazil, Paraguay, Uruguay

NORTH AMERICAN FREE TRADE AGREEMENT (NAFTA)
An agreement on free trade between the member states that also includes environmental and labour agreements.

Members
Canada, Mexico, USA

ORGANIZATION FOR ECONOMIC CO-OPERATION AND DEVELOPMENT (OECD)
The OECD aims to promote economic and social welfare throughout the OECD area.

Members
Australia, Austria, Belgium, Canada, Czech Republic, Denmark, Finland, France, Germany, Greece, Hungary, Iceland, Ireland, Italy, Japan, South Korea, Luxembourg, Mexico, Netherlands, New Zealand, Norway, Poland, Portugal, Spain, Sweden, Switzerland, Turkey, UK, USA

ORGANIZATION OF THE PETROLEUM EXPORTING COUNTRIES (OPEC)
OPEC's principal aims are: to co-ordinate the petroleum policies of its members; to determine the best means of safeguarding their interests; and to ensure the stable pricing and supply of petroleum.

Members
Algeria, Indonesia, Iran, Iraq, Kuwait, Libya, Nigeria, Qatar, Saudi Arabia, UAE, Venezuela

PREFERENTIAL TRADE AREA FOR EASTERN AND SOUTHERN AFRICA (PTA)

An organization intended to promote regional commercial and economic co-operation.

Members
Angola, Burundi, Comoros, Democratic Republic of Congo, Djibouti, Ethiopia, Kenya, Lesotho, Malawi, Mauritius, Mozambique, Namibia, Rwanda, Somalia, Sudan, Swaziland, Tanzania, Uganda, Zambia, Zimbabwe

WORLD TRADE ORGANIZATION

Established in 1995 as successor to the General Agreement on Tariffs and Trade (GATT), the WTO provides the contractual framework that determines how governments conduct trade, and acts as a forum for the discussion of issues in international trade. A list of the 131 members and the 31 governments that have applied to join can be obtained from the WTO.

DIRECTORY OF MAJOR INTERNATIONAL ORGANIZATIONS

Association of South-East Asian Nations (ASEAN)
70 A. Jl. Sisingamangaraja, Kebayoran Baru, Jakarta Selatan, PO Box 2072 Jakarta, Indonesia

Bank for International Settlements
Centralbahnplatz 2, 4002 Basle, Switzerland
Tel: 00 41 61-280 8080
Fax: 00 41 61-280 9100
Web site: http://www.bis.org

CAB International
Wallingford, Oxon OX10 8DE, UK
Tel: 00 44 (0) 1491-832111
Fax: 00 44 (0) 1491-833508
E-mail: cabi@cabi.org
Web site: http://www.cabi.org

Caribbean Community and Common Market (CARICOM)
PO Box 10827, Georgetown, Guyana
Tel: 00 5922-69281
Fax: 00 5922-67816
E-mail: carisec2@caricom.org
Web site: http://www.caricom.org

The Commonwealth
Secretariat: Marlborough House, Pall Mall, London SW1Y 5HX, UK
Tel: 00 44 (0) 171-839 3411
Fax: 00 44 (0) 171-839 9081
Web site: http://www.tcol.co.uk
and http://www.thecommonwealth.org

Commonwealth of Independent States (CIS)
Minsk, Belarus
Web site: http://www.cis.minsk.by

Council of Europe
67075 Strasbourg, France
Tel: 00 33 3-8841 2000
Fax: 00 33 3-8841 2781/2/3
E-mail: information.point@seddoc.coe.fr
Web site: http://www.coe.fr

Economic Community of West African States (ECOWAS)
Secretariat Building, Asokoro, Abuji, Nigeria
Tel: 00 234 9-523 1858

European Bank for Reconstruction and Development (EBRD)
One Exchange Square, London EC2A 2EH, UK
Tel: 00 44 (0) 171-338 6000
Fax: 00 44 (0) 171-338 6100
Web site: http://www.ebrd.com

European Free Trade Association (EFTA)
Headquarters: 9–11 rue de Varembé, 1211 Geneva 20, Switzerland
Tel: 00 41 22-749 1111
Fax: 00 41 22-733 9291
E-mail: efta-mailbox@secrbru.efta.be
Web site: http://www.efta.int

EEA matters: 74 rue de Trèves, B-1040 Brussels, Belgium
Tel: 00-32 2-286 1726
Fax: 00-32 2-286 1750

European Commission
200 rue de la Loi, 1049 Brussels, Belgium
Web site: http://europa.eu.int/en/comm.html

UK Office
8 Storey's Gate, London SW1P 3AT
Tel: 00 44 (0) 171-973 1992
Fax: 00 44 (0) 171-973 1900/1910

European Parliament
Palais de l'Europe, 67006 Strasbourg, France
Tel: 00 33 3-8817 4001
Fax: 00 33 3-8817 4860
rue Wiertz, 1047 Brussels, Belgium
Web site: http://www.europarl.eu.int

UK Office
2 Queen Anne's Gate, London SW1H 9AA
Tel: 00 44 (0) 171-227 4300
Fax: 00 44 (0) 171-227 4301

European Organization for Nuclear Research (CERN)
CH-1211 Geneva 23, Switzerland
Tel: 00 41 22-767 4101
Fax: 00 41 22-785 0247
Web site: http://www.cern.ch

European Space Agency (ESA)
8–10 rue Mario-Nikis, 75738 Paris, France
Tel: 00-33 1-5369 7654
Fax: 00-33 1-5369 7560
Web site: http://www.esa.int

Food and Agriculture Organization of the United Nations (FAO)
Viale delle Terme di Caracalla, I-00100 Rome, Italy
Tel: 00 39 6-57051
Fax: 00 39 6-5705 3152
E-mail: fao_hq@fao.org
Web site: http://www.fao.org

INMARSAT
99 City Road, London EC1Y 1AX, UK
Tel: 00 44 (0) 171-728 1000
Fax: 00 44 (0) 171-728 1044
Web site: http://www.inmarsat.org/inmarsat/index.html

International Atomic Energy Agency (IAEA)
Vienna International Centre, Wagramerstrasse 5, PO Box 100,
A-1400 Vienna, Austria
Tel: 00 43 1-20600
Fax: 00 43 1-20607
E-mail: official.mail@iaea.org
Web site: http://www.iaea.or.at/worldatom

International Civil Aviation Organization (ICAO)
1000 Sherbrooke Street West, Montreal, Quebec H3A 2R2,
Canada
Tel: 00 1 514-954 8221
Fax: 00 1 514-954 6376
Web site: http://www.icao.org

International Confederation of Free Trade Unions (ICFTU)
Boulevard Emile Jacqmain 155 B1, B-1210 Brussels, Belgium
Tel: 00 32 2-224 0211
Fax: 00 32 2-203 0756/201 5815
E-mail: internetpo@icftu.org
Web site: http://www.icftu.org

International Criminal Police Organization (Interpol)
200 Quai Charles de Gaulle, 69006 Lyon, France
Tel: 00 33 4-7244 7000
Fax: 00 33 4-7244 7163
Web site: http://www.interpol.com

UK Office
NCIS-Interpol, PO Box 8000, Spring Gardens, Tinworth Street,
London SE11 5EN, UK
Tel: 00 44 (0) 171-238 8000
Fax: 00 44 (0) 171-238 8446

International Energy Agency (IEA)
9 rue de la Fédération, 75739 Paris 15, France
Tel: 00 33 1-4057 6554
Fax: 00 33 1-4057 6559
Web site: http://www.iea.org

International Fund for Agricultural Development (IFAD)
107 Via del Serafico, 00142 Rome, Italy
Tel: 00 39 6-54591
Fax: 00 39 6-504 3463
E-mail: ifad@ifad.org
Web site: http://www.ifad.org

International Labour Organization (ILO)
4 route des Morillons, CH-1211 Geneva 22, Switzerland
Tel: 00 41 22-799 6111
Fax: 00 41 22-798 8685
Web site: http://www.ilo.org

UK Office
Millbank Tower, 21–24 Millbank, London SW1P 4QP, UK
Tel: 00 44 (0) 171-828 6401
Fax: 00 44 (0) 171-233 5925

International Maritime Organization (IMO)
4 Albert Embankment, London SE1 7SR, UK
Tel: 00 44 (0) 171-735 7611
Fax: 00 44 (0) 171-587 3210
E-mail: info@imo.org
Web site: http://www.imo.org

International Monetary Fund (IMF)
700 19th Street NW, Washington DC 20431, USA
Tel: 00 1 202-623 7000
Fax: 00 1 202-623 4661
E-mail: publicaffairs@imf.org
Web site: http://www.imf.org

International Red Cross and Red Crescent Movement (ICRC)
17 avenue de la Paix, 1211 Geneva, Switzerland
Web site: http://www.icrc.org

UK Member
British Red Cross Society
9 Grosvenor Crescent, London SW1X 7EJ
Tel: 00 44 (0) 171-235 5454
Fax: 00 44 (0) 171-245 6315
E-mail: information@redcross.org.uk
Web site: http://www.redcross.org.uk/vauxhall.htm

International Telecommunications Satellite Organization (Intelsat)
3400 International Drive NW, Washington DC 20008-3098, USA
Tel: 00 1 202-944 6800
Fax: 00 1 202-944 7898
E-mail: customer.service@intelsat.int
Web site: http://www.intelsat.int

International Telecommunication Union (ITU)
Place des Nations, CH-1211 Geneva 20, Switzerland
Tel: 00 41 22-730 5111
Fax: 00 41 22-733 7256
E-mail: itumail@itu.int
Web site: http://www.itu.org

League of Arab States
Maidane Al-Tahrir, Cairo, Egypt
Tel: 00 20 2-750511
Fax: 00 20 2-574 0331

UK Office
52 Green Street, London W1Y 3RH
Tel: 00 44 (0) 171-629 0044
Fax: 00 44 (0) 171-493 7943

Nordic Council
Secretariat of the Presidium, Tyrgatan 7, PO Box 19506, Stockholm 10432, Sweden
Tel: 00 46 8-414 3420/453 4700
Fax: 00 46 8-411 7536
Web site: http://www.norden.org

North Atlantic Treaty Organization (NATO)
B-1110 Brussels, Belgium
Tel: 00 32 2-707 4111
Fax: 00 32 2-707 4579
E-mail: natodoc@hq.nato.int
Web site: http://www.nato.int

Organization for Economic Co-operation and Development (OECD)
2 rue André-Pascal, 75775 Paris Cedex 16, France
Tel: 00-33 1-4524 8200
Fax: 00-33 1-4524 8500
Web site: http://www.oecd.org

Organization for Security and Co-operation in Europe (OSCE)
Kärntner Ring 5–7, A-1010 Vienna, Austria
Tel: 00 43 1-514 360
Fax: 00 43 1-514 3696
Web site: http://www.osce.org

Organization of African Unity (OAU)
PO Box 3243, Addis Ababa, Ethiopia
Tel: 00 251 1-517700
Fax: 00 251 1-513036

Organization of American States (OAS)
General Secretariat: Pan American Union Building, 17th Street and Constitution Avenue NW, Washington DC 20006, USA
Tel: 00 1 202-458 3000
Fax: 00 1 202-458 6421
E-mail: info@oas.org
Web site: http://www.oas.org

Organization of Arab Petroleum Exporting Countries (OAPEC)
PO Box 20501, Safat 13066, Kuwait City, Kuwait
Tel: 00 965-484 4500
Fax: 00 965-481 5747
E-mail: oapec@kuwait.net
Web site: http://www.kuwait.net/~oapec

Organization of the Islamic Conference (OIC)
Kilo 6, Mecca Road, PO Box 178, Jeddah 21411, Saudi Arabia
Tel: 00 966 2-680 0800
Fax: 00 966 2-687 3568

Organization of the Petroleum Exporting Countries (OPEC)
Obere Donaustrasse 93, A-1020 Vienna, Austria
Tel: 00 43 1-211120
Fax: 00 43 1-214 9827
E-mail: info@opec.org
Web site: http://www.opec.org

Pacific Commission (PC)
Secretariat: BP D5, 98848 Nouméa Cedex, New Caledonia
Tel: 00 687-262000
Fax: 00 687-263818
E-mail: spc@spc.org.nc
Web site: http://www.spc.org.nc

The United Nations (UN)
UN Plaza, New York, NY 10017, USA
Tel: 00 1 212-963 1234
Web site: http://www.un.org

UK Office
United Nations Office and Information Centre
21st Floor, Millbank Tower, 21–24 Millbank, London SW1P
4QH
Tel: 00 44 (0) 171-630 1981
Fax: 00 44 (0) 171-976 6478

**United Nations Educational, Scientific and Cultural
Organization (UNESCO)**
7 place de Fontenoy, 75352 Paris 07SP, France
Tel: 00 33 1-4568 1000
Fax: 00 33 1-4567 1690
Web site: http://www.unesco.org

**United Nations Industrial Development Organization
(UNIDO)**
Vienna International Centre, Wagramerstrasse 5, PO Box 300,
A-1400 Vienna, Austria
Tel: 00 43 1-21131
Fax: 00 43 1-232156
E-mail: UNIDO-PINFO@unido.org
Web site: http://www.unido.org

Universal Postal Union (UPU)
Weltpoststrasse 4, 3000 Berne 15, Switzerland
Tel: 00 41 31-350 3111
Fax: 00 41 31-350 3110
E-mail: ib.info@ib.upu.org
Web site: http://www.ib.upu.org

Western European Union (WEU)
4 rue de la Régence, 1000 Brussels, Belgium
Tel: 00 32 2-500 4455
Fax: 00 32 2-511 3519
E-mail: ueo.presse@skynet.be
Web site: http://www.weu.int

World Bank (IBRD)
1818 H Street NW, Washington DC 20433, USA
Tel: 00 1 202-477 1234
Fax: 00 1 202-477 6391
Web site: http://www.worldbank.org

UK Office
New Zealand House, Haymarket, London SW1Y 4TE
Tel: 00 44 (0) 171-930 8511
Fax: 00 44 (0) 171-930 8515

World Council of Churches (WCC)
Box 2100, 1211 Geneva 2, Switzerland
Tel: 00 41 22-791 6111
Fax: 00 41 22-798 1346
E-mail: info@mail.wcc-coe.org
Web site: http://www.wcc-coe.org

World Health Organization (WHO)
20 avenue Appia, 1211 Geneva 27, Switzerland
Tel: 00 41 22-791 2111
Fax: 00 41 22-791 0746
E-mail: info@who.ch
Web site: http://www.who.ch

World Intellectual Property Organization (WIPO)
34 chemin des Colombettes, 1211 Geneva 20, Switzerland
Tel: 00 41 22-338 9111
Fax: 00 41 22-733 5428
E-mail: publicinf.mail@wipo.int
Web site: http://www.wipo.int

World Meteorological Organization (WMO)
41 avenue Guiseppe Motta, PO Box 2300, 1211 Geneva 20,
Switzerland
Tel: 00 41 22-730 8111
Fax: 00 41 22-734 2326

World Trade Organization
Centre William Rappard, rue de Lausanne 154, 1211 Geneva 21,
Switzerland
Tel: 00 41 22-739 5111
Fax: 00 41 22-739 5458
E-mail: enquiries@wto.org
Web site: http://www.wto.org

DEVELOPED AND DEVELOPING COUNTRIES

The United Nations defines the developed and developing countries as follows:

Developed countries

Albania	Kyrgyzstan
Andorra	Latvia
Armenia	Liechtenstein
Australia	Lithuania
Austria	Luxembourg
Azerbaijan	Moldova
Belarus	Monaco
Belgium	The Netherlands
Bulgaria	New Zealand
Canada	Norway
Czech Republic	Poland
Denmark	Portugal
Estonia	Romania
Faröe Islands	Russia
Finland	San Marino
France	Slovakia
Georgia	Spain
Germany	Sweden
Gibraltar	Switzerland
Greece	Tajikistan
Hungary	Turkmenistan
Iceland	Ukraine
Republic of Ireland	UK
Israel	USA
Italy	Uzbekistan
Japan	Vatican City State
Kazakstan	

Developing countries
All countries excluding the developed countries listed above

Least developed countries

Afghanistan	The Gambia
Bangladesh	Guinea
Benin	Guinea-Bissau
Bhutan	Haiti
Burkina Faso	Kiribati
Burundi	Laos
Cambodia	Lesotho
Cape Verde	Liberia
Central African Republic	Madagascar
Chad	Malawi
Comoros	Maldives
Democratic Republic of Congo	Mali
Djibouti	Mauritania
Equatorial Guinea	Mozambique
Eritrea	Myanmar
Ethiopia	Nepal

Niger	Togo
Rwanda	Tuvalu
Samoa	Uganda
São Tomé and Príncipe	Tanzania
Sierra Leone	Vanuatu
Solomon Islands	Yemen
Somalia	Zambia
Sudan	

Third World countries
This term for developing countries is no longer used

ACRONYMS AND ABBREVIATIONS

AC	Alternating current (electricity)
ACS	Association of Caribbean States
ACT	Australian Capital Territory
AIM	Alternative Investment Market
ALADI	Latin-American Integration Association
ANC	African National Congress
AP	Andean Pact
	Associated Press
APEC	Asia-Pacific Economic Co-operation Group
ASEAN	Association of South-East Asian Nations
BC	British Columbia
BLEU	Belgo-Luxembourg Economic Union
BOTB	British Overseas Trade Board
BSEC	Black Sea Economic Co-operation
BST	British Summer Time
CAP	Common Agricultural Policy
CARICOM	Caribbean Community and Common Market
CBI	Confederation of British Industry
CC	Chamber of Commerce
CET	Central European Time
	Common External Tariff
CD	Diplomatic Corps
CEEAC	Economic Community of Central African States
CEFTA	Central European Free Trade Agreement
CEMAC	Economic and Monetary Community of Central Africa
CEPGL	Economic Community of the Great Lakes Countries
CERN	European Organization for Nuclear Research

CFSP	Common Foreign and Security Policy
CI	Channel Islands
CIA	Central Intelligence Agency
CIS	Commonwealth of Independent States
COMESA	Common Market for Eastern and Southern Africa
COR	Committee of the Regions
DC	Direct current (electricity)
	District of Columbia
DFID	Department for International Development
DTI	Department of Trade and Industry
EBRD	European Bank for Reconstruction and Development
EC	European Community
ECGD	Export Credits Guarantee Department
ECO	Economic Co-operation Organization
ECOWAS	Economic Community of West African States
ECSC	European Coal and Steel Community
ECU	European Currency Unit
EEA	European Economic Area
EEC	European Economic Community
EFTA	European Free Trade Association
EIB	European Investment Bank
EMI	European Monetary Institute
EMS	European Monetary System
EMU	Economic and Monetary Union
EP	European Parliament
ERM	Exchange Rate Mechanism
ESA	European Space Agency
ETA	*Euzkadi ta Askatasuna* (Basque separatist organization)
EU	European Union
EURATOM	European Atomic Energy Commission
EUROPOL	European Drugs Agency
FAO	Food and Agriculture Organization (UN)
FBI	Federal Bureau of Investigation
FCO	Foreign and Commonwealth Office
G3	Group of Three (Columbia, Mexico, Venezuela)
G7	Group of Seven (Canada, France, Germany, Italy, Japan, UK, USA)
G8	Group of Eight (G7 plus Russia)
GATT	General Agreement on Tariffs and Trade
GCHQ	Government Communications Headquarters

GDP	Gross domestic product
GMT	Greenwich Mean Time
GNP	Gross national product
Hz	Hertz
IAEA	International Atomic Energy Agency
IATA	International Air Transport Association
IBRD	International Bank for Reconstruction and Development (more commonly known as the World Bank)
ICAO	International Civil Aviation Organization
ICFTU	International Confederation of Free Trade Unions
ICJ	International Court of Justice
ICRC	International Committee of the Red Cross
IDA	International Development Association
IDD	International direct dialling
IEA	International Energy Agency
IFAD	International Fund for Agricultural Development
IFC	International Finance Corporation
ILO	International Labour Organization
IMF	International Monetary Fund
IMO	International Maritime Organization
INMARSAT	International Maritime Satellite Organization
Intelsat	International Telecommunications Satellite Organization
Interpol	International Criminal Police Organization
IOC	International Olympic Committee
IOM	Isle of Man
IOW	Isle of Wight
IRA	Irish Republican Army
ITU	International Telecommunication Union
km	kilometre
kW	kilowatt
MEP	Member of the European Parliament
MERCOSUR	Common Market of the Southern Cone (of South America)
MLA	Member of Legislative Assembly
MLC	Member of Legislative Council
MoD	Ministry of Defence
MP	Member of Parliament
MRU	Mano River Union

NAFTA	North American Free Trade Agreement
NASA	National Aeronautics and Space Administration
NATO	North Atlantic Treaty Organization
NB	New Brunswick
NI	Northern Ireland
NS	Nova Scotia
NSW	New South Wales
NWT	Northwest Territory
NY	New York
NZ	New Zealand
OAPEC	Organization of Arab Petroleum Exporting Countries
OAS	Organization of American States
OAU	Organization of African Unity
OECD	Organization for Economic Co-operation and Development
OHMS	On Her/His Majesty's Service
OIC	Organization of the Islamic Conference
OPEC	Organization of the Petroleum Exporting Countries
OSCE	Organization for Security and Co-operation in Europe
PA	Press Association
PFP	Partnership for Peace
PLO	Palestine Liberation Organization
PNA	Palestinian National Authority
PTA	Preferential Trade Area for Eastern and Southern Africa
RC	Red Cross
RI	Rhode Island
RSA	Republic of South Africa
SA	South Africa
	South America
	South Australia
SADC	Southern African Development Community
SPC	Pacific Community (formerly South Pacific Commission)
UAE	United Arab Emirates
UDI	Unilateral declaration of independence
UNDP	United Nations Development Programme
UEMOA	West African Economic and Monetary Union
UK	United Kingdom

UN	United Nations
UNESCO	United Nations Educational, Scientific and Cultural Organization
UNHCR	United Nations High Commissioner for Refugees
UNICEF	United Nations Children's Fund
UNIDO	United Nations Industrial Development Organization
UNITA	National Union for the Total Independence of Angola
UPI	United Press International
UPU	Universal Postal Union
US(A)	United States (of America)
USSR	Union of Soviet Socialist Republics
VSO	Voluntary Service Overseas
WCC	World Council of Churches
WEU	Western European Union
WFTU	World Federation of Trade Unions
WHO	World Health Organization
WI	West Indies
WIPO	World Intellectual Property Organization
WMO	World Meteorological Organization
WTO	World Trade Organization

DATA SOURCES

All sovereign states are included, plus the major territories of
sovereign states (i.e. those that are inhabited and economically
significant).

Availability of statistics and the definitions used in compiling
them vary from country to country. Wherever possible, the latest
available statistics from sources that present data on an
internationally comparable basis have been used.

The same data is used in the country profiles and the world
rankings.

Data for Cyprus refers to government controlled areas only.

Data for Jordan refers to the East Bank only.

Data for Palestinian Autonomous Areas is for the West Bank and
Gaza Strip.

In some cases, data for Taiwan is included with data for China.

NOTES

General

Area	Total land area and inland waters
Population	Wherever possible a *de facto* population figure is given, i.e. all persons actually present in the country when the census was taken/estimate was made
Exchange rate	Exchange rate against £ sterling on 29 May 1998; market rate given, except where indicated ★ ★official rate Franc CFA = Franc de la Communauté financière africaine Franc CFP = Franc de Comptoirs français du Pacifique
Public holidays	Dates are those obtaining in 1998
Usual business hours	Wherever possible, business hours are given; where these are not known or vary widely, banking hours are given

Demography

Life expectancy	The average number of years of life for males and females if they continue to be subject to the prevailing mortality rate for their country of birth
Population growth rate	Annual percentage of population growth between 1990 and 1995

Government and diplomacy

Trouble spots — Reflects the situation in the country at the time of going to press (June 1998); information about less recent events is included where it may have some bearing on the current situation or future developments

Defence

Military expenditure — Definitions of what constitutes military expenditure and the transparency of reporting military expenditure by governments vary. Figures given here are based on NATO definitions

Military personnel — Refers to active armed forces (including conscripts) and paramilitary forces; reserves are not included unless specifically stated

Conscription duration — Where service is voluntary, no entry is shown

Economy

Gross national product (GNP) — GDP plus net primary income from non-resident sources

GNP per capita — GNP divided by mid-year population

Gross domestic product (GDP) — Value of final output of goods and services produced by residents of an economy; data at constant 1990 prices (1990=100)

GDP per capita — GDP divided by population, expressed at current prices

Annual average growth in GDP — The rate for the year in question is obtained by dividing the GDP for that year by the GDP of the preceding year

Unemployment — Includes all persons not in paid employment or self-employment but available for and seeking employment; data are annual averages

Total external debt — Total long-term and short-term debt owed to non-residents and repayable in foreign currency, goods or services; data is given for developing countries and former Soviet republics

Education

Enrolment — Net enrolment, i.e. total enrolment at a level of education corresponding to the age group of that level of education